Organizational Behaviour:

Readings and Cases

3rd edition

Edited by
Hugh J. Arnold and
Daniel A. Ondrack

Woodsworth   U of T

TABLE OF CONTENTS

READINGS

CASES

Readings

READING 1

MOTIVATION: A DIAGNOSTIC APPROACH

by

D.A. Nadler & E.E. Lawler, III

Reading 6

Motivation: A Diagnostic Approach
David A. Nadler
Edward E. Lawler III

What makes some people work hard while others do as little as possible?

How can I, as a manager, influence the performance of people who work for me?

Why do people turn over, show up late to work, and miss work entirely?

These important questions about employees' behavior can only be answered by managers who have a grasp of what motivates people. Specifically, a good understanding of motivation can serve as a valuable tool for *understanding* the causes of behavior in organizations, for *predicting* the effects of any managerial action, and for *directing* behavior so that organizational and individual goals can be achieved.

EXISTING APPROACHES

During the past twenty years, managers have been bombarded with a number of different approaches to motivation. The terms associated with these approaches are well known—"human relations," "scientific management," "job enrichment," "need hierarchy," "self-actualization," etc. Each of these approaches has something to offer. On the other hand, each of these different approaches also has its problems in both theory and practice. Running through almost all of the approaches with which managers are familiar are a series of implicit but clearly erroneous assumptions.

Assumption 1: All Employees Are Alike
Different theories present different ways of looking at people, but each of them assumes that all employees are basically similar in their makeup: Employees all want economic gains, or all want a pleasant climate, or all aspire to be self-actualizing, etc.

Assumption 2: All Situations Are Alike Most theories assume that all managerial situations are alike, and that the managerial course of action for motivation (for example, participation, job enlargement, etc.) is applicable in all situations.

Assumption 3: One Best Way Out of the other two assumptions there emerges a basic principle that there is "one best way" to motivate employees.

When these "one best way" approaches are tried in the "correct" situation they will work. However, all of them are bound to fail in some situations. They are therefore not adequate managerial tools.

A NEW APPROACH

During the past ten years, a great deal of research has been done on a new approach to looking at motivation. This approach, frequently called "expectancy theory," still needs further testing, refining, and extending. However, enough is known that many behavioral scientists have concluded that it represents the most comprehensive, valid, and useful approach to understanding motivation. Further, it is apparent that it is a very useful tool for understanding motivation in organizations.

The theory is based on a number of specific assumptions about the causes of behavior in organizations.

Assumption 1: Behavior Is Determined by a Combination of Forces in the Individual and Forces in the Environment Neither the individual nor the environment alone determines behavior. Individuals come into organizations with certain "psychological baggage." They have past experiences and a developmental history which has given them unique sets of needs, ways of looking at the world, and expectations about how organizations will treat them. These all influence how individuals respond to their work environment. The work environment provides structures (such as a pay system or a supervisor) which influence the behavior of people. Different environments tend to produce different behavior in similar people just as dissimilar people tend to behave differently in similar environments.

Assumption 2: People Make Decisions about Their Own Behavior in Organizations While there are many constraints on the behavior of individuals in organizations, most of the behavior that is observed is the result of individuals' conscious decisions. These decisions usually fall into two categories. First, individuals make decisions about *membership behavior*—coming to work, staying at work, and in other ways being a member of the organization. Second, individuals make decisions about the amount of *effort* they will direct *towards performing their jobs*. This includes decisions about how hard to work, how much to produce, at what quality, etc.

Assumption 3: Different People Have Different Types of Needs, Desires and Goals Individuals differ on what kinds of outcomes (or rewards) they desire. These differences are not random; they can be examined systematically by an understanding of the differences in the strength of individuals' needs.

Assumption 4: People Make Decisions among Alternative Plans of Behavior Based on Their Perceptions (Expectancies) of the Degree to Which a Given Behavior will Lead to Desired Outcomes In simple terms, people tend to do those things which they see as leading to outcomes (which can also be called "rewards") they desire and avoid doing those things they see as leading to outcomes that are not desired.

In general, the approach used here views people as having their own needs and mental maps of what the world is like. They use these maps to make decisions about how they will behave, behaving in those ways which their mental maps indicate will lead to outcomes that will satisfy their needs. Therefore, they are inherently neither motivated nor unmotivated; motivation depends on the situation they are in, and how it fits their needs.

THE THEORY

Based on these general assumptions, expectancy theory states a number of propositions about the process by which people make decisions about their own behavior in organizational settings. While the theory is complex at first view, it is in fact made of a series of fairly straightforward observations about behavior. (The theory is presented in more technical terms in Appendix A.) Three concepts serve as the key building blocks of the theory:

Performance-Outcome Expectancy Every behavior has associated with it, in an individual's mind, certain outcomes (rewards or punishments). In other words, the individual believes or expects that if he or she behaves in a certain way, he or she will get certain things.

Examples of expectancies can easily be described. An individual may have an expectancy that if he produces ten units he will receive his normal hourly rate while if he produces fifteen units he will receive his hourly pay rate plus a bonus. Similarly an individual may believe that certain levels of performance will lead to approval or disapproval from members of her work group or from her supervisor. Each performance can be seen as leading to a number of different kinds of outcomes and outcomes can differ in their types.

Valence Each outcome has a "valence" (value, worth, attractiveness) to a specific individual. Outcomes have different valences for different individuals. This comes about because valences result from individual needs and perceptions, which differ because they in turn reflect other factors in the individual's life.

For example, some individuals may value an opportunity for promotion or advancement because of their needs for achievement or power, while others may not want to be promoted and leave their current work group because of needs for affiliation with others. Similarly, a fringe benefit such as a pension plan may have great valence for an older worker but little valence for a young employee on his first job.

Effort-Performance Expectancy Each behavior also has associated with it in the individual's mind a certain expectancy or probability of success. This expectancy represents the individual's perception of how hard it will be to achieve such behavior and the probability of his or her successful achievement of that behavior.

For example, you may have a strong expectancy

that if you put forth the effort, you can produce ten units an hour, but that you have only a fifty-fifty chance of producing fifteen units an hour if you try.

Putting these concepts together, it is possible to make a basic statement about motivation. In general, the motivation to attempt to behave in a certain way is greatest when:

a The individual believes that the behavior will lead to outcomes (performance-outcome expectancy)

b The individual believes that these outcomes have positive value for him or her (valence)

c The individual believes that he or she is able to perform at the desired level (effort-performance expectancy)

Given a number of alternative levels of behavior (ten, fifteen, and twenty units of production per hour, for example) the individual will choose that level of performance which has the greatest motivational force associated with it, as indicated by the expectancies, outcomes, and valences.

In other words, when faced with choices about behavior, the individual goes through a process of considering questions such as, "Can I perform at that level if I try?" "If I perform at that level, what will happen?" "How do I feel about those things that will happen?" The individual then decides to behave in that way which seems to have the best chance of producing positive, desired outcomes.

A General Model

On the basis of these concepts, it is possible to construct a general model of behavior in organizational settings (see Figure 6-1). Working from left to right in the model, motivation is seen as the force on the individual to expend effort. Motivation leads to an observed level of effort by the individual. Effort, alone, however, is not enough. Performance results from a combination of the effort that an individual puts forth *and* the level of ability which he or she has (reflecting skills, training, information, etc.). Effort thus combines with ability to produce a given level of performance. As a result of performance, the individual attains certain outcomes. The model indicates this relationship in a dotted line, reflecting the fact that sometimes people perform but do not get desired outcomes. As this process of performance-reward occurs, time after time, the actual events serve to provide information which influences the individual's perceptions (particularly expectancies) and thus influences motivation in the future.

Outcomes, or rewards, fall into two major categories. First, the individual obtains outcomes from the environment. When an individual performs at a given level he or she can receive positive or negative outcomes from supervisors, co-workers, the organization's rewards systems, or other sources. These environmental rewards are thus one source of outcomes for the individual. A second source of outcomes is the individual. These include outcomes

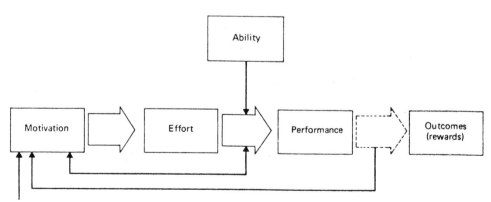

A person's motivation is a function of:

a. Effort-to-performance expectancies
b. Performance-to-outcome expectancies
c. Perceived valence of outcomes

Figure 6-1 The basic motivation-behavior sequence.

which occur purely from the performance of the task itself (feelings of accomplishment, personal worth, achievement, etc.). In a sense, the individual gives these rewards to himself or herself. The environment cannot give them or take them away directly; it can only make them possible.

Supporting Evidence

Over fifty studies have been done to test the validity of the expectancy-theory approach to predicting employee behavior.[1] Almost without exception, the studies have confirmed the predictions of the theory. As the theory predicts, the best performers in organizations tend to see a strong relationship between performing their jobs well and receiving rewards they value. In addition they have clear performance goals and feel they can perform well. Similarly, studies using the expectancy theory to predict how people choose jobs also show that individuals tend to interview for and actually take those jobs which they feel will provide the rewards they value. One study, for example, was able to correctly predict for 80 percent of the people studied which of several jobs they would take.[2] Finally, the theory correctly predicts that beliefs about the outcomes associated with performance (expectancies) will be better predictors of performance than will feelings of job satisfaction since expectancies are the critical causes of performance and satisfaction is not.

Questions about the Model

Although the results so far have been encouraging, they also indicate some problems with the model. These problems do not critically affect the managerial implications of the model, but they should be noted. The model is based on the assumption that individuals make very rational decisions after a thorough exploration of all the available alternatives and on weighing the possible outcomes of all these alternatives. When we talk or observe individuals, however, we find that their decision processes are frequently less thorough. People often stop consid-

[1] For reviews of the expectancy theory research see Mitchell, T. R. Expectancy models of job satisfaction, occupational preference and effort: A theoretical methodological, and empirical appraisal. *Psychological Bulletin*, 1974, **81**, 1053–1077. For a more general discussion of expectancy theory and other approaches to motivation see Lawler, E. E. *Motivation in work organizations*, Belmont, Calif.: Brooks/Cole, 1973.

[2] Lawler, E. E., Kuleck, W. J., Rhode, J. G. & Sorenson, J. E. Job choice and post-decision dissonance. *Organizational Behavior and Human Performance*, 1975, **13**, 133–145.

ering alternative behavior plans when they find one that is at least moderately satisfying, even though more rewarding plans remain to be examined.

People are also limited in the amount of information they can handle at one time, and therefore the model may indicate a process that is much more complex than the one that actually takes place. On the other hand, the model does provide enough information and is consistent enough with reality to present some clear implications for managers who are concerned with the question of how to motivate the people who work for them.

Implications for Managers

The first set of implications is directed towards the individual manager who has a group of people working for him or her and is concerned with how to motivate good performance. Since behavior is a result of forces both in the person and in the environment, you as manager need to look at and diagnose both the person and the environment. Specifically, you need to do the following:

Figure Out What Outcomes Each Employee Values As a first step, it is important to determine what kinds of outcomes or rewards have valence for your employees. For each employee you need to determine "what turns him or her on." There are various ways of finding this out, including (a) finding out employees' desires through some structured method of data collection, such as a questionnaire, (b) observing the employees' reactions to different situations or rewards, or (c) the fairly simple act of asking them what kinds of rewards they want, what kind of career goals they have, or "what's in it for them." It is important to stress here that it is very difficult to change what people want, but fairly easy to find out what they want. Thus, the skillful manager emphasizes diagnosis of needs, not changing the individuals themselves.

Determine What Kinds of Behavior You Desire Managers frequently talk about "good performance" without really defining what good performance is. An important step in motivating is for you yourself to figure out what kinds of performances are required and what are adequate measures or indicators of performance (quantity, quality, etc.). There is also a need to be able to define those performances in fairly specific terms so that observable and measurable behavior can be defined and subordinates can understand what is desired of them (e.g., produce ten .products of a certain quality standard—rather than only produce at a high rate).

Make Sure Desired Levels of Performance are Reachable The model states that motivation is determined not only by the performance-to-outcome expectancy, but also by the effort-to-performance expectancy. The implication of this is that the levels of performance which are set as the points at which individuals receive desired outcomes must be reachable or attainable by these individuals. If the employees feel that the level of performance required to get a reward is higher than they can reasonably achieve, then their motivation to perform well will be relatively low.

Link Desired Outcomes to Desired Performances The next step is to directly, clearly, and explicitly link those outcomes desired by employees to the specific performances desired by you. If your employee values external rewards, then the emphasis should be on the rewards systems concerned with promotion, pay, and approval. While the linking of these rewards can be initiated through your making statements to your employees, it is extremely important that employees see a clear example of the reward process working in a fairly short period of time if the motivating "expectancies" are to be created in the employees' minds. The linking must be done by some concrete public acts, in addition to statements of intent.

If your employee values internal rewards (e.g., achievement), then you should concentrate on changing the nature of the person's job, for he or she is likely to respond well to such things as increased autonomy, feedback, and challenge, because these things will lead to a situation where good job performance is inherently rewarding. The best way to check on the adequacy of the internal and external reward system is to ask people what their perceptions of the situation are. Remember it is the perceptions of people that determine their motivation, not reality. It doesn't matter for example whether you feel a subordinate's pay is related to his or her performance. Motivation will be present only if the subordinate sees the relationship. Many managers are misled about the behavior of their subordinates because they rely on their own perceptions of

the situation and forget to find out what their subordinates feel. There is only one way to do this: ask. Questionnaires can be used here, as can personal interviews. (See Appendix B for a short version of a motivation questionnaire.)

Analyze the Total Situation for Conflicting Expectancies Having set up positive expectancies for employees, you then need to look at the entire situation to see if other factors (informal work groups, other managers, the organization's reward systems) have set up conflicting expectancies in the minds of the employees. Motivation will only be high when people see a number of rewards associated with good performance and few negative outcomes. Again, you can often gather this kind of information by asking your subordinates. If there are major conflicts, you need to make adjustments, either in your own performance and reward structure, or in the other sources of rewards or punishments in the environment.

Make Sure Changes in Outcomes Are Large Enough In examining the motivational system, it is important to make sure that changes in outcomes or rewards are large enough to motivate significant behavior. Trivial rewards will result in trivial amounts of effort and thus trivial improvement in performance. Rewards must be large enough to motivate individuals to put forth the effort required to bring about significant changes in performance.

Check the System for Its Equity The model is based on the idea that individuals are different and therefore different rewards will need to be used to motivate different individuals. On the other hand, for a motivational system to work it must be a fair one—one that has equity (not equality). Good performers should see that they get more desired rewards than do poor performers, and others in the system should see that also. Equity should not be confused with a system of equality where all are rewarded equally, with no regard to their performance. A system of equality is guaranteed to produce low motivation.

Implications for Organizations

Expectancy theory has some clear messages for those who run large organizations. It suggests how organizational structures can be designed so that they increase rather than decrease levels of motivation of organization members. While there are many different implications, a few of the major ones are as follows:

Implication 1: The Design of Pay and Reward Systems Organizations usually get what they reward, not what they want. This can be seen in many situations, and pay systems are a good example.[3] Frequently, organizations reward people for membership (through pay tied to seniority, for example) rather than for performance. Little wonder that what the organization gets is behavior oriented towards "safe," secure employment rather than effort directed at performing well. In addition, even where organizations do pay for performance as a motivational device, they frequently negate the motivational value of the system by keeping pay secret, therefore preventing people from observing the pay-to-performance relationship that would serve to create positive, clear, and strong performance-to-reward expectancies. The implication is that organizations should put more effort into rewarding people (through pay, promotion, better job opportunities, etc.) for the performances which are desired, and that to keep these rewards secret is clearly self-defeating. In addition, it underscores the importance of the frequently ignored performance evaluation or appraisal process and the need to evaluate people based on how they perform clearly defined specific behaviors, rather than on how they score on ratings of general traits such as "honesty," "cleanliness," and other, similar terms which frequently appear as part of the performance appraisal form.

Implication 2: The Design of Tasks, Jobs, and Roles One source of desired outcomes is the work itself. The expectancy-theory model supports much of the job enrichment literature, in saying that by designing jobs which enable people to get their needs fulfilled, organizations can bring about higher levels of motivation.[4] The major difference between

[3]For a detailed discussion of the implications of expectancy theory for pay and reward systems, see Lawler, E. E. *Pay and organizational effectiveness: A psychological view.* New York: McGraw-Hill, 1971.

[4]A good discussion of job design with an expectancy theory perspective is in Hackman, J. R., Oldham, G. R., Janson, R., & Purdy, K. A new strategy for job enrichment. *California Management Review,* Summer, 1975, p. 57.

the traditional approaches to job enlargement or enrichment and the expectancy-theory approach is the recognition by the expectancy theory that different people have different needs and, therefore, some people may not want enlarged or enriched jobs. Thus, while the design of tasks that have more autonomy, variety, feedback, meaningfulness, etc., will lead to higher motivation in some, the organization needs to build in the opportunity for individuals to make choices about the kind of work they will do so that not everyone is forced to experience job enrichment.

Implication 3: The Importance of Group Structures Groups, both formal and informal, are powerful and potent sources of desired outcomes for individuals. Groups can provide or withhold acceptance, approval, affection, skill training, needed information, assistance, etc. They are a powerful force in the total motivational environment of individuals. Several implications emerge from the importance of groups. First, organizations should consider the structuring of at least a portion of rewards around group performance rather than individual performance. This is particularly important where group members have to cooperate with each other to produce a group product or service, and where the individual's contribution is often hard to determine. Second, the organization needs to train managers to be aware of how groups can influence individual behavior and to be sensitive to the kinds of expectancies which informal groups set up and their conflict or consistency with the expectancies that the organization attempts to create.

Implication 4: The Supervisor's Role The immediate supervisor has an important role in creating, monitoring, and maintaining the expectancies and reward structures which will lead to good performance. The supervisor's role in the motivation process becomes one of defining clear goals, setting clear reward expectancies, and providing the right rewards for different people (which could include both organizational rewards and personal rewards such as recognition, approval, or support from the supervisor). Thus, organizations need to provide supervisors with an awareness of the nature of motivation as well as the tools (control over organizational rewards, skill in administering those rewards) to create positive motivation.

Implication 5: Measuring Motivation If things like expectancies, the nature of the job, supervisor-controlled outcomes, satisfaction, etc., are important in understanding how well people are being motivated, then organizations need to monitor employee perceptions along these lines. One relatively cheap and reliable method of doing this is through standardized employee questionnaires. A number of organizations already use such techniques, surveying employees' perceptions and attitudes at regular intervals (ranging from once a month to once every year-and-a-half) using either standardized surveys or surveys developed specifically for the organization. Such information is useful both to the individual manager and to top management in assessing the state of human resources and the effectiveness of the organization's motivational systems.[5] (Again, see Appendix B for excerpts from a standardized survey.)

Implication 6: Individualizing Organizations Expectancy theory leads to a final general implication about a possible future direction for the design of organizations. Because different people have different needs and therefore have different valences, effective motivation must come through the recognition that not all employees are alike and that organizations need to be flexible in order to accommodate individual differences. This implies the "building in" of choice for employees in many areas, such as reward systems, fringe benefits, job assignments, etc., where employees previously have had little say. A successful example of the building in of such choice can be seen in the experiments of

TRW and the Educational Testing Service with "cafeteria fringe-benefits plans" which allow employees to choose the fringe benefits they want, rather than taking the expensive and often unwanted benefits which the company frequently provides to everyone.[6]

SUMMARY

Expectancy theory provides a more complex model of man for managers to work with. At the same time, it is a model which holds promise for the more effective motivation of individuals and the more effective design of organizational systems. It implies, however, the need for more exacting and thorough diagnosis by the manager to determine (a) the relevant forces in the individual, and (b) the relevant forces in the environment, both of which combine to motivate different kinds of behavior. Following diagnosis, the model implies a need to act—to develop a system of pay, promotion, job assignments, group structures, supervision, etc.—to bring about effective motivation by providing different outcomes for different individuals.

Performance of individuals is a critical issue in making organizations work effectively. If a manager is to influence work behavior and performance, he or she must have an understanding of motivation and the factors which influence an individual's motivation to come to work, to work hard, and to work well. While simple models offer easy answers, it is the more complex models which seem to offer more promise. Managers can use models (like expectancy theory) to understand the nature of behavior and build more effective organizations.

[5]The use of questionnaires for understanding and changing organizational behavior is discussed in Nadler, D. A. *Feedback and organizational development: Using data-based methods.* Reading, Mass.: Addison-Wesley, 1977.

[6]The whole issue of individualizing organizations is examined in Lawler, E. E. The individualized organization: Problems and promise. *California Management Review,* 1974, **17**(2), 31–39.

APPENDIX A: The Expectancy Theory Model in More Technical Terms

A person's motivation to exert effort towards a specific level of performance is based on his or her perceptions of associations between actions and outcomes. The critical perceptions which contribute

to motivation are graphically presented in Figure 6-2. These perceptions can be defined as follows:

a The effort-to-performance expectancy $(E \rightarrow P)$:

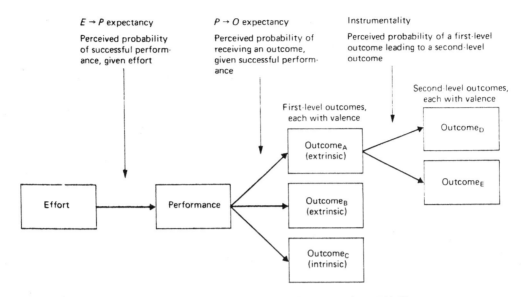

Motivation is expressed as follows: $M = [E \rightarrow P] \times \Sigma [(P \rightarrow O) (V)]$

Figure 6-2 Major terms in expectancy theory.

This refers to the person's subjective probability about the likelihood that he or she can perform at a given level, or that effort on his or her part will lead to successful performance. This term can be thought of as varying from 0 to 1. In general, the less likely a person feels that he or she can perform at a given level, the less likely he or she will be to try to perform at that level. A person's $E \rightarrow P$ probabilities are also strongly influenced by each situation and by previous experience in that and similar situations.

b The performance-to-outcomes expectancy $(P \rightarrow O)$ and valence (V): This refers to a combination of a number of beliefs about what the outcomes of successful performance will be and the value or attractiveness of these outcomes to the individual. Valence is considered to vary from +1 (very desirable) to −1 (very undesirable) and the performance-to-outcomes probabilities vary from +1 (performance sure to lead to outcome) to 0 (performance not related to outcome). In general, the more likely a person feels that performance will lead to valent outcomes, the more likely he or she will be to try to perform at the required level.

c Instrumentality: As Figure 6-2 indicates, a single level of performance can be associated with a number of different outcomes, each having a certain degree of valence. Some outcomes are valent because they have direct value or attractiveness. Some

outcomes, however, have valence because they are seen as leading to (or being "instrumental" for) the attainment of other "second level" outcomes which have direct value or attractiveness.

d Intrinsic and extrinsic outcomes: Some outcomes are seen as occurring directly as a result of performing the task itself and are outcomes which the individual thus gives to himself (i.e., feelings of accomplishment, creativity, etc.). These are called "intrinsic" outcomes. Other outcomes that are associated with performance are provided or mediated by external factors (the organization, the supervisor, the work group, etc.). These outcomes are called "extrinsic" outcomes.

Along with the graphic representation of these terms presented in Figure 6-2. there is a simplified formula for combining these perceptions to arrive at a term expressing the relative level of motivation to exert effort towards performance at a given level. The formula expresses these relationships:

a The person's motivation to perform is determined by the $P \rightarrow O$ expectancy multiplied by the valence (V) of the outcome. The valence of the first order outcome subsumes the instrumentalities and valences of second order outcomes. The relationship is multiplicative since there is no motivation to perform if either of the terms is zero.

11

b Since a level of performance has multiple outcomes associated with it, the products of all probability-times-valence combinations are added together for all the outcomes that are seen as related to the specific performance.

c This term (the summed $P \rightarrow O$ expectancies times valences) is then multiplied by the $E \rightarrow P$ expectancy. Again the multiplicative relationship indicates that if either term is zero, motivation is zero.

d In summary, the strength of a person's motivation to perform effectively is influenced by (1) the person's belief that effort can be converted into performance, and (2) the net attractiveness of the events that are perceived to stem from good performance.

So far, all the terms have referred to the individual's perceptions which result in motivation and thus an intention to behave in a certain way. Figure 6-3 is a simplified representation of the total model, showing how these intentions get translated into actual behavior.[7] The model envisions the following sequence of events:

a First, the strength of a person's motivation to

perform correctly is most directly reflected in his or her effort—how hard he or she works. This effort expenditure may or may not result in good performance, since at least two factors must be right if effort is to be converted into performance. First, the person must possess the necessary abilities in order to perform the job well. Unless both ability and effort are high, there cannot be good performance. A second factor is the person's perception of how his or her effort can best be converted into performance. It is assumed that this perception is learned by the individual on the basis of previous experience in similar situations. This "how to do it" perception can obviously vary widely in accuracy, and—where erroneous perceptions exist—performance is low even though effort or motivation may be high.

b Second, when performance occurs, certain amounts of outcomes are obtained by the individual. Intrinsic outcomes, not being mediated by outside forces, tend to occur regularly as a result of performance, while extrinsic outcomes may or may not accrue to the individual (indicated by the wavy line in the model).

c Third, as a result of the obtaining of outcomes and the perceptions of the relative value of the outcomes obtained, the individual has a positive or negative affective response (a level of satisfaction or dissatisfaction).

d Fourth, the model indicates that events which

[7]For a more detailed statement of the model see Lawler, E. E. Job attitudes and employee motivation: Theory, research and practice. *Personnel Psychology*, 1970, **23**, 223–237.

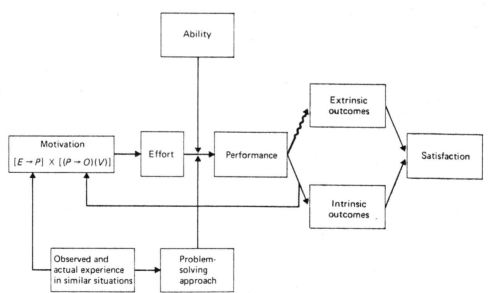

Figure 6-3 Simplified expectancy-theory model of behavior.

occur influence future behavior by altering the $E{\rightarrow}P$, $P{\rightarrow}O$, and V perceptions. This process is represented by the feedback loops running from actual behavior back to motivation.

APPENDIX B: Measuring Motivation Using Expectancy Theory

Expectancy theory suggests that it is useful to measure the attitudes individuals have in order to diagnose motivational problems. Such measurement helps the manager to understand why employees are motivated or not, what the strength of motivation is in different parts of the organization, and how effective different rewards are for motivating performance. A short version of a questionnaire used to measure motivation in organizations is included here.[8] Basically, three different questions need to be asked (see Tables 6-1, 6-2, and 6-3).

Using the Questionnaire Results

The results from this questionnaire can be used to calculate a *work-motivation score*. A score can be

[8]For a complete version of the questionnaire and supporting documentation see Nadler, D. A., Cammann, C., Jenkins, G. D., & Lawler, E. E. (Eds.) *The Michigan organizational assessment package* (Progress Report II). Ann Arbor: Survey Research Center, 1975.

calculated for each individual and scores can be combined for groups of individuals. The procedure for obtaining a work-motivation score is as follows:

a For each of the possible positive outcomes listed in questions 1 and 2, multiply the score for the outcome on question 1 ($P{\rightarrow}O$ expectancies) by the corresponding score on question 2 (valences of outcomes). Thus, score 1a would be multiplied by score 2a, score 1b by score 2b, etc.

b All of the 1 times 2 products should be added together to get a total of all expectancies times valences _____.

c The total should be divided by the number of pairs (in this case, eleven) to get an average expectancy-times-valence score _____.

d The scores from question 3 ($E{\rightarrow}P$ expectancies) should be added together and then divided by three to get an average effort-to-performance expectancy score _____.

Table 6-1 *Question 1:* Here are some things that could happen to people if they do their jobs *especially well*. How likely is it that each of these things would happen if you performed your job *especially well*?

	Not at all likely		Somewhat likely		Quite likely		Extremely likely
a You will get a bonus or pay increase	(1)	(2)	(3)	(4)	(5)	(6)	(7)
b You will feel better about yourself as a person	(1)	(2)	(3)	(4)	(5)	(6)	(7)
c You will have an opportunity to develop your skills and abilities	(1)	(2)	(3)	(4)	(5)	(6)	(7)
d You will have better job security	(1)	(2)	(3)	(4)	(5)	(6)	(7)
e You will be given chances to learn new things	(1)	(2)	(3)	(4)	(5)	(6)	(7)
f You will be promoted or get a better job	(1)	(2)	(3)	(4)	(5)	(6)	(7)
g You will get a feeling that you've accomplished something worthwhile	(1)	(2)	(3)	(4)	(5)	(6)	(7)
h You will have more freedom on your job	(1)	(2)	(3)	(4)	(5)	(6)	(7)
i You will be respected by the people you work with	(1)	(2)	(3)	(4)	(5)	(6)	(7)
j Your supervisor will praise you	(1)	(2)	(3)	(4)	(5)	(6)	(7)
k The people you work with will be friendly with you	(1)	(2)	(3)	(4)	(5)	(6)	(7)

Table 6-2 *Question 2:* Different people want different things from their work. Here is a list of things a person could have on his or her job. How *important* is each of the following to you?

How Important Is . . . ?	Moderately important or less			Quite important			Extremely important
a The amount of pay you get	(1)	(2)	(3)	(4)	(5)	(6)	(7)
b The chances you have to do something that makes you feel good about yourself as a person	(1)	(2)	(3)	(4)	(5)	(6)	(7)
c The opportunity to develop your skills and abilities	(1)	(2)	(3)	(4)	(5)	(6)	(7)
d The amount of job security you have	(1)	(2)	(3)	(4)	(5)	(6)	(7)
How Important Is . . . ?							
e The chances you have to learn new things	(1)	(2)	(3)	(4)	(5)	(6)	(7)
f Your chances for getting a promotion or getting a better job	(1)	(2)	(3)	(4)	(5)	(6)	(7)
g The chances you have to accomplish something worthwhile.	(1)	(2)	(3)	(4)	(5)	(6)	(7)
h The amount of freedom you have on your job.	(1)	(2)	(3)	(4)	(5)	(6)	(7)
How Important Is . . . ?							
i The respect you receive from the people you work with	(1)	(2)	(3)	(4)	(5)	(6)	(7)
j The praise you get from your supervisor.	(1)	(2)	(3)	(4)	(5)	(6)	(7)
k The friendliness of the people you work with	(1)	(2)	(3)	(4)	(5)	(6)	(7)

e Multiply the score obtained in step c (the average expectancy times valence) by the score obtained in step d (the average $E \rightarrow P$ expectancy score) to obtain a total work-motivation score

Additional Comments on the Work-Motivation Score

A number of important points should be kept in mind when using the questionnaire to get a work-motivation score. First, the questions presented here are just a short version of a larger and more comprehensive questionnaire. For more detail, the articles and publications referred to here and in the text should be consulted. Second, this is a general questionnaire. Since it is hard to anticipate in a general questionnaire what may be valent outcomes in each situation, the individual manager may want to add additional outcomes to questions 1 and 2. Third, it is important to remember that questionnaire results can be influenced by the feelings people have when they fill out the questionnaire. The use of the questionnaire as outlined above assumes a certain level of trust between manager and subordinates. People filling out questionnaires need to know what is going to be done with their answers and usually need to be assured of the confidentiality of their responses. Finally, the research indicates that, in many cases, the score obtained by simply averaging all the responses to question 1 (the $P \rightarrow O$ expectancies) will be as useful as the fully calculated work-motivation score. In each situation, the manager should experiment and find out whether the additional information in questions 2 and 3 aid in motivational diagnosis.

Table 6-3 *Question 3:* Below you will see a number of pairs of factors that look like this:

Warm weather→sweating   (1) (2) (3) (4) (5) (6) (7)

You are to indicate by checking the appropriate number to the right of each pair how often it is true for *you* personally that the first factor leads to the second on *your job*. Remember, for each pair, indicate how often it is true by checking the box under the response which seems most accurate.

	Never		Sometimes		Often		Almost always
a Working hard → high productivity	(1)	(2)	(3)	(4)	(5)	(6)	(7)
b Workind hard → doing my job well	(1)	(2)	(3)	(4)	(5)	(6)	(7)
c Working hard → good job performance	(1)	(2)	(3)	(4)	(5)	(6)	(7)

READING 2

SATISFACTION AND BEHAVIOR

by

E.E. Lawler, III

From: Motivation in Work Organizations by Edward E Lawler,
         III. ©1973 by Wadsworth Publishing Company Inc.
         Reprinted by permission of Brooks/Cole Publishing Co.,
         Monterey, CA.

Reading 7

Satisfaction and Behavior
Edward E. Lawler III

Compared to what is known about motivation, relatively little is known about the determinants and consequences of satisfaction. Most of the psychological research on motivation simply has not been concerned with the kinds of affective reactions that people experience in association with or as a result of motivated behavior. No well-developed theories of satisfaction have appeared and little theoretically based research has been done on satisfaction. The influence of behaviorism on the field of psychology had a great deal to do with this lag in research. While psychology was under the influence of behaviorism, psychologists avoided doing research that depended on introspective self-reports. Behaviorists strongly felt that if psychology were to develop as a science, it had to study observable behavior. Since satisfaction is an internal subjective state that is best reported by the people experiencing it, satisfaction was not seen as a proper subject for study. Psychologists thought they should concentrate on those aspects of motivation that are observable (for exam-

ple, performance, hours of deprivation, strength of response, and so on).

Most of the research on the study of satisfaction has been done by psychologists interested in work organizations. This research dates back to the 1930s. Since that time, the term "job satisfaction" has been used to refer to affective attitudes or orientations on the part of individuals toward jobs. Hoppock published a famous monograph on job satisfaction in 1935, and in 1939 the results of the well-known Western Electric studies were published. The Western Electric studies (Roethlisberger & Dickson, 1939) emphasized the importance of studying the attitudes, feelings, and perceptions employees have about their jobs. Through interviews with over 20,000 workers, these studies graphically made the point that employees have strong affective reactions to what happens to them at work. The Western Electric studies also suggested that affective reactions cause certain kinds of behavior, such as strikes, absenteeism, and turnover. Although the studies

Excerpt from chap. 4 of E. E. Lawler III, *Motivation in work organizations.* Monterey, Calif.: Brooks/Cole, 1973.

failed to show any clear-cut relationship between satisfaction and job performance, the studies did succeed in stimulating a tremendous amount of research on job satisfaction. During the last 30 years, thousands of studies have been done on job satisfaction. Usually these studies have not been theoretically oriented; instead, researchers have simply looked at the relationship between job satisfaction and factors such as age, education, job level, absenteeism rate, productivity, and so on. Originally, much of the research seemed to be stimulated by a desire to show that job satisfaction is important because it influences productivity. Underlying the earlier articles on job satisfaction was a strong conviction that "happy workers are productive workers." Recently, however, this theme has been disappearing, and many organizational psychologists seem to be studying job satisfaction simply because they are interested in finding its causes. This approach to studying job satisfaction is congruent with the increased prominence of humanistic psychology, which emphasizes human affective experience.

The recent interest in job satisfaction also ties in directly with the rising concern in many countries about the quality of life. There is an increasing acceptance of the view that material possessions and economic growth do not necessarily produce a high quality of life. Recognition is now being given to the importance of the kinds of affective reactions that people experience and to the fact that these are not always tied to economic or material accomplishments. Through the Department of Labor and the Department of Health, Education, and Welfare, the United States government has recently become active in trying to improve the affective quality of work life. Job satisfaction is one measure of the quality of life in organizations and is worth understanding and increasing even if it doesn't relate to performance. This reason for studying satisfaction is likely to be an increasingly prominent one as we begin to worry more about the effects working in organizations has on people and as our humanitarian concern for the kind of psychological experiences people have during their lives increases. What happens to people during the work day has profound effects both on the individual employee's life and on the society as a whole, and thus these events cannot be ignored if the quality of life in a society is to be high. As John Gardner has said:

Of all the ways in which society serves the individual, few are more meaningful than to provide him with a decent job. . . . It isn't going to be a decent society for any of us until it is for all of us. If our sense of responsibility fails us, our sheer self-interest should come to the rescue [1968, p. 25].

As it turns out, satisfaction is related to absenteeism and turnover, both of which are very costly to organizations. Thus, there is a very "practical" economic reason for organizations to be concerned with job satisfaction, since it can influence organizational effectiveness. However, before any practical use can be made of the finding that job dissatisfaction causes absenteeism and turnover, we must understand what factors cause and influence job satisfaction. Organizations can influence job satisfaction and prevent absenteeism and turnover only if the organizations can pinpoint the factors causing and influencing these affective responses.

Despite the many studies, critics have legitimately complained that our understanding of the causes of job satisfaction has not substantially increased during the last 30 years (for example, see Locke, 1968, 1969) for two main reasons. The research on job satisfaction has typically been atheoretical and has not tested for causal relationships. Since the research has not been guided by theory, a vast array of unorganized, virtually uninterpretable facts have been unearthed. For example, a number of studies have found a positive relationship between productivity and job satisfaction, while other studies have found no evidence of this relationship. Undoubtedly, this disparity can be explained, but the explanation would have to be based on a theory of satisfaction, and at present no such theory exists. One thing the research on job satisfaction has done is to demonstrate the saying that "theory without data is fantasy; but data without theory is chaos!"

Due to the lack of a theory stating causal relationships, the research on job satisfaction has consistently looked simply for relationships among variables. A great deal is known about what factors are related to satisfaction, but very little is known about the causal basis for the relationships. This is a serious problem when one attempts to base change efforts on the research. This problem also increases the difficulty of developing and testing theories of satisfaction. Perhaps the best example of the resulting dilemma concerns the relationship between satisfaction and performance. If satisfaction causes performance, then organizations should try to see that their employees are satisfied; however, if performance causes satisfaction, then high satisfaction is not necessarily a goal but rather a by-product of an effective organization.

A MODEL OF FACET SATISFACTION

Figure 7-1 presents a model of the determinants of facet satisfaction. The model is intended to be applicable to understanding what determines a person's satisfaction with any facet of the job. The model assumes that the same psychological processes operate to determine satisfaction with job factors ranging from pay to supervision and satisfaction with the work itself. The model in Figure 4-1 is a discrepancy model in the sense that it shows satisfaction as the difference between a, what a person feels he should receive, and b, what he perceives that he actually receives. The model indicates that when the person's perception of what his outcome level is and his perception of what his outcome level should be are in agreement, the person will be satisfied. When a person perceives his outcome level as falling below what he feels it should be, he will be dissatisfied. However, when a person's perceived outcome level exceeds what he feels it should be, he will have feelings of guilt and

inequity and perhaps some discomfort (Adams, 1965). Thus, for any job factor, the assumption is that satisfaction with the factor will be determined by the difference between how much of the factor there is and how much of the factor the person feels there should be.

Present outcome level is shown to be the key influence on a person's perception of what rewards he receives, but his perception is also shown to be influenced by his perception of what his "referent others' receive. The higher the outcome levels of his referent others, the lower his outcome level will appear. Thus, a person's psychological view of how much of a factor he receives is said to be influenced by more than just the objective amount of the factor. Because of this psychological influence, the same amount of reward often can be seen quite differently by two people; to one person it can be a large amount, while to another person it can be a small amount.

The model in Figure 7-1 also shows that a person's perception of what his reward level should be is influenced by a number of factors. Perhaps the most important influence is perceived job inputs. These inputs include all of the skills, abilities, and training a person brings to the job as well as the behavior he exhibits on the job. The greater he perceives his inputs to be, the higher will be his perception of

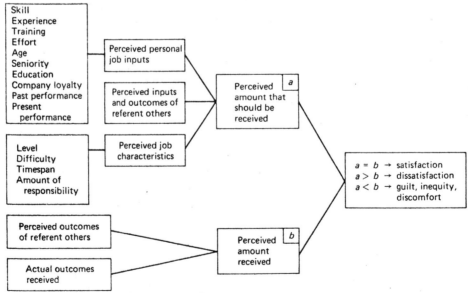

Figure 7-1 Model of the determinants of satisfaction.

19

what his outcomes should be. Because of this relationship, people with high job inputs must receive more rewards than people with low job inputs or they will be dissatisfied. The model also shows that a person's perception of what his outcomes should be is influenced by his perception of the job demands. The greater the demands made by the job, the more he will perceive he should receive. Job demands include such things as job difficulty, responsibilities, and organization level. If outcomes do not rise along with these factors, the clear prediction of the model is that the people who perceive they have the more difficult, higher level jobs will be the most dissatisfied.

The model shows that a person's perception of what his outcomes should be is influenced by what the person perceives his comparison-other's inputs and outcomes to be. This aspect of the model is taken directly from equity theory and is included to stress the fact that people look at the inputs and outcomes of others in order to determine what their own outcome level should be. If a person's comparison-other's inputs are the same as the person's inputs but the other's outcomes are much higher, the person will feel that he should be receiving more outcomes and will be dissatisfied as a result.

The model allows for the possibility that people will feel that their outcomes exceed what they should be. The feelings produced by this condition are quite different from those produced by under-reward. Because of this difference, it does not make sense to refer to a person who feels over-rewarded as being dissatisfied. There is considerable evidence that very few people feel over-rewarded, and this fact can be explained by the model. Even when people are highly rewarded, the social-comparison aspect of satisfaction means that people can avoid feeling over-rewarded by looking around and finding someone to compare with who is doing equally well. Also, a person tends to value his own inputs much higher than they are valued by others (Lawler, 1967). Because of this discrepancy, a person's perception of what his outcomes should be is often not shared by those administering his rewards, and is often above what he actually receives. Finally, the person can easily increase his perception of his inputs and thereby justify a high reward level.

As a way of summarizing some of the implications of the model, let us briefly make some statements about who should be dissatisfied if the model is correct. Other things being equal:

1 People with high perceived inputs will be more dissatisfied with a given facet than people with low perceived inputs.
2 People who perceive their job to be demanding will be more dissatisfied with a given facet than people who perceive their jobs as undemanding.
3 People who perceive similar others as having a more favorable input-outcome balance will be more dissatisfied with a given facet than people who perceive their own balance as similar to or better than that of others.
4 People who receive a low outcome level will be more dissatisfied than those who receive a high outcome level.
5 The more outcomes a person perceives his comparison-other receives, the more dissatisifed he will be with his own outcomes. This should be particularly true when the comparison-other is seen to hold a job that demands the same or fewer inputs.

OVERALL JOB SATISFACTION

Most theories of job satisfaction argue that overall job satisfaction is determined by some combination of all facet-satisfaction feelings. This could be expressed in terms of the facet-satisfaction model in Figure 7-1 as a simple sum of, or average of, all $a - b$ discrepancies. Thus, overall job satisfaction is determined by the difference between all things a person feels he should receive from his job and all the things he actually does receive.

A strong theoretical argument can be made for weighting the facet-satisfaction scores according to their importance. Some factors do make larger contributions to overall satisfaction than others. Pay satisfaction, satisfaction with the work itself, and satisfaction with supervision seem to have particularly strong influences on overall satisfaction for most people. Also, employees tend to rate these factors as important. Thus, there is a connection between how important employees say job factors are and how much job factors influence overall job satisfaction (Vroom, 1964). Conceptually, therefore, it seems worthwhile to think of the various job-facet-satisfaction scores as influencing total satisfaction in terms of their importance. One way to express this relationship is by defining overall job satisfaction as being equal to Σ (facet satisfaction $\times$ facet importance). However, as stressed earlier, actually measuring importance and multiplying it by measured facet satisfaction often isn't necessary because the satisfaction scores themselves seem to take importance into account. (The most important items tend to be scored as either very satisfactory or very dissatisfactory; thus, these items have the most influence on any sum score.) Still, on a conceptual level, it is important to remember that facet-satisfaction scores do differentially contribute to the feeling of overall job satisfaction.

A number of studies have attempted to determine how many workers are actually satisfied with their jobs. Our model does not lead to any predictions in this area. The model simply gives the conditions that lead to people experiencing feelings of satisfaction or dissatisfaction. Not surprisingly, the studies that have been done do not agree on the percentage of dissatisfied workers. Some suggest figures as low as 13 percent, others give figures as high as 80 percent. The range generally reported is from 13 to 25 percent dissatisfied. Herzberg et al. (1957) summarized the findings of research studies conducted from 1946 through 1953. The figures in their report showed a yearly increase in the median percentage of job-satisfied persons (see Table 7-1). Figure 7-2 presents satisfaction-trend data for 1948 through 1971. These data also show an overall increase in the number of satisfied workers, which is interesting because of recent speculation that satisfaction is

decreasing. However, due to many measurement problems, it is impossible to conclude that a real decline in number of dissatisfied workers has taken place.

The difficulty in obtaining meaningful conclusions from the data stems from the fact that different questions yield very different results. For example, a number of studies, instead of directly asking workers "How satisfied are you?," have asked "If you had it to do over again, would you pick the same job?" The latter question produces much higher dissatisfaction scores than does the simply "how satisfied are you" question. One literature review showed that 54 percent of the workers tended to say that they were sufficiently dissatisfied with their jobs that they would not choose them again. On the other hand, the straight satisfaction question shows between 13 and 25 percent dissatisfied. However, even this figure is subject to wide variation depending on how the question is asked. When the question is asked in the simple form, "Are you satisfied, yes or no?," the number of satisfied responses is large. When the question is changed so that the employees can respond yes, no, or undecided—or satisfied, dissatisfied, or neutral—the number of satisfied responses drops.

Because of these methodological complexities, it is difficult to draw conclusions about the number of workers who are or are not satisfied with their jobs or with some facet of their jobs. This drawback does not mean, however, that meaningful research on satisfaction is impossible. On the contrary, interesting and important research has been and can be done on the determinants of job satisfaction. For example, the relationship between personal-input factors—such as education level, sex, and age and seniority—and job or facet satisfaction can be ascertained by simply comparing those people who report they are satisfied with those people who report they are dissatisfied and checking the results to see if the two groups differ in any systematic manner. The number of people reporting satisfaction is not crucial for this purpose. What is important is that we distinguish those people who tend to be more satisfied from those people who tend to be less satisfied. This distinction can be made with many of the better-known satisfaction-measuring instruments, such as the Job Description Index (Smith, Kendall, & Hulin, 1969) and Porter's (1961) need-satisfaction instrument.

Table 7-1 Median Percentage of Job-dissatisfied Persons Reported from 1946–1953
(From Herzberg et al., *Job Attitudes: Review of Research and Opinion.* Copyright 1957 by the Psychological Service of Pittsburgh. Reprinted by permission.)

Year	Median percentage of job dissatisfied
1953	13
1952	15
1951	18
1949	19
1948	19
1946–1947	21

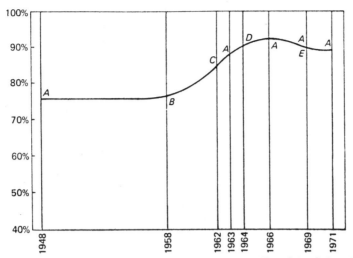

Figure 7-2 Percentage of "satisfied" workers, 1948–1971. *(From Quinn Staines, & McCollough, 1973.) Note:* "Don't know" and "uncertain" have been excluded from the base of the percentages. *Sources: A* = Gallup, or Gallup as reported by Roper; *B* = Survey Research Center (Michigan); *C* = NORC; *D* = Survey Research Center (Berkeley); *E* = 1969–1970 Survey of Working Conditions.

A number of studies have tried to determine the amount of employee dissatisfaction that is associated with different job facets. Although these studies have yielded interesting results, some serious methodological problems are involved in this work. As with overall job satisfaction, factors such as type of measurement scale used and manner of wording questions seriously affect the number of people who express dissatisfaction with a given facet. For example, a question about pay satisfaction can be asked in a way that will cause few people to express dissatisfaction, while a question about security satisfaction can be asked in a way that will cause many people to express dissatisfaction. In this situation, comparing the number of people expressing security satisfaction with the number of people expressing pay dissatisfaction might produce very misleading conclusions. This problem is always present no matter how carefully the various items are worded because it is impossible to balance the items so they are comparable for all factors.

Despite methodological problems, the data on relative satisfaction levels with different job factors are interesting. These data show that the factors mentioned earlier as being most important—that is, pay, promotion, security, leadership, and the work itself—appear in these studies as the major sources of dissatisfaction. Porter (1961) designed items using Maslow's needs as a measure of satisfaction. With these items, he collected data from various managers. The results of his study (see Table 7-2) show that more managers express higher order need dissatisfaction than express lower order need dissatisfaction. The results also show that a large number of managers are dissatisfied with their pay and with the communications in their organizations and that middle level managers tend to be better satisfied in all areas than lower level managers.

Porter's data also show that managers consider the areas of dissatisfaction to be the most important areas. It is not completely clear whether the dissatisfaction causes the importance or the importance causes the dissatisfaction. The research reviewed earlier suggests that the primary causal direction is from dissatisfaction to importance, although there undoubtedly is a two-way-influence process operating. The important thing to remember is that employees do report varying levels of satisfaction with different job factors, and the factors that have come out high on dissatisfaction have also been rated high in importance and have the strongest influence on overall job satisfaction.

A study by Grove and Kerr (1951) illustrates how strongly organizational conditions can affect factor satisfaction. Grove and Kerr measured employee satisfaction in two plants where normal work condi-

Table 4-2 Differences between Management Levels in Percentage of Subjects Indicating Need-Fulfillment Deficiencies (Adapted from Porter, 1961)

Questionnaire items	% Bottom management (N = 64)	% Middle management (N = 75)	% Difference
Security needs	42.2	26.7	15.5
Social needs	35.2	32.0	3.2
Esteem needs	55.2	35.6	19.6
Autonomy needs	60.2	47.7	12.5
Self-actualization needs	59.9	53.3	6.6
Pay	79.7	80.0	−0.3
Communications	78.1	61.3	16.8

tions prevailed and found that 88 percent of the workers were satisfied with their job security, which indicated that security was one of the least dissatisfying job factors for employees in these two plants. In another plant where layoffs had occurred, only 17 percent of the workers said they were satisfied with the job security, and job security was one of the most dissatisfying job factors for this plant's employees.

The research on the determinants of satisfaction has looked primarily at two relationships: (1) the relationship between satisfaction and the characteristics of the job, and (2) the relationship between satisfaction and the characteristics of the person. Not surprisingly, the research shows that satisfaction is a function of both the person and the environment. These results are consistent with our approach to thinking about satisfaction, since our model (shown in Figure 7-1) indicates that personal factors influence what people feel they should receive and that job conditions influence both what people perceive they actually receive and what people perceive they should receive.

The evidence on the effects of personal-input factors on satisfaction is voluminous and will be only briefly reviewed. The research clearly shows that personal factors do affect job satisfaction, basically because they influence perceptions of what outcomes should be. As predicted by the satisfaction model in Figure 7-1, the higher a person's perceived personal inputs—that is, the greater his education, skill, and performance—the more he feels he should receive. Thus, unless the high-input person receives

more outcomes, he will be dissatisfied with his job and the rewards his job offers. Such straightforward relationships between inputs and satisfaction appear to exist for all personal-input factors except age and seniority. Evidence from the study of age and seniority suggests a curvilinear relationship (that is, high satisfaction among young and old workers, low satisfaction among middle-age workers) or even a relationship of increasing satisfaction with old age and tenure. The tendency of satisfaction to be high among older, long-term employees seems to be produced by the effects of selective turnover and the development of realistic expectations about what the job has to offer.

CONSEQUENCES OF DISSATISFACTION

Originally, much of the interest in job satisfaction stemmed from the belief that job satisfaction influenced job performance. Specifically, psychologists thought that high job satisfaction led to high job performance. This view has now been discredited, and most psychologists feel that satisfaction influences absenteeism and turnover but not job performance. However, before looking at the relationship among satisfaction, absenteeism, and turnover, let's review the work on satisfaction and performance.

Job Performance

In the 1950s, two major literature reviews showed that in most studies only a slight relationship had been found between satisfaction and performance.

A later review by Vroom (1964) also showed that studies had not found a strong relationship between satisfaction and performance; in fact, most studies had found a very low positive relationship between the two. In other words, better performers did seem to be slightly more satisfied than poor performers. A considerable amount of recent work suggests that the slight existing relationship is probably due to better performance indirectly causing satisfaction rather than the reverse. Lawler and Porter (1967) explained this "performance causes satisfaction" viewpoint as follows:

If we assume that rewards cause satisfaction, and that in some cases performance produces rewards, then it is possible that the relationship found between satisfaction and performance comes about through the action of a third variable—rewards. Briefly stated, good performance may lead to rewards, which in turn lead to satisfaction; this formulation then would say that satisfaction rather than causing performance, as was previously assumed, is caused by it.

[Figure 7-3] shows that performance leads to rewards, and it distinguishes between two kinds of rewards and their connection to performance. A wavy line between performance and extrinsic rewards indicates that such rewards are likely to be imperfectly related to performance. By extrinsic rewards is meant such organizationally controlled rewards as pay, promotion, status, and security—rewards that are often referred to as satisfying mainly lower-level needs. The connection is relatively weak because of the difficulty of tying extrinsic rewards directly to performance. Even though an organization may have a policy of rewarding merit, performance is difficult to measure, and in dispensing rewards like pay, many other factors are frequently taken into consideration.

Quite the opposite is likely to be true for intrinsic rewards, however, since they are given to the individual by himself for good performance. Intrinsic or internally mediated rewards are subject to fewer disturbing influences and thus are likely to be more directly related to good performance. This connection is indicated in the model by a semi-wavy line. Probably the best example of an intrinsic reward is the feeling of having accomplished something worthwhile. For that matter any of the rewards that satisfy self-actualization needs or higher order growth needs are good examples of intrinsic rewards [p. 23–24].[1]

Figure 7-3 shows that intrinsic and extrinsic rewards are not directly related to job satisfaction, since the relationship is moderated by perceived equitable rewards (what people think they should receive). The model in Figure 7-3 is similar to the model in Figure 7-1, since both models show that satisfaction is a function of the amount of rewards a person receives and the amount of rewards he feels he should receive.

Because of the imperfect relationship between performance and rewards and the important effect of perceived equitable rewards, a low but positive relationship should exist between job satisfaction and job performance in most situations. However, in certain situations, a strong positive relationship may exist; while in other situations, a negative relationship may exist. A negative relationship would be expected where rewards are unrelated to performance or negatively related to performance.

[1]Lawler, E. E., and Porter, L. W. The effect of performance on job satisfaction. *Industrial Relations*, 1967, **7**, 20–28. Reprinted by permission of the publisher, Industrial Relations.

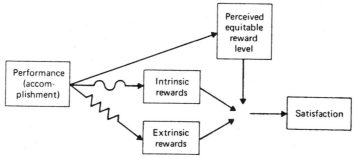

Figure 7-3 Model of the relationship of performance to satisfaction. *(From Lawler and Porter, The effect of performance on job satisfaction. Industrial Relations, 1967, 7, 20–28. Reprinted by permission of the publisher, Industrial Relations.)*

To have the same level of satisfaction for good performers and poor performers, the good performers must receive more rewards than the poor performers. The reason for this, as stressed earlier, is that performance level influences the amount of rewards a person feels he should receive. Thus, when rewards are not based on performance—when poor performers receive equal rewards or a larger amount of rewards than good performers—the best performers will be the least satisfied, and a negative satisfaction-performance relationship will exist. If, on the other hand, the better performers are given significantly more rewards, a positive satisfaction-performance relationship should exist. If it is assumed that most organizations are partially successful in relating rewards to performance, it follows that most studies should find a low but positive relationship between satisfaction and performance. Lawler and Porter's (1967) study was among those that found this relationship; their study also found that, as predicted, intrinsic-need satisfaction was more closely related to performance than was extrinsic-need satisfaction.

In retrospect, it is hard to understand why the belief that high satisfaction causes high performance was so widely accepted. There is nothing in the literature on motivation that suggests this causal relationship. In fact, such a relationship is opposite to the concepts developed by both drive theory and expectancy theory. If anything, these two theories would seem to predict that high satisfaction might reduce motivation because of a consequent reduction in the importance of various rewards that may have provided motivational force. Clearly, a more logical view is that performance is determined by people's efforts to obtain the goals and outcomes they desire, and satisfaction is determined by the outcomes people actually obtain. Yet, for some reason, many people believed—and some people still do believe—that the "satisfaction causes performance" view is best.

Turnover

The relationship between satisfaction and turnover has been studied often. In most studies, researchers have measured the job satisfaction among a number of employees and then waited to see which of the employees studied left during an ensuing time period (typically, a year). The satisfaction scores of the employees who left have then been compared with the remaining employees' scores. Although relationships between satisfaction scores and turnover have not always been very strong, the studies in this area have consistently shown that dissatisfied workers are more likely than satisfied workers to terminate employment; thus, satisfaction scores can predict turnover.

A study by Ross and Zander (1957) is a good example of the kind of research that has been done. Ross and Zander measured the job satisfaction of 2680 female workers in a large company. Four months later, these researchers found that 169 of these employees had resigned; those who left were significantly more dissatisfied with the amount of recognition they received on their jobs, with the amount of achievement they experienced, and with the amount of autonomy they had.

Probably the major reason that turnover and satisfaction are not more strongly related is that turnover is very much influenced by the availability of other positions. Even if a person is very dissatisfied with his job, he is not likely to leave unless more attractive alternatives are available. This observation would suggest that in times of economic prosperity, turnover should be high, and a strong relationship should exist between turnover and satisfaction; but in times of economic hardship, turnover should be low, and little relationship should exist between turnover and satisfaction. There is research evidence to support the argument that voluntary turnover is much lower in periods of economic hardship. However, no study has compared the relationship between satisfaction and turnover under different economic conditions to see if it is stronger under full employment.

Absenteeism

Like turnover, absenteeism has been found to be related to job satisfaction. If anything, the relationship between satisfaction and absenteeism seems to be stronger than the relationship between satisfaction and turnover. However, even in the case of absenteeism, the relationship is far from being isomorphic. Absenteeism is caused by a number of factors other than a person's voluntarily deciding not to come to work; illness, accidents, and so on can prevent someone who wants to come to work from actually coming to work. We would expect satisfaction to affect only voluntary absences; thus, satisfaction can never be strongly related to a measure of overall absence rate. Those studies that have separated voluntary absences from overall absences have, in fact, found that voluntary absence rates are much more closely related to satisfaction than are overall absence rates (Vroom, 1964). Of course, this outcome would be expected if satisfaction does influence people's willingness to come to work.

Organization Effectiveness

The research evidence clearly shows that employees' decisions about whether they will go to work on any given day and whether they will quit are affected by their feelings of job satisfaction. All the literature reviews on the subject have reached this conclusion. The fact that present satisfaction influences future absenteeism and turnover clearly indicates that the causal direction is from satisfaction to behavior. This conclusion is in marked contrast to our conclusion with respect to performance—that is, behavior causes satisfaction.

The research evidence on the determinants of satisfaction suggests that satisfaction is very much influenced by the actual rewards a person receives; of course, the organization has a considerable amount of control over these rewards. The research also shows that, although not all people will react to the same reward level in the same manner, reactions are predictable if something is known about how people perceive their inputs. The implication is that organizations can influence employees' satisfaction levels. Since it is possible to know how employees will react to different outcome levels, organizations can allocate outcomes in ways that will either cause job satisfaction or job dissatisfaction.

Absenteeism and turnover have a very direct influence on organizational effectiveness. Absenteeism is very costly because it interrupts scheduling, creates a need for overstaffing, increases fringe-benefit costs, and so on. Turnover is expensive because of the many costs incurred in recruiting and training replacement employees. For lower-level jobs, the cost of turnover is estimated at $2000 a person; at the managerial level, the cost is at least five to ten times the monthly salary of the job involved. Because satisfaction is manageable and influences absenteeism and turnover, organizations can control absenteeism and turnover. Generally,

by keeping satisfaction high and, specifically, by seeing that the best employees are the most satisfied, organizations can retain those employees they need the most. In effect, organizations can manage turnover so that, if it occurs, it will occur among employees the organization can most afford to lose. However, keeping the better performers more satisfied is not easy, since they must be rewarded very well.

REFERENCES

Adams, J. S. Injustice in social exchange. In L. Berkowitz (Ed.), *Advances in experimental social psychology*, Vol. 2. New York, Academic Press, 1965.

Gardner, J. W. *No easy victories*. New York, Harper & Row, 1968.

Grove, E. A., & Kerr, W. A. Specific evidence on origin of halo effect in measurement of employee morale. *Journal of Social Psychology*, 1951, **34**, 165–170.

Herzberg, F., Mausner, B., Peterson, R. O., & Capwell, D. I. *Job attitudes: Review of research and opinion*. Pittsburgh, Psychological Service of Pittsburgh, 1957.

Lawler, E. E. The multitrait multirater approach to measuring managerial job performance. *Journal of Applied Psychology*, 1967, **51**, 369–381.

Lawler, E. E., & Porter, L. W. The effect of performance on job satisfaction. *Industrial Relations*, 1967, **7**, 20–28.

Locke, E. A. What is job satisfaction? Paper presented at the APA Convention, San Francisco, September 1968.

Locke, E. A. What is job satisfaction? *Organizational Behavior and Human Performance*, 1969, **4**, 309–336.

Porter, L. W. A study of perceived need satisfactions in bottom and middle management jobs. *Journal of Applied Psychology*, 1961, **45**, 1–10.

Quinn, R. P., Staines, G., & McCullough, M. Job satisfaction in the 1970's. Recent history and a look to the future. *Manpower Monograph*, 1973.

Roethlisberger, F. I., & Dickson, W. I. *Management and the worker*. Cambridge, Mass., Harvard University Press, 1939.

Ross, I. E., & Zander, A. F. Need satisfaction and employee turnover. *Personnel Psychology*, 1957, **10**, 327–338.

Smith, P., Kendall, I., & Hulin, C. *The measurement of satisfaction in work and retirement*. Chicago, Rand McNally & Company, 1969.

Vroom, V. H. *Work and motivation*. New York, John Wiley & Sons, 1964.

READING 3

LEADERS AND LEADERSHIP: OF SUBSTANCE AND SHADOW

by

Morgan W. McCall, Jr.

Reading 45

Leaders and Leadership: Of Substance and Shadow

Morgan W. McCall, Jr.

There are at least two ways to approach the topic of leadership. The first is from the emotional, experiential frame of reference which captures the colorful and dramatic flavor of myth and legend—of the fate of nations and the course of history. The second is an empirical approach based on research about this nebulous topic. If the former is bright orange, the latter is decidedly slate gray.

The bright orange side of leadership emerges when people are asked to name highly effective leaders. The most frequently mentioned—Hitler, Churchill, Kennedy, Roosevelt, Eisenhower, Gandhi—all played a significant part in world history. The characteristics attributed to such effective leaders—charisma, intelligence, persuasiveness, dynamism, energy—also reflect the almost mystical power of central figures in world events.

The essence of the powerful leader's impact has been captured in song, poem, and novel. One example is Tolstoy's description of Napoleon:

> Napoleon was standing a little in front of his marshals, on a little grey horse, wearing the same blue overcoat he had worn throughout the Italian campaign. He was looking intently and silently at the hills, which stood up out of the sea of mist, and the Russian troops moving across them in the distance, and he listened to the sounds of firing in the valley. His face—still thin in those days—did not stir a single muscle: his gleaming eyes were fixed intently on one spot. . . .
>
> When the sun had completely emerged from the fog, and was glittering and dazzling brilliance over the fields and the mist (as though he had been waiting for that to begin the battle), he took his glove off his handsome white hand, made a signal with it to his marshals, and gave orders for the battle to begin. (From *War and Peace*)

Given the emotional power of leadership, it is no surprise that social scientists have devoted massive amounts of time and resources to studying it. Researchers have looked at leadership in almost every conceivable setting, from army squads to executives; they have examined personality traits, leadership styles, situational contingencies, and a multitude of other topics pertinent to leadership. With leadership studies appearing at a rate of more than 170 a year,[1] it seems reasonable to ask what we know about this elusive topic.

SKIPPING THROUGH A MINEFIELD

At a recent conference on the "frontiers" of leadership research, the concluding speaker made the following comment:

> The heresy I propose is that the concept of leadership itself has outlived its usefulness. Thus I suggest we abandon it in favor of some other more fruitful way of cutting up the theoretical pie. (Miner, 1975, p. 5)

After over forty years of empirical investigation, leadership remains an enigma. In 1959, Warren Bennis suggested reasons for this state of affairs, and over twenty years later his points still seem valid.

First, the term "leadership" has never been clearly defined. Ralph Stogdill, in a mammoth review of the leadership research, pointed out that "there are almost as many different definitions of leadership as there are persons who have attempted to define the concept" (1974, p. 7). Perhaps the closest thing to a consensus on a definition for leadership is that it is a social-influence process. Since most interactions involve social influence, such categorizations of leadership have not helped much.

The lack of a generally agreed upon definition of the central concept has led to a proliferation of terms to deal with leadership phenomena. The last fifteen years have seen the appearance of at least four different "contingency" models, as well as path-goal and open system models, not to mention transactional and vertical dyad approaches, normative and integrative models, four-factor and behavioral theories, and attribution explanations.

Second, the "growing mountain" of research data

[1] Based on a search of *Psychological Abstracts*.

A version of this paper was presented at the annual meeting of the British Psychological Society, Occupational Psychology Section, Keefe, Staffordshire, England, January 1976. Copyrighted by Morsau W. McCall, Jr. Used with permission.

has produced an impressive mass of contradictions. The dimensions of the mountain were suggested by Stogdill's (1974) review of the leadership literature which covered over 3,000 studies. While numerous models, theories, and approaches exist, the accumulated research has not yet produced a unified and generally accepted paradigm for research on the topic, much less a clear understanding of the phenomenon. In fact, Warren Bennis's summary is even more accurate today:

> Of all the hazy and confounding areas in social psychology, leadership theory undoubtedly contends for top nomination. And, ironically, probably more has been written and less known about leadership than about any other topic in the behavioral sciences. (1959)

Naturally enough, much of the early work on leadership attempted to isolate the characteristics of people, distinguishing leaders from nonleaders, or successful from unsuccessful leaders. Almost every conceivable trait and characteristic, from activity to weight, have been examined, but the results have been equivocal. The initial hope that leaders shared common characteristics across situations has not been borne out, and it now appears that personal characteristics are related to leadership outcomes only in the context of specific situations (Gibb, 1969; Campbell, Dunnette, Lawler, & Weick, 1970). Unfortunately, it is not yet clear which aspects of the situation are most critical.

Another major approach to leadership involves the "style" a leader uses in dealing with subordinates. Many different labels have been generated to describe essentially two styles of leadership (the number of "styles" ranges from two to five): (1) task oriented and (2) person (consideration) oriented. While initially intended to reflect the *behavior* of leaders, styles are most commonly measured by one of several paper-and-pencil questionnaires; thus, they represent self- or others' reported perceptions rather than actual behavior.

The human-relations school at first contended that leaders should emphasize considerate, participative styles. Consideration of employees' feelings and allowing employees' participation in decision making would result in increased satisfaction which, it was thought, would improve performance. While considerate behavior by leaders did generally lead to increased satisfaction, satisfaction did not necessarily lead to improved performance. Equivocal and sometimes negative results (Stogdill, 1974) indicated that this normative approach was not the answer in all situations.

Other researchers (e.g., Blake & Mouton, 1964) argued that an effective leader must be high on structuring *and* high on consideration. Again, the data did not clearly conform to the normative prescriptions (e.g., Larson, Hunt, & Osborn, 1975). Further refinements aimed at isolating the specific situations in which certain styles are effective (e.g., Vroom & Yetton, 1973) have replaced the earlier, simpler models, but as yet no adequate taxonomy of situational components exists. In fact, recent theorizing suggests that leader style says more about follower attributions than it does about leaders (Calder, 1977; Pfeffer, 1978).

Data do exist, however, which indicate that leaders change their behavior in response to situational conditions (Hill & Hughes, 1974) and to subordinates' behaviors (Lowin & Craig, 1968; Farris & Lim, 1969; Greene, 1975). Leaders are not perceived by subordinates as having "one style" (Hill, 1973), nor do they treat all subordinates the same way (Graen & Cashman, 1975). Thus, the search for invariant truth—the one-best-way approach—may not hold answers, even when the model includes situational moderators. Leaders may have numerous behaviors to choose from (not two or three) and may face a wide variety of different situations. A number of leadership behaviors may be equally effective in the same situation. As researchers include task structures, power, hierarchical level, subordinate expectations, and other organizational characteristics in their models, predictive power and model complexity increase. But only one thing is clear—no one leadership style is effective in all situations.

Thus early work made an important contribution to understanding leadership. It showed that neither personal characteristics nor styles of leadership behavior could predict leadership effectiveness across situations. More importantly, these findings steered researchers toward identifying the characteristics of situations which might interact with personality or style dimensions to generate positive outcomes.

Most of the current theories have retained the basic ingredients of the earlier models while adding situational contingencies. Although the specific variables included vary, the basic contingency approach is illustrated in Table 45-1.

The relationships studied in contingency frameworks still reflect leadership's research origins in individual and group psychology. The focal unit is the leader and a group of followers. The outcomes (dependent variable) generally represent an index of the performance or satisfaction of the follower group, and the independent variables are still characteristics or "behaviors" of the leader. The relationships between the leader and group outcomes are contingent on some aspect of the situation.

Fiedler's (1967) contingency theory has been a focus for many current researchers and provides a good example of the contingency approach. Fiedler postulated that the effectiveness of a group depends on the leader's motivational orientation (person versus task) and on the nature of the situation (determined by the structuredness of the task, the position of power of the leader, and the quality of leader-member relations). The elaborate model contains a continuum of situational favorableness (from highly favorable to highly unfavorable) and postulates that task-motivated leaders are effective in both highly favorable and unfavorable situations, while person-motivated leaders are effective in the moderate situations.

The path-goal model (Evans, 1970; House, 1971) provides another example of the contingency approach. Built on an expectancy-theory framework, the path-goal model argues that a leader's style (task or person orientation) is effective when it clarifies linkages between subordinate effort and valued outcomes. Thus, leaders' behavior has contingent effects on group outcomes depending upon the presence or absence of performance-outcome linkages.

In spite of their logical appeal, the contingency models have still yielded contradictory research results. As Korman (1974) has pointed out, the contingency approach "has been a great leap forward in the complexity and sophistication of theoretical formulations and the range of variables which have come under consideration," but he adds, "There has also been a neglect of some basic considerations." Included in such considerations are issues of measurement, the continued focus on personality constructs, a static rather than dynamic view of leadership processes, and a failure to extend situational factors beyond those relevant to the immediate work group.

In the long run, the test of leadership theory is its utility for those individuals who find themselves in leadership roles. The bulk of current research has made some contribution by sensitizing practitioners to the differences among leadership styles and, in general, to the complexity of the leadership process. But researchers are still a long way from an integrated understanding of leadership processes, and equally far from providing organizational leaders with integrated and validated models of leadership.

Relative to the bulk of research on styles, characteristics, and contingencies, a small number of studies have examined what organizational leaders actually do (McCall, Morrison, & Hannan, 1978). Many researchers dismiss the results of such studies because, it is argued, leadership and management (or headship) are different things. Unfortunately, the lack of consensus about the meaning of "leadership" makes it difficult to find leaders and follow them around. People who occupy leadership roles in organizations (foremen, managers, executives), however, can be identified and studied. The results of such efforts have produced some thought-provoking approaches which might clarify some of the confusion in the more traditional leadership literature.

DEMANDS OF THE LEADERSHIP ROLE

No es lo mismo hablar de toros, que estar en el redondel.[2]

[2]This is an old Spanish proverb which means, "It is not the same to talk of bulls as to be in the bullring."

Table 45-1 The Basic Model for Contingency Approaches to Leadership

Characteristic of leader (e.g., style, personality)	Characteristic of situation (e.g., group task, members' expectations)	Relationship with group outcome (e.g., performance or satisfaction)
A	X	Positive
A	Y	Negative or unrelated
B	X	Negative or unrelated
B	Y	Positive

Data on the day-to-day activities of those who occupy leadership roles shed some light on (a) the pace of management work, (b) the degree to which the work group itself is a focus of managerial interaction, (c) the kinds of media central to managerial activity, and (d) a global picture of what life is like in the leadership bullring. These, in turn, challenge several assumptions which seemingly underlie leadership theories based on the leader-group paradigm.

The Pace of Managerial Work

Many models of leadership, particularly those advocating participative management or situational determination of an appropriate leadership style, seem to assume that leaders have (a) a relatively small number of events about which style decisions must be made, and (b) enough time to analyze the situation and choose a style.

Two studies of foremen provide an interesting insight into these assumptions. In one study, foremen engaged in an average of 583 activities in a day (Guest, 1955–56); and in another, foremen averaged between 200 and 270 activities per eight-hour day. Other studies of higher level managers confirm the unrelenting pace of managerial work. One study of a Swedish top executive found that he was undisturbed for twenty-three minutes or more only twelve times in thirty-five days (Carlson, 1951). Mintzberg (1973), in a study of five top executives, found that half of their activities lasted nine minutes or less, and only a tenth lasted more than one hour. Mintzberg's observations led him to conclude that a manager's activities are "characterized by brevity, variety, and fragmentation" (1973, p. 31).

The hectic pace of managerial work is exacerbated by the manager's relative lack of control over it. Mintzberg (1975) found, for example, that the managers in his study initiated only 32 percent of their contacts and that 93 percent of the contacts were arranged on an "ad hoc" basis.

The pace of the work has implications for training, research, and practice. Because there are so many activities in a day and because there is so little uninterrupted time, the occupant of a formal leadership role must be, as Mintzberg (1973) calls it, "proficient at superficiality." Training models which advocate "rational" decision strategies (e.g., analyzing each situation to determine the appropriate decision style) make sense, but they are extremely difficult for a manager to implement. Research approaches which ignore the day-to-day process of leading are missing what may be critical dimensions —the crunch of the pace and the breadth of the activities. Finally, managers themselves can be easily overwhelmed. The work is demanding and largely reactive. Activities that require little time and are relatively routine may postpone other activities that are ambiguous and have no routine solution. Thus, larger decisions may be made by default.

Time with the Work Group

The fact that almost all current models of leadership focus on the leader and the immediate work group suggests that the relationship between leader and led is the most important aspect of the leadership process. Translated into what managers do, one might expect that almost all of a manager's time is spent with members of the group.

Dubin's (1962) review indicates that foremen spend between 34 and 60 percent of their *interaction* time with subordinates. Mintzberg's (1973) executives spent only 48 percent of their *contact time* with subordinates, even though the subordinate groups contained most of their respective organizational memberships. Managers, then, spend about a third of their total time and roughly half their contact time with subordinates. About an equal amount of interaction is with nonsubordinates—a group including superiors, peers, professional colleagues, members of other departments and units, and outsiders. Dubin concluded in his review:

> It cannot be too strongly emphasized that horizontal relations among peers in management and the nonformal behavior systems through which such interactions are carried out constitute a dimension of organizational behavior long neglected and probably as important as authority relations. (1962, p. 15)

Surprisingly, managers spend relatively little of their interaction time with their superiors (Brewer & Tomlinson, 1963–64); seldom more than one fifth and usually closer to one tenth (according to Mintzberg, 1973).

The mosaic of available data shows that there is considerable variability in the amount of time a manager spends in contact with subordinates. While it is generally true that interactions with subordinates consume the largest single block of a manager's time, it should not be concluded that leader-subordinate relationships are the only—or even the most important—aspect of the leadership process. In one study of sixty managers, group members accounted for an average of only 23.4 percent of the total number of information sources listed by the leader (McCall, 1974).

More research on leadership needs to focus on the leader-system relationship and how the organizational leader fits into the interaction matrix. Sayles (1964, 1979) and Mintzberg (1973), among others, have emphasized the major importance and complexity of the managers' information network. Unfortunately, empirical investigation of the impact of nonsubordinates' interactions on leadership effectiveness is sorely lacking.

Many leadership development programs also suffer because of narrow leader-follower paradigms. Since there are few data on the impact and nature of other relationships, it is not surprising that few training programs deal with them. One cannot help wondering, though, if we are creating a generation of managers who believe that their style with their immediate subordinates is the only matter of concern.

Managers and Media

Studies of what managers do consistently find that their work is primarily oral. Dubin and Spray (1964), Mintzberg (1973), Brewer and Tomlinson (1963–64), Kurke & Aldrich (1979), and Dubin (1962) all cite evidence emphasizing the high percentage of managerial time spent talking. Much of this talk is directed at exchanging information (Mintzberg, 1973; Horne & Lupton, 1965), and very little of it is spent giving orders or issuing instructions (Horne & Lupton, 1965).

With between 60 and 80 percent of their time spent in oral exchanges, formal leaders cannot spend too much time with written communications (Dubin, 1962). A successful leader, therefore, must have the ability to selectively "hear," retain, and transmit vast quantities of oral information and, perhaps even more difficult, selectively utilize a vast volume of written information provided routinely by the organization.[3] In communicating with others,

the manager would do well to remember that other managers, too, are focusing on the spoken word—things in writing just do not get the time, in general, that is available for an oral communication.

What Leaders Do: An Integration

For formal leaders in organizations, the data indicate that the world consists of many activities (most of them of short duration), frequent interruptions, a large network of contacts extending far beyond the immediate work group, and a preponderance of oral interaction. How do these characteristics fit in with the mythology and empirical work on leadership?

First, notice that these dimensions of leadership represent the day-to-day processes that go on between the leader's "moments of glory." It is easy to latch onto the "Ich bin ein Berliner" and "I have nothing to offer but blood, toil, tears and sweat," thereby ignoring what Kennedy or Churchill did in the daily conduct of their leadership roles. To the extent that we do know what these leaders were like, we owe that knowledge to journalists and not to the empirical leadership literature.[4] Most of the leaders with whom we have direct contact—our bosses, politicians, community figures, and gang leaders—have less grandiose moments of glory, but they too engage in the process of leading. What observational studies have shown us is that the leadership we react to—the inspiration, or lack of it, the autocratic behavior—is only a part of the larger and more complex set of phenomena comprising the role of leader.

Second, leadership models which emphasize the "style" of a leader vis-à-vis the follower group have limited utility, even when they introduce situational contingencies. They have no explanatory power when it comes to nonsubordinate interactions, and it is difficult to understand the relationship between some global measure of a leader's style and the literally hundreds of activities that are part of the daily life of a manager. The concentration on leadership style that pervades all of the mainstream leadership research reminds one of what Omar Bradley once said in a different context: "This strategy would involve us in the wrong war, at the wrong place, at the wrong time, and with the wrong enemy."

Third, the results of observational studies suggest

---

[3]Ackoff (1967) has discussed the problems managers face with one type of written information—that provided by managerial information systems. One of his conclusions is that managers have too much, rather than too little, information.

[4]Vaill (1978) made this point by arguing that the *New Yorker* is the best social science journal.

a host of different variables and questions that might direct future leadership research and which pose challenges for leadership development. The presence of nonauthority relationships and the emphasis on oral communication, coupled with the nonrational way decisions get made (e.g., Cyert & March, 1963; March & Simon, 1958; Katz & Kahn, 1966; Pettigrew, 1973), suggest that a major element of the leadership process is political. While social scientists have advocated the inclusion of political activity in studies of leadership (e.g., Lundberg, 1978, has talked about coalitions, lieutenants, and shadows), little empirical work *in leadership* has confronted these issues directly.

Another approach involves looking systematically at the impact of oral communication on leadership processes and outcomes. Skill in oral communication is measured routinely in some assessment center operations (Bray, Campbell, & Grant, 1974), but it has not received adequate attention as a variable in leadership (except in some small group studies where total talk time has been related to the group's nomination of a leader, e.g., Jaffee & Lucas, 1969). Related to the communication dimension are the cognitive processes wherein individuals in leadership roles somehow retain the information transmitted in oral interactions. Unlike the written word, which automatically creates a record for future reference, the spoken word is easily lost.

More intriguing yet is Mintzberg's notion of proficient superficiality. Plagued by interruptions and activities of short duration, how do leaders synthesize, integrate, and understand the larger picture? Direct observation of behavior can produce a catalog of activities, but it cannot shed much light on the actor's mediation of events. How do all those activities fit together for the leader? One interpretation of the huge number of activities in the manager's day is that each activity represents a different situation. Most current leadership theories would imply that the manager should apply the correct style in each situation and thereby achieve the greatest effectiveness. Another way of looking at the problem is to say that leaders face a near-infinite set of situations and engage in a near-infinite set of behaviors. Many different combinations of behaviors may be effective in a given situation, so there may not be any one best way of responding. If so, the search for invariant truth is an academic exercise and any real understanding of leadership will involve a more holistic approach—one that looks beyond superficial behaviors and simplified taxonomies of situations.

TRAINING AND LEADERSHIP

If our understanding of leadership is less than adequate, then we might predict that training based on that knowledge would produce equivocal research results. Campbell reviewed the empirical literature on training and development and concluded, "In sum, we know a few things but not very much" (1971, p. 593). Stogdill also reviewed the leadership training literature and reached a similar concise conclusion: "It must be concluded that the research on leadership training is generally inadequate in both design and execution. It has failed to address itself to the most crucial problems of leadership" (1974, p. 199).

Most leadership training based on the behavioral-science approach to leadership repeats the mistakes of leadership research: (a) It tends to focus quite narrowly on the relationship between the leader and the group, and specifically on the issue of leadership style. (b) It fails to take into account the nature of managerial work—many activities, fragmentation, variety, nonhierarchical relationships, etc. (c) When situational considerations are including in training, they tend to be limited to the situation of the immediate work group (e.g., the task of the group or the nature of the immediate problem).

It may be useful for leaders to develop a knowledge of leadership styles and a sensitivity to their contingent application, but applying such learning on the job is a different matter. Instead of teaching content. leadership training courses might better focus on creating situations reflecting the daily demands of the leadership role, and, through the use of extensive feedback, allow the trainees to study their performances and their impact. While the value of simulations for research and training purposes has been articulated for some time (e.g., Weick, 1965), few *organizational* simulations have been designed and utilized.[5]

One result of the hectic pace of managerial work is that managers seldom have time to reflect on their behavior. On-the-job feedback is likely to be fragmented, badly timed, vague, or even entirely lack-

[5]One review of the literature turned up only two organizational simulations used for leadership assessment (Omstead et al., 1973).

ing. One valuable outcome of a training experience is that it can provide the time for reflection on the process of being a leader. To maximize this potential, the training must generate behaviors approximating those of the organizational role and must provide valid feedback on what the behaviors were and what their impact was. T-groups are high in generating feedback, but they create a situation with few parallels in the organizational setting. Thus, transfer of learning from the training situation to the job is difficult (Campbell & Dunnette, 1968). Simulations, too, can only be approximations of reality, but we do know enough about the context of managerial work to create reasonable approximations.

TAKING PROCESS SERIOUSLY

In 1970, Campbell et al. depicted the leadership process as a function of the person, the behavior, the outcomes of behavior, environmental influences, and feedback. Advocacy of a "systems" perspective on organizations and the leadership process within them is not new (e.g., Katz & Kahn, 1966; Weick, 1969; Rosen, 1970; Rubin & Goldman, 1968), and the current abundance of contingency models of leadership is a sign that researchers are moving more in that direction. Still, a number of current trends in leadership research seem to be holding back progress: (1) attempting to categorize a wide range of leadership behaviors into a few simple categories (e.g., structure and consideration), (b) defining the situation as a few simple categories focused on only the immediate situation (e.g., the task of the group) and the interpersonal relations between leader and led, (c) measuring leadership outcomes solely on the basis of group effectiveness, and (d) emphasizing static rather than dynamic components of the organizational context (i.e., assuming that the situation stays the same over time).

While it is relatively easy to be critical of social science, it is more challenging to offer alternative approaches. Fortunately, there are alternatives for looking at leadership.

First, Mintzberg (1973) has shown that the classification of leaders' behaviors can be extended beyond the two basic styles of structure and consideration. Drawing on his observations of managerial work, he generated ten basic roles which he argued are typical of most managerial jobs. Only one, what he calls "leader," focuses exclusively on the leader-subordinate interaction, while the other nine encompass such activities as monitoring and disseminating information, acting as a figurehead, negotiating, handling disturbances, etc. Mintzberg's work is only a beginning, but breaking the set of leadership styles—and moving toward a more representative sampling of the behaviors involved in leadership—heralds a productive advance in research and training.

Second, the introduction of environmental (as opposed to situational) variables into the leadership context has yielded some interesting results. Pfeffer (1978), for example, has argued that leadership doesn't matter as much as we think it does. Reviewing a number of studies which examined the impact of such things as budgets, economic conditions, changes in top executive positions, and role-set expectations, he found that these and similar factors frequently override the effects of leadership on organizational outcomes.

To date, most leadership theories make the implicit assumption that the leader has a great deal of unilateral control: if the leader only used the appropriate style, the group would be more productive; if the leader understood group processes, the group would be more cohesive, creative, and effective. Understanding how nonleader variables influence such outcomes would help both researchers and leaders by providing a more realistic perspective on just what the leader can and cannot hope to achieve.

Third, the measure of a leader's effectiveness is not and cannot be a simple index of group productivity or satisfaction. While group-level variables are important, there are too many factors mitigating the effects of the leader's behavior on work-group outcomes; and there are many leadership roles for which the "work group" cannot be identified precisely (for example, the role of senator) or for which group output is heavily determined by some factor such as technology (for example, on the assembly line). At a minimum, both researchers and practitioners must realize that leadership effectiveness involves a number of areas of functioning—including how well the leader deals with nonsubordinate relationships, how structures are designed and modified, development of human resources in the organization, utilization and dissemination of knowledge, creating and coping with change, and actual task performance by the leader. The point is that simplified criteria are misleading, and breaking the rut of current leadership research will require increasing emphasis on the development of realistic performance measures.

Fourth, in most leadership research (and training) the situation is treated as a given. The technology is this, the climate is that, the task is something else. In reality, these and other components of a system are constantly changing. New machinery, new policies, new people are always entering systems (though the rate of change may vary), and the degree to which organizational components are interdependent is itself a variable (Weick, 1974). Leaders, then, do not simply face a number of different situations, but the situations themselves are changing. Part of the leadership process is clearly the leader's attempt to map the organizational dynamics which influence his or her functioning in the leadership role. Another component is how leaders influence the dynamics of their organizational environments by using, modifying, and implementing structure.

SOME CONCLUDING REMARKS

When managers are told that their work is characterized by brevity, variety, fragmentation, a lot of activities, and oral communication, they frequently respond, "You didn't have to tell us that." But these characteristics of managerial work, coupled with the organizational and environmental context within which the work takes place, suggest some new ways of focusing on leadership processes.

First, it is a mistake for leaders or researchers to assume that "the situation" is composed of a small number of fixed parts. The organization, and its environment, are dynamic. An act of Congress, a new invention, or a new corporate president may change all existing cause and effect relationships overnight. Effective leadership behavior must involve flexibility in thinking about the givens of organizational life. Fire-fighting is the bane of many a manager's existence, but the ability of a leader to negotiate successfully through a constant barrage of changes and incongruities is an important component of the leadership process.

Second, it is a mistake to assume that a leadership role, even with its trappings of authority, implies unilateral control by the leader. Organizational rewards and structures, as well as external forces, limit both the leader's and the group's flexibility. Another important component of leadership, then, is how the role occupants create, modify, work around, or ignore the structures imposed on them and their followers. Kerr (1975) has provided numerous examples of how organizations (and the leaders in them) hope for one behavior and get another by inadvertently rewarding the wrong things. DeVries (1978) has shown that relatively simple structures used by a teacher can facilitate classroom learning. These two examples indicate that leaders can succeed not just because of personal charisma or social influence, but because of a sensitivity to, and awareness of, organizational structures and reward systems.

Third, much of human learning is dependent on the receipt of valid and timely feedback on the results of behavior. With all its variety and fragmentation, managerial work provides inadequate feedback—and sometimes none at all. Occupants of leadership roles carry a double burden because they must not only assure themselves of adequate feedback, but also must facilitate feedback to their subordinates (and to other units or individuals working with the unit). Since much of managerial communication is oral, the job of obtaining and transmitting feedback requires substantial effort. No individual in a leadership role can hope to take full responsibility for providing feedback for all who need it. While the personal element cannot be ignored, the leader's use of structural (e.g., designing tasks to provide feedback or *using* an appraisal system to generate valid data) and reward (e.g., basing part of promotion or salary on feedback generation) systems may be a critical component.

Fourth, political activity—in the sense of developing and maintaining a network of contacts throughout the organization and its environment (Mintzberg, 1973)—is a real part of managerial work. Research has not revealed much about how these networks are created and used, but most people in leadership roles know how important contacts can be. Many of the contacts are in nonauthority relationships with the leader, and this may be the arena where the critical social and political influence aspects of leadership are played out (Pettigrew, 1973).

Certainly, leadership research and theory should begin including this dimension, and practitioners might look at some of their problems in "getting things done" in light of their own interconnectedness with key people in the organization.

The four areas outlined above by no means cover all of the possibilities for expanding thinking about leadership processes. They do reflect some areas which have received insufficient attention in leadership research and training. In sum, the focus on leader-group interactions has yielded some useful information, but much remains to be learned about the leadership processes going on outside of the immediate work setting. By learning more about what leaders actually do, researchers can expose themselves to numerous activities not considered by most traditional approaches to the topic. It is in the day-to-day activities of leaders that the situational-organizational context of leadership is sharply reflected.

Peter Vaill, (1978), has defined an art as "the attempt to wrest more coherence and meaning out of more reality than we ordinarily try to deal with." In this context, he has described management as a performing art (1974). The analogy of leaders as artists is potent because effective leaders orchestrate a complex series of processes, events, and systems. Understanding bits and pieces—using a stop-frame on Nureyev—can never capture the whole. Perhaps neither researchers nor practitioners will ever understand the particular magic that makes the legends of leadership. To the extent that constant practice makes the artist more than he or she might have been, expanding our knowledge of the complex processes involved in leadership may, one day, provide part of that magic formula for success.

REFERENCES

Ackoff, R. L. Management misinformation systems. *Management Science*, 1967, **14**, B147–B156.

Bennis, W. G. Leadership theory and administrative behavior: The problem of authority. *Administrative Science Quarterly*, 1959, **4**, 259–301.

Blake, R. R., & Mouton, J. S. *The managerial grid*. Houston: Gulf, 1964.

Bray, D. W., Campbell, R. J., & Grant, D. L. *Formative years in business*. New York: Wiley, 1974.

Brewer, E., & Tomlinson, J. W. C. The manager's working day. *Journal of Industrial Economics*, 1963–64, **12**, 191–197.

Calder, B. J. An attribution theory of leadership. In B. M. Staw & G. R. Salancik (Eds.), *New directions in organizational behavior*. Chicago: St. Clair Press, 1977.

Campbell, J. P. Personnel training and development. In P. Mussen & M. Rosenzweig (Eds.), *Annual Review of Psychology*, 1971, **22**, 565–602.

———, & Dunnette, M. D. Effectiveness of T-group experiences in managerial training and development. *Psychological Bulletin*, 1968, **70**, 73–104.

———, Dunnette, M. D., Lawler, E. E., III, & Weick, K. E., Jr. *Managerial behavior, performance, and effectiveness*. New York: McGraw-Hill, 1970.

Carlson, S. *Executive behaviour*. Stockholm: Strombergs, 1951.

Cyert, R. M., & March, J. G. *A behavioral theory of the firm*. Englewood Cliffs, N.J.: Prentice-Hall, 1963.

De Vries, D. L., & Slavin, R. E. Teams-Games-Tournaments (TGT): Review of ten classroom experiments. *Journal of Research and Development in Education*, 1978, **12**, 28–38.

Dubin, R. Business behavior behaviorally viewed. In G. B. Strother (Ed.), *Social science approaches to business behavior*. Homewood, Ill.: Dorsey, 1962.

———, & Spray, S. L. Executive behavior and interaction. *Industrial Relations*, 1964, **3**(2), 99–108.

Evans, M. The effects of supervisory behavior on the path-goal relationship. *Organizational Behavior and Human Performance*, 1970, **5**, 277–298.

Farris, G. F., & Lim, F., Jr. Effects of performance on leadership, cohesiveness, influence, satisfaction, and subsequent performance. *Journal of Applied Psychology*, 1969, **53**, 490–497.

Fiedler, F. E. *A theory of leadership effectiveness*. New York: McGraw-Hill, 1967.

Gibb, C. A. Leadership. In G. Lindzey & E. Aronson (Eds.), *The handbook of social psychology*, 2d ed., Vol. 4. Reading, Mass.: Addison-Wesley, 1969.

Graen, G., & Cashman, J. F. A role-making model of leadership in formal organizations: A developmental approach. In J. G. Hunt & L. L. Larson (Eds.), *Leadership frontiers*. Kent, Ohio: Kent State University Press, Comparative Administration Research Institute, 1976.

Greene, C. N. The reciprocal nature of influence between leader and subordinate. *Journal of Applied Psychology*, 1975, **60**, 187–193.

Guest, R. H. Of time and the foreman. *Personnel*, 1955–56, **32**, 478–486.

Hill, W. Leadership style: Rigid or flexible. *Organizational Behavior and Human Performance*, 1973, **9**, 35–47.

———, & Hughes, D. Variations in leader behavior as a

READING 4

SUBSTITUTES FOR LEADERSHIP: SOME IMPLICATIONS FOR ORGANIZATION DESIGN

by

Steven Kerr

Reading 50

Substitutes for Leadership: Some Implications for Organizational Design
Steven Kerr

The design of tasks, jobs, and organizations—which began so long ago with Durkheim, Smith, Weber, and Taylor (or was it with Cyrus in 400 B.C.?)—has now come full circle. The early concern was with tasks which *all men* could perform in the "one best way" and with organizational forms which might protect us from our own vices and limitations. Consistent with the engineering and mass-production manufacturing backgrounds of so many of its apostles, classical management considered individual worker differences primarily as something to be overcome. It was hoped that, with careful attention to detail, impersonality could be achieved, and our organizations made to operate efficiently. During this phase selection techniques were emphasized, although training was conducted to accomplish standardization.

Soon afterward we heard from the humanists, who were not at all reluctant to acquaint us with *their* orientations and value systems. We were informed that our methods were inhuman and our results dehumanizing, and that we ought to be more concerned with worker health and morale, and less obsessed with efficiency. Even those in the movement who were of good business background sought to persuade us that it was not only nice to be nice, but profitable as well, that we could (in Tom Lehrer's words) "do well by doing good." The emphasis then was not on job but on people design, i.e., training, the object of which was not to eliminate but to accentuate people's differences. Now we would develop people's potentialities, help them to "find" themselves, and prepare them for the psychological as well as physiological demands of the workplace.

In the most recent phase, now in vogue, if the worker cannot be so prepared, the workplace simply must adjust to him. Some small part of this adjustment has taken the form of job enrichment programs for low-level workers; however, the primary thrust has been the rearrangement of ground-rules, tasks, and reporting relationships so as to provide

From *Organization and Administrative Sciences*, **8**, 135–146.

managerial-level employees the challenge, freedom, recognition, and responsibility required for self-actualization. Many job enrichment programs are of this nature, for example, and so are most approaches to management by objectives. Once again the emphasis is on task, job, and organizational design, but now the value orientation of the engineer has been replaced by that of the behavioral scientist.

The phases described above are pertinent to organization theory in general but have their counterpart in leadership theory and practice. Research on leadership was guided mainly by trait theories until the late 1940s and was accompanied by great interest in selection techniques. Behavioral leadership theories came into prominence in the 1950s and generated considerable interest in training methods since leader behaviors, unlike traits, are amenable to change through training. Currently the emphasis is on situational (contingency) approaches to leadership, which are attractive to the practicing manager because they increase his options. Certainly he may still attempt selection or training, and all presently popular situational theories permit him to do so. In addition, however, he may elect to change the situation—that is, in Fiedler's terms the job may be engineered to fit the hierarchical superior. When we consider the lackluster records compiled by most available selection and training techniques, this is no small incremental benefit.

The problem though, is that current approaches to leadership and organizational design are as enmeshed in their promoters' beliefs and value systems, and are as influenced by the selective perceptions of those who espouse them, as were the earlier ones. The internal consistency which is an attractive feature of many (though by no means all) of our theories and models is often achieved at the expense of external validity, and many prescriptions and principles which permeate the organizational design and leadership literature may, therefore, be said to contradict a considerable body of existing data.

This paper seeks to identify and re-evaluate some of these principles in the light of existing research evidence and to make recommendations for organizational design consistent with leadership research, and with what is generally known about organizations and about people. The framework within which this re-evaluation is attempted can best be understood in terms of the concept of "substitutes for leadership."

HIERARCHICAL LEADERSHIP

A number of theories and models of leadership presently exist, each seeking to most clearly identify and best explain the supposedly powerful effects of hierarchical leadership upon the satisfaction, morale, and performance of subordinates. While failing to agree in many important respects, almost all modern leadership theories and models assume that no leadership trait or behavioral style exists strong enough to be effective in all situations. The focus of present-day theory and research is, therefore, primarily upon identification and analysis of *situational contingencies* under which different leader characteristics contribute toward improved subordinate performance and satisfaction. For example:

Path-goal theory asserts that leader behavior will be acceptable to subordinates to the extent that subordinates see such behavior as either an immediate source of satisfaction or as instrumental to future satisfaction. . . . A second characteristic of subordinates on which the effects of leader behavior are contingent is subordinates' perception of their own ability with respect to their assigned tasks. The higher the degree of perceived

ability relative to task demands, the less the subordinate will view leader directiveness and coaching behavior as acceptable. . . . The theory [also] asserts that effects of the leader's behavior on the psychological states of subordinates are contingent on other parts of the subordinates' environment . . . (House and Mitchell, 1974).

Based upon a comprehensive review, Kerr et al. (1974), summarized the voluminous literature on leader consideration (leader-subordinate relations which feature mutual trust and respect for subordinates' ideas and feelings) and initiating structure (structuring by the leader of his or her own role and subordinates' roles toward goal attainment—Fleishman and Peters, 1962). Kerr et al. also put forth ten propositions which were consistent with, and in many cases similar to, hypotheses described in House's (1971) path-goal theory. These propositions are summarized in Table 50-1.

SUBSTITUTES FOR HIERARCHICAL LEADERSHIP

Present-day theories and models of leadership share another important assumption—that hierarchical leadership is always important. Even those models most concerned with situational contingencies assume that while the style of leadership most likely to be effective will vary with the situation, *some* leadership style will be effective regardless of the situation. Of course, the extent to which this assumption is explicated varies greatly: for example, the vertical dyad linkage model developed by Graen and his associates (cf. Graen et al., 1972) is fairly explicit in

Table 50-1 Situational Propositions From the Consideration—Initiating Structure Literature

1. The greater the pressure, the greater will be subordinate tolerance of leader initiating structure, and the greater will be the positive relationships between structure and satisfaction and performance criteria.

2. The greater the intrinsic satisfaction from the task, the less positive will bé relationships between consideration and satisfaction and performance criteria, the less negative will be relationships between structure and subordinate satisfaction, and the less positive will be relationships between structure and performance.

3. The smaller the informational needs of subordinates, the lower will be their tolerance for leader initiating structure, and the less positive will be relationships between structure and satisfaction criteria.

4. The greater the task certainty, the greater will be the positive relationships between leader consideration and subordinate satisfaction.

5. The less the agreement between subordinate expectations of leader consideration and structure and their observations of these behaviors, the lower will be the levels of subordinate satisfaction and performance.

6. The less higher management is perceived by subordinates to exhibit consideration, the lower will be the positive relationships between lower-level supervisors' consideration and subordinate satisfaction.

7. The greater the perceived organizational independence of subordinates, the greater will be the positive relationships between leader behavior and subordinate satisfaction and performance criteria.

8. The greater the perceived upward influence of the leader, the greater will be the positive relationships between consideration and subordinate satisfaction.

Note: adapted from Kerr, et al., 1974:73–74.

its attribution of importance to hierarchical leadership without concern for the situation, while House's path-goal theory is considerably less so. Path-goal theory does, however, predict that even unnecessary and redundant leader behaviors will affect subordinate satisfaction, morale, motivation, performance, and acceptance of the leader (House and Mitchell, 1974; House and Dessler, 1974). While leader attempts to clarify paths and goals are therefore recognized by path-goal theory to be unnecessary and redundant in certain situations, in no situation are they explicitly hypothesized by path-goal (or any other leadership theory) to be irrelevant.

This lack of recognition is unfortunate. As has been pointed out by Woodward (1973:66):

In the earliest and simplest kinds of work organization and control, the subordinate has tasks allocated to him by his superior, is accountable to him for end results, and refers back to him problems which he cannot solve. The spheres of influence and authority and the size of the area of discretion become larger as the individual moves up the hierarchical pyramid. This concept of a pyramid of authority and influence is so much a part of both management ideology and sociological conceptualization, that it is almost impossible to think about management control in any other way. . . . This picture of control, however, is an over-simplified one.

As Woodward suggests, we must abandon the over-simplified picture that control is exercised almost exclusively through the personal hierarchy of the organization's structure. Once we do, we are forced to recognize that many individual, task, and organizational characteristics have the capacity to act as "substitutes for hierarchical leadership," in that they often serve to neutralize or substitute for the formal leader's ability to influence work group satisfaction and performance for either better or worse. Such substitutes for leadership are apparently prominent in a wide variety of modern organizational settings and may help to account for the fact that data from many studies suggest that in some situations hierarchical leadership per se does not seem to matter.

What is clearly needed is a taxonomy of situations where we should probably not be studying "leadership" (in the formal sense) at all. Development of such a taxonomy is still at an early stage, but Woodward (1973) and Miner (1975) have laid important groundwork by providing classifications of systems of control, and some research into the effects of nonleader sources of clarity has been conducted by Hunt (1975) and Hunt and Osborne (1975). In addition, the previously cited reviews of the leadership literature by House and Mitchell (1974) and Kerr et al. (1974) suggest that characteristics such as those in Table 50-2 will help to determine whether or not hierarchical leadership is likely to make an important difference.

The leadership substitutes construct has potential importance not only for the study of leadership, but also for organizational design and development. If the existence of substitutes for hierarchical leader-

Table 50-2 Potential Substitutes for Hierarchical Leadership

Subordinate	Task	Organization
Ability	Repetitiveness and unambiguity	Formalization
Experience	Methodological invariance	Inflexibility
Training	Intrinsic satisfaction	Highly-specified, active advisory and staff functions
Knowledge	Task-provided feedback concerning accomplishment	
"Professional" orientation		Closely-knit, cohesive work groups
Need for independence		Rewards not within the leader's control
Indifference toward organizational rewards		Spatial distance between leader and subordinates

ship is ignored, then efforts at leadership training, organizational development, and task design may well result in ineffectiveness for the organization and frustration for its members, as they come to realize that inflexible policies, invariant work methodologies, or other barriers mentioned in Table 50-2 are interfering with intended changes and preventing desired benefits.

LEADER BEHAVIORS AS CAUSE AND EFFECT

It is now evident from a variety of field and laboratory studies (e.g., Lowin and Craig, 1968; Lowin et al., 1969; Greene, 1973) that leader behavior may result from as well as cause subordinate attitudes and performance. In some studies reciprocal causality has been found to exist to such an extent that determination of any primary thrust was impossible. Other investigations have concluded that causation was primarily in one direction (in some studies from leader behaviors to subordinate outcomes, in other the reverse). Even in these instances, however, chain reactions were apparently formed which affected both predictors and criteria in subsequent time periods.

In retrospect, it is not surprising that leader behaviors and subordinate attitudes and activities have been found to exert reciprocal influence. What is surprising is that so many prescriptions, both for leadership and for organizational design, continue to be founded upon outmoded and over-simplified notions of one-way causation. Numerous design and developmental efforts have been undertaken as though we knew for a fact that broad delegation of authority, task design (e.g., MBO and job enrichment), and supervisory training in PERT-CPM (structure) and human relations (consideration) logically precede and consistently result in high member satisfaction and work group performance. It has also often been assumed that this would be the case regardless of the situation, i.e., irrespective of whether substitutes for leadership exist.

However unsubstantiated, this assumption underlies many currently popular approaches to training and organizational design. When initiated without adequate attention being paid to the probable direction of causation, such approaches may prove costly and irrelevant. For example, it is well established that a strong positive relationship exists between leader consideration egalitarianism and subordinate

satisfaction. It might, therefore, seem logical to undertake job design or management training such that low-level subordinates are provided greater opportunities to participate in the planning process, thereby enhancing their satisfaction. Let us assume, however, that important substitutes for leadership exist, in the form of highly formalized policies and objectives and highly invariant work methodologies. As has already been mentioned, the effect of such factors should be to reduce sharply the extent to which the (newly) egalitarian leader can implement his changed behaviors or attitudes. On the other hand, there seems no reason why leadership substitutes should prevent changes in leader behaviors and attitudes which *result* from different levels of subordinate satisfaction. Under such circumstances it is most likely that either no important changes at all would result, or that subordinate satisfaction might change due to circumstances unrelated to the design or training program, and leader egalitarianism might then change in the same direction.

EGALITARIANISM AMONG HIERARCHICAL UNEQUALS

Many leadership training programs, and several major approaches to job redesign (for example, management by objectives), depend for their internal consistency upon the assumption that egalitarianism is possible among employees who are at different levels of the organizational hierarchy. It is claimed of one participative system, for example, that even that most sensitive of interactions, the formal appraisal interview between superior and subordinate, can be "strictly man-to-man in character. . . . In listening to the subordinate's review of performance, problems, and failings, the manager is automatically cast in the role of counselor. This role for the manager, in turn, results naturally in a problem-solving discussion" (Meyer et al., 1965:129).

There are probably many situations where substitutes for leadership are strong or numerous enough to neutralize the usual inequality of superior-subordinate authority. It is possible, for example, that where subordinates possess unique and critical job knowledge, or are indifferent toward rewards within the leader's control, the kind of relationship described by Meyer et al. may be attained. In general, however, the research literature (cf., Blau and Scott, 1962) clearly suggests that hierarchical inequalities produce very predictable effects upon interaction patterns, subordinate anxiety and defensiveness, and quality and quantity of communications, and that these effects seriously interfere with "joint" goal-setting, problem-solving, etc., by unequals. Bennis has succinctly summarized some of these difficulties:

> Two factors seem to be involved. . . . The superior as a helper, trainer, consultant, and coordinator, and the superior as an instrument and arm of reality, a man with power over the subordinate. . . . For each actor in the relationship, a *double reference* is needed. . . . The double reference approach requires a degree of maturity, more precisely a commitment to maturity, on the part of both the superior and subordinate that exceeds that of any other organizational approach. . . . It is suggestive that psychiatric patients find it most difficult to see the psychiatrist both as a human being and helper and an individual with certain perceived powers. The same difficulty exists in the superior-subordinate relationship (1960:285–287).

As a general rule, then, it may be said that leader training and organizational design programs which depend for their success upon democracy and egalitarianism among hierarchical unequals are unlikely to be successful. This will tend to be true unless such programs are able simultaneously to increase the strength and number of available substitutes for leadership and by so doing minimize the leader's dominant position. One method for accomplishing this is to increase the work group's ability to serve as a substitute and formalize its function in that regard. For example, it has been recommended by several MNO theorists that subordinates meet and set objectives with their superior *as a group*, since "status differentials are likely to be less important, freeing individuals of the need to be cautious and deferential. . . . Successful negotiation with the boss should be easier, since group support would tend to offset the boss's higher rank" (Kerr, 1976:17).

STABILITY OF LEADER BEHAVIORS

As already mentioned, the emphasis today in leadership theory and research is upon situational approaches, which supposedly increase the alternatives available to the practicing manager by encouraging adjustments to job content, reporting requirements, task structure, etc., so as to provide a better fit between the leader's behavioral style and his work situation. Fiedler (1967), Chemers and Rice (1974), and others have suggested situational change as a workable alternative to traditional selection and training techniques.

This approach to leader effectiveness and job design depends, however, upon the assumption that while task demands and the working environments of leaders are amenable to conscious and systematic manipulation, such manipulation will not simultaneously alter their behavioral patterns and leadership styles. This approach further assumes that the leader's behavioral style will not change easily by itself, i.e., without conscious and systematic manipulation. Only by accepting such assumptions can we remain untroubled by Chemers and Rice's reminder that the Fiedler Contingency Model "makes its predictions on the basis of a static LPC store" (1974:114) and acquiescent toward Fiedler's (1973) argument that leadership training and experience will typically change the leader's situation, but not his LPC score.

Such assumptions and arguments are inconsistent, however, with a growing and increasingly-convincing body of research which shows leader behavior and personality measures to be quite unstable over time and across situations. Leader LPC scores, for example, have often been found to change dramatically over relatively short periods of time, whether or not accompanied by planned change (cf., Stinson and Tracy, 1973; Farris, 1975). Similar changes in leader behavior patterns after training (as evidenced by test-retest correlations of .54 and .49 for LOQ consideration and structure, and .27 and .22 for SBDQ consideration and structure) have also been observed (Fleishman et al., 1955; Harris and Fleishman, 1955, respectively).

Only by disregarding such accumulating evidence are proponents of situational engineering able to seriously recommend the redesign of jobs and work environments so as to better "fit" the manager. More careful attention to existing data would probably lead to the less decisive but more accurate conclusion that planned change may under different conditions affect leader behavior, the working environment, both, or neither. Certainly there will be instances where training will result in an altered work situation, while leaving unchanged the leader's personality and behavioral style. On other occasions, however, particularly when strong substitutes for leadership exist, leadership training or experience may succeed in changing the leader but not the situation, as characteristics of the organization, tasks, or subordinates prevent the "changed" leader from influencing his or her environment.

While organizational and task design may, therefore, be highly appropriate in some cases to improve the fit between the leader and his or her work situation, such efforts should not be undertaken in situations where the leader's attitudes and behaviors are themselves subject to subsequent change, lest continual redesign be necessary. The accumulating research evidence suggests that Fiedler's (1965) recommendation that we "engineer the job to fit the manager" may be impractical in all but a few special cases.

EFFECTS OF "PROFESSIONAL" NORMS AND STANDARDS

There are several reasons why the working environment of professionals employed in organizations presents special opportunities for leadership substitutes to flourish and hierarchical leadership to be consequently less important. The professional's expertise, normally acquired as a result of specialized training in a body of abstract knowledge, often serves to reduce the need for structuring information; furthermore, a belief in peer review and collegial maintenance of standards often causes the professional to look to fellow professionals rather than to the hierarchical leader for what informational needs remain. Even concerning performance feedback, which was described earlier as typically transmitted from formal superior to subordinates, substitutes for leadership may exist:

> First, professionals may deny that their hierarchical superiors have the skills to determine whether performance standards are being met. From the professional's viewpoint, only fellow professionals know enough about their work to evaluate it competently. Second, professionals may deny that their superior's performance standards are even relevant. Such attributes as knowledge of the specialty, originality of approach, and impact upon the professional community may seem reasonable criteria for performance evaluation to the professional, but may not even be a part of the organiza-

tion's formal evaluation procedure (Filley et al., 1976:385).

Clearly, many of the substitutes for hierarchical leadership mentioned in Table 50-2 (e.g., knowledge, training, group cohesiveness) are pertinent to professionals in organizations. Yet despite the frequent tendency for such substitutes to exist and exert influence in professional settings, leadership research has seldom taken systematic cognizance of this influence. One consequence is that data obtained from professionals in hospitals, R&D laboratories, and other settings often diverge from patterns of data obtained in non-professional work sites.

Perhaps the most important deficiency of research conducted in settings where hierarchical supervision was found to be inconsequential has been the failure of researchers to investigate the kinds, strength, and effects of those substitutes for leadership which exist. In the same vein, designers of tasks and jobs in professional organizations have inadequately attended to matters pertaining to the creation, maintenance, and institutionalization of professional norms and standards. Certainly it is true that such norms and standards are generally derived from formal academic training prior to employment; nonetheless, they tend to be maintained subsequent to employment, if necessary through informal means in organizations which do not provide for them formally. It is, therefore, likely that important advantages would accrue to organizations the tasks, reporting arrangements, and evaluation procedures of which were designed to be supportive of, not antagonistic toward, professional norms and standards.

For example, despite professionals' interest in collegial maintenance of standards, and although research has shown peer ratings to be attractive in many situations as a supplement (even an alternative) to traditional leader-rating systems, very few organizations have designed and made use of peer evaluation processes. This is even the case in professionally oriented settings where substitutes for leadership flourish. Nor are professionals organized so that they are encouraged or required to develop goals and work objectives as a group. This is true despite some evidence that such collegial activities can facilitate communications and help to reduce inequities of power and status.

As noted above, collegial activities and lateral relationships will manifest themselves to some extent in any organization where professionals are employed. If necessary these processes will occur informally, even in opposition to the formal structure. However, "their use can be substantially improved by designing them into the formal organization. At the very least, organizations can be designed so as not to prevent these processes from arising spontaneously, and reward systems can be designed to encourage such processes" (Galbraith, 1973:47; see also Farris, 1971).

SUMMARY

I have suggested that a number of individual, task, and organizational characteristics often act as substitutes for hierarchical leadership, impairing the leader's ability to influence the attitudes and performance of his work group for either better or worse. I have also argued here that the leadership substitutes construct, though important, has been underattended by both leadership theorists and organizational designers, and this lack of attention has been to the detriment of organization theory, research, and practice.

It follows that greater attention needs to be paid to the identification of substitutes for hierarchical leadership, and to the design of authority, control, evaluation, and reward systems which are explicitly cognizant of their existence. Such an approach will require greater imagination and creativity than has been evident in the past and will require us to abandon naive assumptions which have served us poorly (for example, those concerning stable personality measures and one-way causation) in favor of what research evidence is available.

It also follows that we should begin to think seriously about not only the identification, but the systematic *creation,* of substitutes for hierarchical leadership. In particular, to the extent that we value and wish to promote egalitarianism and subordinate participation in organizational planning, control, and goal-setting activities, it may be absolutely essential that we build group MBO, task provided feedback, peer evaluation systems, and other potential substitutes for leadership into our typically autocratic organizations, so as to permit communications among hierarchical unequals to flow more freely and collegial norms to flourish.

REFERENCES

Bennis, Warren G. "Leadership Theory and Administrative Behavior: The Problem of Authority." *Administrative Science Quarterly,* 1960, **4:**259–301.

Blau, Peter M., and W. Richard Scott. *Formal Organizations.* San Francisco, Ca.: Chandler, 1962.

Chemers, Martin M., and Robert W. Rice. "A Theoretical and Empirical Examination of Fiedler's Contingency Model of Leadership Effectiveness." In James G. Hunt and Lars L. Larson (eds.), *Contingency Approaches to Leadership.* Carbondale, Ill.: Southern Illinois University Press, 1974.

Farris, George F. "Organizing Your Informal Organization," *Innovation,* 1971.

———. "Does Performance Affect LPC?" unpublished manuscript, 1975.

Fiedler, Fred E. "Engineer the Job to Fit the Manager." *Harvard Business Review,* 1965, **43:**115–122.

———. *A Theory of Leadership Effectiveness.* New York: McGraw-Hill, 1967.

———. "Predicting the Effects of Leadership Training and Experience From the Contingency Model: A Clarification." *Journal of Applied Psychology,* 1973, **57:**110–13.

Filley, Alan C., Robert J. House, and Steven Kerr. *Managerial Process and Organizational Behavior* (2nd. ed.). Glenview, Ill.: Scott, Foresman, 1976.

Fleishman, Edwin A., E. F. Harris, and Harold E. Burtt. *Leadership and Supervision in Industry.* Columbus: Bureau of Educational Research, The Ohio State University, 1955.

Fleishman, Edwin A., and D. R. Peters. "Interpersonal Values, Leadership Attitudes and Managerial Success." *Personnel Psychology,* 1962, **5:**127–43.

Galbraith, Jay. *Designing Complex Organizations.* Reading, Mass.: Addison-Wesley, 1973.

Graen, George, Fred Dansereau, Jr., and Takao Minami. "Dysfunctional Leadership Styles." *Organizational Behavior and Human Performance,* 1972, **7:**216–36.

Greene, Charles N. "A Longitudinal Analysis of Relationships Among Leader Behavior and Subordinate Performance and Satisfaction." *Academy of Management Proceedings,* 1973, 433–40.

Harris, E. G., and Edwin A. Fleishman. "Human Relations Training and the Stability of Leadership Patterns." *Journal of Applied Psychology,* 1955, **39:**20–25.

House, Robert J. "A Path-Goal Theory of Leader Effectiveness." *Administrative Science Quarterly,* 1971, **16:** 321–38.

House, Robert J., and Gary Dessler. "The Path-Goal Theory of Leadership: Some Post Hoc and A Priori Tests." In James G. Hunt and Lars L. Larson (eds.), *Contingency Approaches to Leadership.* Carbondale: Southern Illinois University Press, 1974.

House, Robert J., and Terence R. Mitchell. "Path-Goal

READING 5

DECISION MAKING BY CONSENSUS

by

J.J. Holder

From: Business Horizons, April 1972, pp. 47-54.
Used by Permission.

JACK J. HOLDER, JR.

DECISION MAKING BY CONSENSUS

The experience at Yellow Freight

Jack J. Holder, Jr. is assistant vice-president/director of management development at Yellow Freight System, Inc.

Decision making by consensus has been practiced at Yellow Freight System, Inc. since the early 1950's. This article, written by an officer of the company, supports the policy and refers to various studies that explain the process. Work groups, which extend from top officers to the dock crews, are important in Yellow Freight's operation. They encourage individual motivation, and, because they incorporate the linking pin function, allow a manager to exert upward influence. The advantages of group decision making by consensus are cited and examples given of the application of this management philosophy at Yellow Freight. If a group fails to reach a consensus, action should be deferred; subsequent events will make the decision easier to reach.

Consensus is defined basically as agreement by all parties involved in some group decision or action; it occurs only after deliberation and discussion of pros and cons of the issues, and when all (not a majority) of the managers are in agreement. Each member of the group must be satisfied as to the ultimate course of action to be taken.

Decision making by consensus has been a common practice at Yellow Freight System, Inc. since the early 1950's, especially among the top management group of the company. The process is not a simple one. Some of the more important variables include the leader, the followers, the organizational structure, communications, leadership styles, motivation of group members, and the group itself. Many additional factors could be listed. This article will attempt to provide academic support for the present company policy of management decision making by consensus. An attempt will be made to cover the necessary supplemental information and studies one must understand in order to fully comprehend the process.

PARTICIPATIVE MANAGEMENT

Likert has reported in detail on his research into participative management, which is basically the process of involving people in decisions that affect them. In one experiment, two groups were established and closely observed. One group was involved in a participative program and the other in a hierarchically controlled program, where the management relied on authority to get the work done.

Although both programs achieved increases in productivity, they yielded significantly different results in other respects. The productivity increases in the hierarchically controlled program were accompanied by shifts in an *adverse* direction in such factors as loyalty, attitudes, interest, and involvement in the work. Just the opposite was true in the participative program. For example, when more general supervision and increased participation were provided, the employee's feeling of responsibility to see that the work got done increased. Observations showed that when the supervisor was away, the employees kept on working. In the hierarchically controlled program, however, the feeling of responsibility decreased and when the supervisor was absent the work tended to stop.[1]

Likert emphasized most of the ingredients involved in decision making by consensus:

[He] has focused on the problem of interdepartmental communications and group relationships; his thesis is that factors promoting internalization of objectives can be realized by involving all subgroups of the organization in group decision making of a task-oriented character. Separate organizational groups with overlapping common members (linking pins) serve to provide vertical and horizontal communications as well as a task orientation toward common organizational goals. The linking pin concept will be covered in detail at a later point in this article. Specific responsibility for decision making is delegated to each organizational group.[2]

Decision making by consensus requires knowledgeable and well-oriented managers as well as a strong leader.

The most effective leaders are those who best meet and fulfill the needs of their organizations. The use of management committees and other necessary integrating mechanisms does not mitigate the need for a strong executive presence. A strong leader will produce a strong organization. Conceptually, the problem has been that power equalization techniques, such as participative management and management teams, have implied that those who use them must abdicate their leadership role.

Operationally, nothing can be further from reality. What is needed is a different team of strong leadership calling for presence rather than prominence. By presence, we mean that state of leadership which permits a manager to achieve a close relationship with his people. He does this by building a climate in which people are free to reach their potential and to grow along with the organization. Two-way communication, participation techniques, and the tools of an "environmental creator" require strong leadership presence, primarily because in a dynamic organization the emphasis is on lack of structure.

In operational matters, the participative approach presupposes that the chief executive cannot run the organization alone, and that those on whom he depends must have free access to information and decisions if they are to personally develop and the organization is to maximize its growth potential.[3]

In addition, the participative program produced more favorable attitudes, a closer relationship between supervisors and employees, greater upwards communications, and greater employee satisfaction with supervisors as their representatives.

Effects on Productivity

Both Likert and Odiorne have commented on the effect of participative management on productivity:

Research findings do not support the conclusion that every organization in which there are high levels of confidence and trust, favorable attitudes, and high levels of job satisfaction will be highly productive. Even though a manager may have built his department into an organization with these qualities his department will not achieve high productivity unless his leadership and the decision-making process used by the organization result in the establishment of high performance goals by the members for themselves. High performance goals as well as favorable attitudes must be present if an organization is to achieve a high degree of productivity.

The conclusion to be reached is that neither tightness of supervision nor looseness is a sole controlling variable, and that participation of itself has no claim to being the core of a new pattern of managing that will guarantee high productivity if universally adopted by managers. There is some evidence, however, that a strong orientation toward goals, coupled with leader enthusiasm, ample rewards for achieving them, and the uniting of people in moving toward them does have a beneficial effect.[4]

Research findings indicate that the general pattern of operations of the highest producing managers tends to differ from that of the managers of mediocre and low-producing units by more often showing certain characteristics. *First*, according to Likert, favorable attitudes tend to prevail on the part of each

1. Rensis Likert, *New Patterns of Management* (New York: McGraw-Hill Book Company, 1971), p. 65.
2. George H. Labovitz, "Organizing for Adaptation: the Case for a Behavioral View," *Business Horizons* (June, 1971), p. 21.
3. George H. Labovitz, "Organizing for Adaptation," p. 25, p. 26.
4. First paragraph from Rensis Likert, *New Patterns*, p. 59; second paragraph from George S. Odiorne, *Management by Objectives* (New York: Pitman Publishing Corp., 1970), p. 145.

member of the organization toward all the other members, toward supervisors, toward the work, toward the organization—toward all aspects of the job. These attitudes reflect a high level of mutual confidence and trust, as well as identification with the organization and its objectives and a high sense of involvement in achieving them.

Second, this highly motivated, cooperative orientation toward the organization and its objectives is achieved by harnessing effectively such major forces as motives related to the ego and security, and economic motives.

Third, the organization consists of a tightly knit, effectively functioning social system. This system is made up of interlocking work groups with a high degree of group loyalty, participation, and communication. *Finally,* the leadership acts habitually to tap the motives that produce cooperative and favorable attitudes, participation, and involvement in decisions.[5]

Management Perceptions

Participative management requires a leader who is interested in listening to ideas and suggestions from others in order to reach the best possible decision. Some guides to help the action-oriented manager determine when to listen to others include:

Listening is cheap. The best rule to guide decision making is that listening won't hurt anybody. Even when the aurally received material goes in one ear and out the other, it doesn't harm anything, and helps the person talking. It always opens the possibility that something useful might be said.

When listening makes the program stronger. There are some decisions that will depend upon support and teamwork for the execution. If listening to others' suggestions adds impetus to the execution and gains acceptance for the final decision, it's worthwhile.

When it wins over hostile forces. One of the best ways of gaining an ally is to ask an enemy for assistance and advice. He'll say things that make him part of the decision as it's finally made and will be identified with it.

When the decision to be made is already decided.

5. Rensis Likert, *New Patterns,* pp. 98-99.

During the Korean War one firm had decided to go into defense work up to 20 per cent of its sales volume. Numerous suggestions were made and arguments given for and against going into defense work for several weeks after the decision was made. . . . 'It didn't hurt us to listen, and we got a lot of our people involved in what was going to happen. . . . they almost all recommended that we do what we were going to do anyhow.'

When the person talking is an expert. At many stages in the decision making process, careful listening to all ideas and especially from people who know some special facet can improve the decision considerably.[6]

Widespread participation is one of the more important approaches employed by the high-producing managers in their efforts to get full benefit from the technical resources and knowledgeability of other managers. Participation also applies to all aspects of the job including decision making in setting goals, controlling costs, organizing the work, personnel changes, and general policy matters.

Manager and Employee Reaction

Research studies show that employees react favorably to experiences that they feel support and contribute to their sense of importance and personal worth. Similarly, persons react unfavorably to experiences that are threatening and decrease or minimize their sense of dignity and personal worth.

With this thought in mind, our management leadership

. . . and other processes of the organization must be such as to insure a maximum probability that in all interactions and all relationships with the organization each member will, in the light of his background, values, and expectations, view the experiences as supportive and one which builds and maintains his sense of personal worth and importance. . . .each member of the organization must feel that the organization's objectives are of significance and that his own particular task contributes in an indispensable manner to the organization's achievement of its objectives. He should see his role as difficult, important and meaningful.[7]

6. George S. Odiorne, *"How People Make Things Happen* (Englewood Cliffs, N.J.: Prentice-Hall, Inc., 1969), pp. 202-203.
7. Rensis Likert, *New Patterns,* p. 103.

Participation in decision making fosters greater commitment on the part of the individual to the company's goals and objectives, as well as to his own goals and objectives.

Commitment is more than participation. It is not unlike a personal bond—a bond between the individual and his own goals, and/or between the individual and the company goals. A definite quid pro quo relationship must exist. Commitment is specifically a personal nature between the individual's own feelings and his attitude or concern for company goals and objectives.

Ideally, the individual goal and the company goal should be the same, or one is achieved by the achievement of the other. Company goals of long run growth and profitability are achieved only on the basis of a number of individual goals and objectives being achieved.[8]

Management By Objectives

The process of management by objectives is basically one whereby

. . . the superior and the subordinate managers of an enterprise jointly, identify its common goals, define each individual's major areas of responsibility in terms of the results expected of him and use these measures as guides for operating the unit and assessing the contribution of each of its members.

We realize that it is not an easy task to integrate the goals and objectives of all individuals with the goals of the organization. Yet it is not an impossible task. An approach to this problem which has been used successfully in some organizations in our culture is a process called management by objectives.[9]

Management by objectives should be employed throughout a company, from the top to the lower management levels. Corporate officers and operations division vice-presidents meet each year to formulate the goals and objectives for Yellow Freight. By the same token, branch managers should meet with their operating and sales supervisors to map out the branch goals in a management by objectives fashion.

8. Jack J. Holder, Jr., "Achieving Goals and Objectives in the Motor Carrier Industry," *Transportation Journal* (Spring, 1971), pp. 51-59.

9. Paul Hersey and Kenneth H. Blanchard, *Management of Organizational Behavior* (Englewood Cliffs, N.J.: Prentice-Hall, Inc., 1969), p. 118.

THE WORK GROUP

The various work groups at Yellow Freight extend from the top company officers to the dock foreman and his crew of dock workers. Our work groups are important to us, and as a result we are highly motivated to behave in ways consistent with the goals and values of the group in order to obtain recognition, support, security, and favorable reactions. We can conclude that "Management will make full use of the potential capacities of its human resources only when each person in an organization is a member of one or more effective functioning work groups that have a high degree of group loyalty, effective skills of interaction, and high performance goals.[10]

As managers we should strive to build strong work groups that merit attention and loyalty from their members. The individual who has a strong loyalty is motivated to:

Accept the goals and decisions of the group
Attempt to influence the group's goals and decisions
Communicate fully to other members
Welcome communication and attempts to persuade from other members
Help implement the goals and decisions that are seen as most important
Behave in ways calculated to receive support and favorable recognition from members.

The Linking Pin Function

The capacity to exert influence upward is essential if a manager is to perform his supervisory functions well. Work groups will provide this capacity if they are linked into an over-all organization through overlapping group memberships. The supervisor in one group is a subordinate in the next, and so on throughout the organization. This process is known as the linking pin function. Its application to the operations function in Yellow Freight is shown in the accompanying figure.

In order to be effective the linking pin

10. Rensis Likert, *New Patterns*, p. 104.

Company Organization—Linking Pin Concept

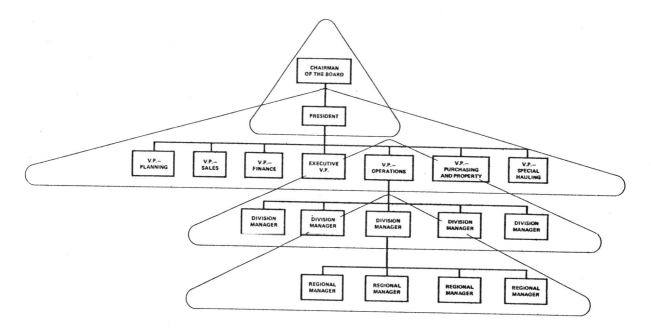

function requires effective group processes. The following characteristics should be present:

If an organization is to derive the full benefit from its highly effective group they must be linked to the total organization by means of overlapping groups.

The potential power of the overlapping group form of organization will not be approached until all of the groups of the organization are functioning reasonably well.

The higher an ineffective group in the hierarchy, the greater the adverse effect of its failure on the performance of the organization.

To help maintain an effective organization, it is desirable for superiors not only to hold group meetings of their own subordinates, but also to have occasional meetings over two hierarchical levels.

An organization takes a serious risk when it relies on a single linking pin or single linking process to tie the organization together.[11]

Man-to-Man Organization Structure

The effective group organization structure is highly superior to the typical man-to-man organizational structure. The man-to-man arrangement is structured this way:

11. Rensis Likert, *New Patterns*, pp. 114-15.

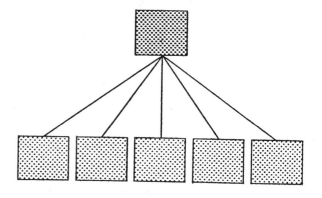

Several inadequacies can be noted in the man-to-man organizing structure. For example, meetings are primarily held for sharing of information and not decision making. Communication is quite difficult and usually filtered or inaccurate; in fact, individuals benefit by keeping as much information as possible to themselves.

In addition, problems are solved from a departmental point of view and not always in the company's best interest, and each manager attempts to enlarge his area of responsibility. Finally, hostilities increase as decisions are made at the top and flow downward.

CONSENSUS DECISION MAKING

Now that we have covered the basic ingredients of participative management, effects on productivity, work groups, the linking pin concept, and management by objectives, we are ready to examine decision making by consensus. Such a background is necessary to obtain more than a token understanding of the subject.

Decisions can be made on a consensus basis in effective work groups that have the characteristics previously discussed. Consensus, again, means 100 percent agreement to a course of action by members of the group.

The work group provides several advantages in the decision-making process. For example, technical knowledge and expertise may be shared; in fact, in an effective group the motivation is high to communicate accurately all relevant and important information. In addition, individual contributions make the group do a rigorous job of sifting ideas; members become experienced in effective group functioning and leadership; and group regulation of individual members can be exercised. Finally, each member is highly motivated to do his best to implement decisions and to achieve group goals. There are indications that an organization operating in a group fashion can be staffed for less than peak loads at each point.

One can realize the importance of group decision making when observing the basic steps in making a decision. These steps include determination of goals and objectives; proper diagnosis of the problem; conception of one or more good solutions; projection and comparison of the consequences of such alternatives; and selection of a course of action.

The most important advantage of group decision making by consensus, in addition to the opportunity for knowledgeable managers to combine all their efforts to reach a decision, is that the members of the group have an ego identification with the goals. A

manager's involvement in decision making in this manner makes him work hard to follow through with the decision; because he helped to make the decision he will help make it succeed.

Decision making by consensus may take more time than decision making by majority. However, in the long run, as has been proven by Yellow Freight's past operations, the best decisions are made by consensus of all parties involved.

Examples at Yellow Freight

Decision making by consensus has been practiced at Yellow Freight since the present management assumed control of the company in the early 1950's. On important matters, the chairman of the board never took action without first discussing the decision with the president; the reverse was also true. Complete agreement was necessary before any action was taken. In later years, and after organizational changes, a new president and executive vice-president joined the chairman and honorary chairman of the board to form a decision-making group for major decisions.

The proper implementation of participative management for consensus decisions can be illustrated in some examples. In these examples, attempts have been made to point out how a manager should formulate a decision-making group and then reach a consensus decision.

First, company officers and division managers decide jointly each year, and on a consensus basis, the goals and objectives for the company during the coming year. In a management by objectives process, the division managers have a voice in establishing the goals against which they will be judged.

Second, when a consensus decision is being sought regarding the opening of a new terminal, the division manager should utilize the ability of a number of people. Through his own expert ability, and with a regional and branch manager, sufficient data can be generated indicating whether customer potential is present. Since the opening of a new terminal affects the entire system, the division manager would necessarily have to work with a number of people before a decision could be made. Other managers who should be involved in this decision would include the vice-president of sales, the vice-president of operations, and president of the company, and the chairman of the board.

Third, personnel promotions and shifts at all levels of the company should definitely involve consensus decisions by the appropriate management. When a new branch manager is being selected, a regional manager should work with his division manager, who may involve the vice-presidents of sales and operations, and the president of the company. The regional manager should also look to other branch managers for their opinions and reactions to his suggestion regarding the vacancy.

Fourth, if a branch manager is making a decision to establish or terminate an agreement with an interline carrier, he should involve a number of people in this decision-making group because of their various levels of expertise. The regional manager, the salesman, and, possibly, the office manager (because of accounts receivable) should be involved. It would also be appropriate for the city dispatcher to be included.

When a new account is obtained, the branch manager should involve several people in the terminal in a participative management process. In deciding how this account is to be handled, he should involve the salesman, the operations manager, and the city dispatcher in all aspects of the new account and the procedures necessary to handle that account properly.

Any personnel shift in the terminal should involve several people related to the departments involved. For example, suppose the branch manager wants to move a dock foreman into the position of city dispatcher. The dock foreman's immediate supervisor, the present city dispatcher, the regional manager,

the division manager, and other relevant individuals should be a part of the decision-making group. In case a branch manager wants to promote a shift supervisor to operations manager, the group should include city dispatch, line dispatch, office manager, regional manager, division manager, and others in the terminal.

When dock foremen and dispatchers are working with nonmanagement groups, it is not always possible or practical to strive for decision making by consensus. However, they can allow union employees to participate in the implementation measures relating to the decision. For example, a dock foreman can utilize participative management. If a terminal wants to increase its load average by 500 pounds, the foreman can involve his crew; since the dock workers will actually be loading the trailers, they probably will have a number of suggestions about how to increase the load average.

If a terminal is spending too much money in overtime for the city drivers, and their pick-ups have not been at a satisfactory level, their dispatcher could join in participative management with his drivers. He could call them together and discuss possible alternatives regarding work procedures that would be more efficient.

Failure to Reach a Consensus

If a consensus cannot be reached by the group they should forego a decision at that time. Time as a prime consideration for a decision should be minimized. The group's decision not to make a specific decision on an important question may, or may not, be a consensus decision. Yellow Freight's experience has proven that when a decision cannot be reached, action should be deferred. Subsequent events will make a consensus decision easier to achieve because the action requiring a decision will have changed one way or the other.

Hasty decisions, made without a consensus, have proven unprofitable. This is true in many areas, but is especially true in matters relating to operating changes, terminal openings or closings, personnel changes and promotions, and general policy matters.

The Japanese Experience

In Japan most institutions, including governmental agencies and businesses, make decisions on a consensus basis after extensive debate within their organization. This approach is not too practical in the United States because of the likelihood of indecision, lost time, compromise or politicking.

In a recent article, Drucker focused on Japanese management procedures and made some interesting observations about decision by consensus:

... the Westerner and the Japanese mean something different when they talk of 'making a decision.' With us in the West, all the emphasis is on the answer to the question. Indeed, our books on decision making try to develop systematic approaches to giving an answer. To the Japanese, however, the important element in decision making is defining the question. The important and crucial steps are to decide whether there is a need for a decision and what the decision is about. And it is in this step that the Japanese aim at attaining 'consensus.' Indeed, it is this step that, to the Japanese, is the essence of the decision. . . .

During this process that precedes the decision, no mention is made of what the answer might be. This is done so that people will not be forced to take sides; once they have taken sides, a decision would be a victory for one side and a defeat for the other. Thus, the whole process is focused on finding out what the decision is really about, not what the decision should be.

In this country, we spend a great deal of time "selling" decisions. For the Japanese, this is not necessary.

Everybody has been presold. Also, their process makes it clear where in the organization a certain answer to a question will be welcomed and where it will be resisted. Therefore, there is penty of time to work on persuading the dissenters, or on making small concessions to them which will win them over without destroying the integrity of the decision.

In this country we are continually spending a great deal of time making small

decisions. In contrast, the Japanese system forces them to make the big decisions, and they may simply neglect many small ones.

The following paragraph summarizes Drucker's analysis of the Japanese approach to consensus decision making:

The Japanese process is focused on understanding the problem. The desired end result is certain action and behavior on the part of people. This almost guarantees that all the alternatives will be considered. It rivets management attention to essentials. It does not permit commitment until management has decided what the decision is all about. Japanese managers may come up with the wrong answer to the problem (as was the decision to go to war against the United States in 1941), but they rarely come up with the right answer to the wrong problem.[12]

Effective work groups of supervisors and subordinates, structured in a linking pin fashion throughout the organization, should be able to make good decisions through participation and to reach decisions on a consensus basis. Managers and employees are committed to decisions when they have helped make decisions. Managers must make every effort to establish effective work groups at the top organizational levels; once these groups have been established, others can be set up throughout the organization, all the way to dock foremen and dispatchers working with dock workers and drivers.

Naturally, a consensus decision cannot be reached on every administrative and day-to-day decision. The make-up of the decision-making group will vary, but should involve all those individuals immediately related to the problem area. Once the group is formed, all must have a voice in the decision, and all must agree on the course of action to be taken. With most companies experiencing high rates of change and increased growth, it is important that we continue to make decisions by consensus. Our management groups throughout the company must remain cohesive.

12. This and preceding quotations from Peter F. Drucker, "What We Can Learn from Japanese Management," *U.S./Japan Outlook, a Digest of American View of Japan,* I (Fall, 1971).

READING 6

A GENERAL DIAGNOSTIC MODEL FOR ORGANIZATIONAL BEHAVIOR

by

David A. Nadler & Michael Tushman

Reading 11

A General Diagnostic Model for Organizational Behavior: Applying a Congruence Perspective

David A. Nadler
Michael L. Tushman

Most of the job of management is the struggle to make organizations function effectively. The work of society gets done through organizations, and the function of management is to get those organizations to perform that work.

The task of getting organizations to function effectively is a difficult one, however. Understanding one individual's behavior is a challenging problem in and of itself. A group, made up of different individuals and multiple relationships among those individuals, is even more complex. Imagine, then, the mind-boggling complexity inherent in a large organization made up of thousands of individuals, hundreds of groups, and relationships among individuals and groups too numerous to count.

In the face of this overwhelming complexity, organizational behavior must be managed. Ultimately the work of organizations gets done through the behavior of people, individually or collectively, on their own or in collaboration with technology. Thus, central to the management task is the management of organizational behavior. To do this, there must be the capacity to *understand* the patterns of behavior at individual, group, and organizational levels, to *predict* what behavioral responses will be elicited by different managerial actions, and finally to use understanding and prediction to achieve *control*.

How can one achieve understanding, prediction, and control of organizational behavior? Given its inherent complexity and enigmatic nature, one needs tools to help unravel the mysteries, paradoxes, and apparent contradictions that present themselves in the everyday life of organizations. One kind of tool is the conceptual framework or model. A model is a theory which indicates which factors (in an organization, for example) are most critical or important. It also indicates how these factors are related, or which factors or combination of factors cause other factors to change. In a sense, then, a

Article prepared especially for this book.

model is a road map that can be used to make sense of the terrain of organizational behavior.

The models we use are critical because they guide our analysis and action. In any organizational situation, problem solving involves the collection of information about the problem, the interpretation of that information to determine specific problem types and causes, and the development of action plans. The models that individuals hold influence what data they collect and what data they ignore; models guide how people attempt to analyze or interpret the data they have; finally models aid people in choosing action plans.

Indeed, anyone who has been exposed to an organization already has some sort of implicit model. People develop these road maps over time, building on their own experiences. These implicit models (they usually are not explicitly written down or stated) guide behavior (Argyris & Schon, 1974). These models also vary in quality, validity, and sophistication depending on the nature and extent of the model builder's experience, as well as the model builder's perceptiveness, ability to conceptualize and generalize from experience, etc.

We are not solely dependent, however, on the implicit and experienced-based models that individuals develop. The last four decades have witnessed intense work including research and theory development related to organization behavior (see, for example, Dunnette. 1976). It is therefore possible to think about scientifically developed explicit models for the analysis of organizational behavior and for use in organizational problem solving.

This paper will present one particular research- and theory-based model. It is a general model of organizations. Rather than describe a specific phenomenon or aspect of organizational life (such as a model of motivation or a model of organizational design) it attempts to provide a framework for thinking about the organization as a total system. The major thrust of the model is that for organizations to be effective, their subparts or components must be consistently structured and managed—they must approach a state of congruence.

The paper will be organized into several sections. In the first section we will discuss the basic view of organizations which underlies the model—systems theory. In the second section, we will present and discuss the model itself. In the third section, we will present an approach to using the model for organizational problem analysis. Finally, we will discuss some of the implications of this model for thinking about organizations.

A BASIC VIEW OF ORGANIZATIONS

There are many different ways of thinking about organizations. Typically a manager who is asked to "draw a picture of an organization" will respond with some version of a pyramidal organizational chart. The model this rendition reflects is one which views the most critical factors as the stable formal relationships among the jobs and formal work units that make up the organization. While this clearly is one way to think about organizations, it is a very limited view. It excludes such factors as leader behavior, the impact of the environment, informal relations, power distribution, etc. Such a model can only capture a small part of what goes on in an organization. It is narrow and static in perspective.

Over the past twenty years there has been a growing consensus that a viable alternative to the static classical models of organizations is to think about organizations as social systems. This approach stems from the observation that social phenomena display many of the characteristics of natural or mechanical systems (Von Bertalanffy, 1968; Buckley, 1967). In particular it is argued that organizations can be better understood if they are considered as dynamic and open social systems (Katz & Kahn, 1966, 1978).

What is a system? In the simplest of terms, a system is a set of interrelated elements. These elements are related; thus change in one element may lead to changes in other elements. An *open system* is one that interacts with its environment. Thus it is more than just a set of interrelated elements. Rather, these elements make up a mechanism that takes input from the environment, subjects it to some form of transformation process, and produces output (Figure 11-1). At the most general

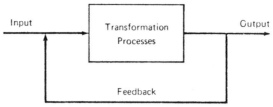

Figure 11-1 The basic systems model.

level, it should be easy to visualize organizations as systems. Let us consider a manufacturing plant, for example. It is made up of different related components (different departments, jobs, technologies, etc.). It receives input from the environment, including labor, raw materials, production orders, etc., and subjects those inputs to a transformation process to produce products.

Organizations as systems display a number of basic systems characteristics. Katz and Kahn (1966, 1978) discuss these in detail, but a few of the most critical characteristics will be mentioned here. First, organizations display degrees of internal *interdependence* (Thompson, 1967). Changes in one component or subpart of an organization frequently have repercussions for other parts—the pieces are interconnected. Returning to our manufacturing plant example, if changes are made in one element (for example, the skill levels of the people hired to do jobs), other elements will be affected (the productiveness of the equipment used, the speed or quality of production activities, the nature of supervision needed, etc.). Second, organizations have the capacity for *feedback* (see Figure 11-1). Feedback is information about the output of a system that can be used to control the system (Weiner, 1950). Organizations can correct errors and indeed change themselves because of this characteristic (Bauer, 1966). If, in our plant example, the plant management receives information about the declining quality of its product, it can use this information to identify factors in the system itself that contribute to this problem. It is important to note that unlike mechanized systems, feedback information does not always lead to correction. Organizations have the potential to use feedback and be self-correcting systems, but they do not always realize this potential.

A third characteristic of organizations as systems is *equilibrium*. Organizations develop energy to move toward states of balance. When an event occurs that puts the system out of balance, it reacts and moves toward a balanced state. If one work group in our plant example were suddenly to increase its performance dramatically, it would throw the system out of balance. This group would be making increasing demands on the groups that supply it with information or materials to give it what it needs. Similarly, groups that work with the output of the high-performing group would feel the pressure of work-in-process inventory piling up in front of them. Depending on the pay system used, other groups might feel inequity as this one group begins to earn more. We would predict that some actions would be taken to put the system back into balance. Either the rest of the plant would be changed to increase production and thus be back in balance with the single group or (more likely) actions would be taken to get this group to modify its behavior to be consistent with the levels of performance of the rest of the system (by removing workers, limiting supplies, etc.). The point is that somehow the system would develop energy to move back toward a state of equilibrium or balance.

Fourth, open systems display *equifinality*. In other words, different system configurations can lead to the same end or lead to the same type of input-output conversion. This means there is not a universal way, or "one best way," to organize. Finally, open systems need to display *adaptation*. For a system to survive, it must maintain a favorable balance of input and output transactions with the environment or it will run down. If our plant produces a product for which there are decreasing applications, it must adapt to the environmental changes and develop new products or ultimately the plant will simply have to close its doors. Any system, therefore, must adapt by changing as environmental conditions change. The consequences of not adapting to the environment can be seen in the demise of many once-prosperous organizations (such as the Eastern railroads) which did not alter in response to environmental changes.

Thus systems theory provides a different way of thinking about the organization, in more complex and dynamic terms. While systems theory is a valuable basic perspective on organizations, it is limited as a problem-solving tool. The reason is that as a model systems theory is too abstract to be used for day-to-day organizational behavior-problem

analysis. Because of the level of abstraction of systems theory, we need to develop a more specific and pragmatic model based on the concepts of the open-systems paradigm.

A CONGRUENCE MODEL OF ORGANIZATIONAL BEHAVIOR

Given the level of abstraction of open-systems theory, our job is to develop a model which reflects the basic systems concepts and characteristics, but which will also be more specific and thus more usable as an analytic tool. In this section, we will describe a model which attempts to specify in more detail the critical inputs, the major outputs, and the transformation processes that characterize organizational functioning.

The model puts its greatest emphasis on the transformation process and in particular reflects the critical system property of interdependence. It views organizations as made up of components or parts which interact with each other. These components exist in states of relative balance, consistency, or "fit" with each other. The different parts of an organization can fit well together and thus function effectively, or fit poorly, thus leading to problems, dysfunctions, or performance below potential. Given the central nature of these "fits" among components in the model, we will talk about it as a *congruence model of organizational behavior,* since effectiveness is a function of the congruence among the various components.

The concept of congruence is not a new one. Homans (1952) in his pioneering work on social processes in organizations emphasized the interaction and consistency among key elements of organizational behavior. Leavitt (1965), for example, identified the four major components of organizations as people, tasks, technology, and structure. The model we will present here builds on these views and also draws from fit models developed and used by Seiler (1967), Lawrence and Lorsch (1969), and Lorsch & Sheldon (1972).

It is important to remember that we are concerned about modeling the *behavioral* system of the organization—the system of elements that ultimately produce patterns of behavior and thus performance of the organizations. In its simplest form we need to deal with the question of what inputs the system has to work with, what outputs it needs to and actually produces, and how the major components of the transformation process interact with each other.

Inputs

Inputs are those factors that are, at any one point in time, the "givens" that face the organization. They are the materials that the organization has to work with. There are several different types of inputs, each of which presents a different set of "givens" to the organization. (See Figure 11-2 for an overview of inputs.)

The first input is the *environment*, or all of those factors outside of the boundaries of the organization being examined. Every organization exists within the context of a larger environment which includes individuals, groups, other organizations, and even larger social forces, all of which have a potentially powerful impact on how the organization performs (Pfeffer & Salancik, 1978). Specifically, the environ-

ment includes markets (clients or customers), suppliers, governmental and regulatory bodies, labor unions, competitors, financial institutions, special-interest groups, etc. The environment is critical to organizational functioning (Aldrich & Pfeffer, 1976). In particular, for purposes of organizational analysis, the environment has three critical features. First, the environment makes demands on the organization. For example, it may require the provision of certain products or services, at certain levels of quality or quantity. Market pressures are particularly important here. Second, the environment may place constraints on organizational action. It may limit the types or kinds of activities in which an organization can engage. These constraints could range from limitations imposed by scarce capital all the way to governmental regulatory prohibitions. Third, the environment provides opportunities which the organization can explore. In total, then, the analysis of an organization needs to consider

Input	Environment	Resources	History	Strategy
DEFINITION	All factors, including institutions, groups, individuals, events, etc. outside of the boundaries of the organization being analyzed, but having a potential impact on that organization.	Various assets that organization has access to, including human resources, technology, capital, information, etc. as well as less tangible resources (recognition in the market, etc.).	The patterns of past behavior, activity, and effectiveness of the organization which may have an effect on current organizational functioning.	The stream of decisions made about how organizational resources will be configured against the demands, constraints, and opportunities, within the context of history.
CRITICAL FEATURES OF THE INPUT FOR ANALYSIS	— What demands does the environment make on the organization? — environment puts constraints on organizational action.	— What is the relative quality of the different resources that the organization has access to? — To what extent are resources fixed, as opposed to flexible in their configuration?	— What have been the major stages or phases of development of the organization? — What is the current impact of historical factors such as — strategic decisions — acts of key leaders — crises — core values & norms	— How has the organization defined its core mission, including: — What markets it serves. — What products/services it provides to these markets. — On what basis does it compete? — What supporting strategies has the organization employed to achieve the core mission? — What specific objectives have been set for organizational output?

Figure 11-2 Key organizational inputs.

what factors are present in the environment of the organization and how those factors individually or in relation to each other create demands, constraints, or opportunities.

The *resources* of the organization are the second input. Any organization faces its environment with a range of different assets to which it has access and which it can employ. These include human beings, technology, capital, information, etc. Resources can also include certain less tangible assets, such as the perception of the organization in the marketplace or a positive organizational climate. A set of resources can be shaped, deployed, or configured in different ways by an organization. For analytic purposes, there are two features that are of primary interest. One aspect of resources concerns the relative quality of those resources, or the value they have in light of the nature of the environment. The second factor concerns the extent to which resources can be reconfigured, or how fixed or flexible different resources are.

The third input is the *history* of the organization. There is growing evidence that the contemporary functioning of many organizations is greatly influenced by events in the past (see Levinson, 1972, 1976). In particular, it is important to understand the major stages or phases of development of the organization over time (Galbraith & Nathanson, 1978) as well as the current impact of events that occurred in the past, such as key strategic decisions that were made, the acts or behavior of key leaders in the past, the nature of past crises and the organizational responses to them, and the evolution of core values and norms of the organization.

The final input is somewhat different than the others in that it in some ways reflects some of the factors in the environment, resources, and history of the organization. The fourth input is *strategy*. We will use this term in its most global and broad context (Hofer & Schendel, 1978) to describe the whole set of decisions that are made about how the organization will configure its resources against the demands, constraints, and opportunities of the environment within the context of its history. Strategy refers to the issue of matching the organization's resources to its environment, or making the fundamental decision of "what business are we in?" For analytic purposes, it is important to identify several aspects of strategy (Katz, 1970). First is the core mission of the organization, or what the organiza-

tion has defined as its basic purpose or function within the larger system or environment. The core mission includes decisions about what markets the organization will serve, what products or services it will provide to those markets, or what basis it will use to compete in those markets. Second, strategy includes the specific supporting strategies (or tactics) that the organization will employ or is employing to achieve its core mission. Third, the specific performance or output objectives that have been established.

Strategy is perhaps the most important single input for the organization (see the discussion in Nadler, Hackman, & Lawler, 1979). On one hand, strategic decisions implicitly determine the nature of the work that the organization should be doing or the tasks that it should perform. On the other hand, strategic decisions, and particularly decisions about objectives, serve as the oasis for determining what the outputs of the system should be. Based on strategy, one can determine what is the desired or intended output of the system.

In summary, there are three basic inputs, environment, resources, and history, and a fourth input, strategy, which reflects how the organization chooses to respond to or deal with those other inputs. Strategy is critical because it determines the work that the organization should be performing and it defines the nature of desired organizational outputs.

Outputs

Outputs describe what the organization produces, how it performs, or globally, how effective it is. There has been a lot of discussion about what makes for an effective organization (see Steers, 1978; Goodman & Pennings, 1978; Van de Ven & Ferry, 1980). For our purposes, however, it is possible to identify a number of key indicators of organizational output. First, we need to think about system output at different levels (see Figure 11-3). Obviously we can think about the output that the system itself produces, but we also need to think about the various other types of output that contribute to organizational performance, such as the functioning of groups or units within the organization as well as the functioning of individual organization members.

At the organizational level, it is important to keep three factors in mind in evaluating organizational performance. The first factor is goal attainment, or how well the organization meets its objectives (usu-

59

Organizational Functioning

- Goal attainment
- Resource utilization
- Adaptability

Group/Unit Functioning

Individual Functioning

- Behavior
- Affective reactions

Figure 11-3 Key organizational outputs.

ally determined by strategy). The second factor is resource utilization, or how well the organization makes use of resources that it has available to it. The question here is not just whether the organization meets its goals but whether it realizes all of the potential performance that is there and whether it achieves its goals by continuing to build resources or by "burning them up" in the process. The final factor is adaptability, or whether the organization continues to position itself in a favorable position vis-à-vis its environment—whether it is capable of changing and adapting to environmental changes.

Obviously, these organizational-level outputs are contributed to by the functioning of groups or units (departments, divisions, or other subunits within the organization). Organizational output also is influenced by individual behavior, and certain individual-level outputs (affective reactions, such as satisfaction, stress, or experienced quality of working life) may be desired outputs in and of themselves.

The Organization as a Transformation Process

So far, we have defined the nature of inputs and outputs for the organizational system. This approach leads us toward thinking about the transformation process. The question that any manager faces, given an environment, a set of resources, and a history, is how to take a strategy and implement it to produce effective organizational, group/unit, and individual performances.

In our framework, the means for implementing strategies, or the transformation mechanism in the system, is the *organization*. We therefore think about the organization and its major component parts as the fundamental means for transforming energy and information from inputs into outputs (see Figure 11-4). The question, then, is to identify the key components of the organization and the critical dynamic which describes how those components interact with each other to perform the transformation function.

Organizational Components

There are many different ways of thinking about what makes up an organization. At this point in the development of a science of organizations, we probably do not know what is the one right or best way to describe the different components of an organization. The question, then, is to find approaches for describing organizations that are useful, help to simplify complex phenomena, and help to identify patterns in what may at first blush seem to be random sets of activities. The particular approach here views organizations as composed of four major components: (1) the task, (2) the individuals, (3) the formal organizational arrangements, and (4) the informal organization. We will discuss each one of these individually. (See Figure 11-5 for overviews of these components.)

The first component is the *task* of the organization. The task is defined as the basic or inherent work to be done by the organization and its subunits. The task (or tasks) is the activity the organization is engaged in, particularly in light of its strategy. The emphasis is on the specific work activities or

Figure 11-4 The organization as a transformation process.

Component	Task	Individual	Formal organizational arrangements	Informal organization
Definition	The basic and inherent work to be done by the organization and its parts.	The characteristics of individuals in the the organization.	The various structures processes, methods, etc. that are formally created to get individuals to perform tasks.	The emerging arrangements including structures, processes, relationships, etc.
Critical features of each component	– The types of skill and knowledge demands the work poses. – The types of rewards the work inherently can provide. – The degree of uncertainty associated with the work, including factors such as interdependence, routineness, etc. – The constraints on performance demands inherent in the work (given a strategy).	– Knowledge and skills individuals have. – Individual needs and preferences. – Perceptions and expectancies. – Background factors.	– Organization design, including grouping of functions, structure of subunits, and coordination and control mechanisms. – Job design – Work environment – Human resource management systems.	– Leader behavior. – Intragroup relations. – Intergroup relations. – Informal working arrangements. – Communication and influence patterns.

Figure 11-5 Key organizational components.

functions that need to be done and their inherent characteristics (as opposed to characteristics of the work created by how the work is organized or structured in this particular organization at this particular time). Analysis of the task would include a description of the basic work flows and functions, with attention to the characteristics of those work flows, such as the knowledge or skill demands made by the work, the kinds of rewards the work inherently provides to those who do it, the degree of uncertainty associated with the work, and the specific constraints inherent in the work (such as critical time demands, cost constraints, etc.). The task is the starting point for the analysis, since the assumption is that a primary (although not the only) reason for the organization's existence is to perform the task consistent with strategy. As we will see, the assessment of the adequacy of other components will be dependent to a large degree on an understanding of the nature of the tasks to be performed.

The second component of organizations concerns the *individuals* who perform organizational tasks.

The issue here is to identify the nature and characteristics of the individuals that the organization currently has as members. The most critical aspects to consider include the nature of individual knowledge and skills, the different needs or preferences that individuals have, the perceptions or expectancies that they develop, and other background factors (such as demographics) that may be potential influences on individual behavior.

The third component is the *formal organizational arrangements*. These include the range of structures, processes, methods, procedures, etc., that are explicitly and formally developed to get individuals to perform tasks consistent with organizational strategy. "Organizational arrangements" is a very broad term which includes a number of different specific factors. One factor of organizational arrangements is organization design—how jobs are grouped together into units, the internal structure of those units, and the various coordination and control mechanisms used to line the units together (see Galbraith, 1977; Nadler, Hackman, & Lawler,

1979). A second factor in organizational arrangements is how jobs are designed within the context of organizational designs (Hackman & Oldham, 1980). A third factor is the work environment, which includes a number of factors characterizing the immediate environment in which work is done, such as the physical working environment, the work resources made available to performers, etc. A final factor includes the various formal systems for attracting, placing, developing, and evaluating human resources in the organization.

Together, these factors combine to create the set of organizational arrangements. It is important to remember that these are the formal arrangements—formal in that they are explicitly designed and specified, usually in writing.

The final component is the *informal organization.* In any organization, while there is a set of formal organizational arrangements, over time another set of arrangements tends to develop or emerge. These arrangements are usually implicit and not written down anywhere, but they influence a good deal of behavior. For lack of a better term, these arrangements are frequently referred to as the "informal organization," and they include the different structures, processes, arrangements, etc., that emerge over time. These arrangements sometimes arise to complement the formal organizational arrangements by providing structures to aid work where none exist. In other situations they may arise in reaction to the formal structure, to protect individuals from it. They may, therefore, either aid or hinder organizational performance.

A number of aspects of the informal organization have a particularly critical effect on behavior and thus need to be considered. The behavior of leaders (as opposed to the formal creation of leader positions) is an important feature of the informal organization, as are the patterns of relationships that develop both within and between groups. In addition, there are different types of informal working arrangements (including rules, procedures, methods, etc.) that develop. Finally, there are the various communication and influence patterns that combine to create the informal organization design (Tushman, 1977).

Organizations can, therefore, be thought of as a set of components: the task, the individuals, the organizational arrangements, and the informal organization. In any system, however, the critical question is not what the components are, but rather the nature of their interaction. The question in this model is, then, What is the dynamic of the relationship among the components? To deal with this issue, we need to return to the concept of congruence or fit.

The Concept of Congruence

Between each pair of inputs, there exists in any organization a relative degree of congruence, consistency, or "fit." Specifically, the congruence between two components is defined as follows: "the degree to which the needs, demands, goals, objectives and/or structures of one component are consistent with the needs, demands, goals, objectives and/or structures of another component."

Congruence, therefore, is a measure of the goodness of fit between pairs of components. For example, consider two components, the task and the individual. At the simplest level, the task can be thought of as inherently presenting some demands to individuals who would perform it (i.e., skill/knowledge demands). At the same time, the set of individuals available to do the tasks have certain characteristics (i.e., levels of skill and knowledge). Obviously, when the individual's knowledge and skill match the knowledge and skill demanded by the task, performance will be more effective.

Obviously, even the individual-task congruence relationship encompasses more factors than just knowledge and skill. Similarly, each congruence relationship in the model has its own specific characteristics. At the same time, in each relationship, there also is research and theory which can guide the assessment of fit. An overview of the critical elements of each congruence relationship is provided in Figure 11-6.

The Congruence Hypothesis

Just as each pair of components has a high or low degree of congruence, so does the aggregate model, or whole organization, display a relatively high or low level of system congruence. The basic hypothesis of the model builds on this total state of congruence and is as follows: "Other things being equal, the greater the total degree of congruence or fit between the various components, the more effective will be the organization, effectiveness being defined as the degree to which actual organization outputs at individual, group, and organizational levels are simi-

Fit	The issues
Individual—organization	To what extent individual needs are met by the organization arrangements. To what extent individuals hold clear or distorted perceptions of organizational structures, the convergence of individual and organizational goals.
Individual—task	To what extent the needs of individuals are met by the tasks, to what extent individuals have skills and abilities to meet task demands.
Individual—informal organization	To what extent individual needs are met by the informal organization, to what extent does the informal organization make use of individual resources, consistent with informal goals.
Task—organization	Whether the organizational arrangements are adequate to meet the demands of the task, whether organization arrangements tend to motivate behavior consistent with task demands.
Task—informal organization	Whether the informal organization structure facilitates task performance or not, whether it hinders or promotes meeting the demands of the task.
Organization—informal organization	Whether the goals, rewards, and structures of the informal organization are consistent with those of the formal organization.

Figure 11-6 Definitions of "fits."

lar to expected outputs, as specified by strategy."

The basic dynamic of congruence thus views the organization as being more effective when its pieces fit together. If we also consider questions of strategy, the argument expands to include the fit between the organization and its larger environment. An organization will be most effective when its strategy is consistent with the larger environment (in light of organizational resources and history) and when the organizational components are congruent with the tasks to be done to implement that strategy.

One important implication of the congruence hypothesis is that organizational problem analysis (or diagnosis) involves description of the system, identification of problems, and analysis of fits to determine the causes of problems. The model also implies that different configurations of the key components can be used to gain outputs (consistent with the systems characteristic of equifinality). Therefore it is not a question of finding the "one best way" of managing, but of determining effective combinations of components that will lead to congruent fits among them.

The process of diagnosing fits and identifying combinations of components to produce congruence

is not necessarily intuitive. A number of situations which lead to congruence have been defined in the research literature. Thus, in many cases fit is something that can be defined, measured, and even quantified. There is, therefore, an empirical and theoretical basis for making an assessment of fit. In most cases, the theory provides considerable guidance about what leads to congruent relationships (although in some areas the research is more definitive and helpful than in others). The implication is that the manager who is attempting to diagnose behavior needs to become familiar with critical aspects of relevant organizational behavior models or theories in order to evaluate the nature of fits in a particular system.

The congruence model is thus a general organizing framework. The organizational analyst will need other, more specific "submodels" to define high and low congruence. Examples of such submodels that might be used in the context of this general diagnostic model would be (1) the Job Characteristics model (Hackman & Oldham, 1980) to assess and explain the fit between individuals and tasks as well as the fit between individuals and organizational arrangements (job design); (2) Expectancy Theory models of motivation (Vroom, 1964; Lawler, 1973) to explain the fit between individuals and the other three components; (3) the Information Processing model of organizational design (Galbraith, 1973; Tushman & Nadler, 1978) to explain the task–formal organization and task–informal organization fits; and (4) an organizational-climate model (Litwin & Stringer, 1968) to explain the fit between the informal organization and the other components. These models and theories are listed in illustrations of how more specific models can be used in the context of the general model. Obviously, those mentioned above are just a sampling of possible tools that could be used.

In summary, then, we have described a general model for the analysis of organizations (see Figure 11-7). The organization is seen as a system which takes inputs and transforms them into outputs. At the core of the model, the transformation process is the organization, seen as composed of four basic components. The critical dynamic is the fit or congruence among the components. We now turn our attention to the pragmatic question of how to use this model for analyzing organizational problems.

A PROCESS FOR ORGANIZATIONAL PROBLEM ANALYSIS

The conditions that face organizations are frequently changing, and as a consequence, managers are required to continually engage in problem identification and problem-solving activities (Schein, 1970).

To do this managers must be involved in gathering data on the performance of their organizations, comparing these data to desired performance levels, identifying the causes of problems. developing and choosing action plans. and finally implementing and evaluating these action plans. These phases can be viewed as a generic problem-solving process. For long-term organizational viability, some sort of problem-solving process needs to continually be in operation (Schein, 1970; Weick, 1969).

Experience with using the congruence model for organizations to do problem analysis in actual organizational settings has led to the development of an approach to using the model. based on the generic problem-solving processes described above (see Figure 11-8). In this section, we will "walk through" the process, describing the different steps and discussing how the model can be used at each stage. There are eight specific steps in the problem-analysis process, and each one will be described separately.

1 *Identify symptoms:* In any situation there is initial information that presents itself as an indication that problems may exist. We can think of this information as symptomatic data. These data tell us that a problem might exist, but they do not usually indicate what the problem is or what the causes are. It is important to note symptomatic data, however, since the symptoms or problems that present themselves may be important indicators of where to look for more complete data.

2 *Specify inputs:* Having noted the symptoms, the starting point for analysis is to identify the system

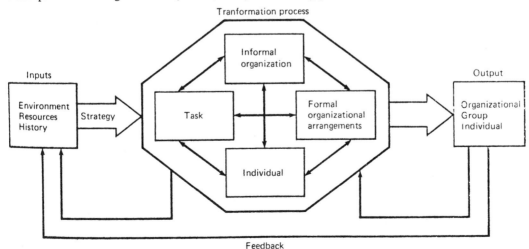

Figure 11-7 A congruence model for organizational analysis.

Step	Explanation
1. Identify symptoms	List data indicating possible existence of problems.
2. Specify inputs	Identify the system Determine nature of environment, resources, and history. Identify critical aspects of strategy
3. Identify outputs	Identify data that define the nature of outputs at various levels (individual, group/unit, organization) should include Desired outputs (from strategy) Actual outputs being obtained.
4. Identify problems	Identify areas where there are significant and meaningful differences between desired and actual outputs. To the extent possible, identify penalties, i.e., specific costs (actual and opportunity costs) associated with each problem.
5. Describe components of the organization	Describe basic nature of each of the four components with emphasis on their critical features.
6. Assessment of congruence (fit)	Do analysis to determine relative congruence among components (draw on submodels as needed)
7. Generate Identify causes	Analyze to associate fit with specific problems.
8. Identify action steps	Indicate what possible actions might deal with causes of problems.

Figure 11-8 Basic problem-analysis steps using the congruence model.

and the environment in which it functions. This means collecting data about the nature of the environment, the type of resources the organization has, and the critical aspects of its history. Input analysis also involves identifying the strategy of the organization, including its core mission, supporting strategies, and objectives.

3 Identify outputs: The third step is an analysis of the outputs of the organization at the individual, group, and organizational levels. Output analysis actually involves two elements. The first is to define the desired or planned output. This usually can be obtained from an analysis of strategy, which should explicitly or implicitly define what the organization is attempting to achieve in terms of output or performance indicators. The second is to collect data that would indicate what type of output the organization is actually achieving.

4 Identify problems: Symptoms indicate the possibility of problems. For our purposes, we will define problems as the differences between expected output and actual output. A problem exists when a significant and meaningful difference is observed between the output (at any level) that is desired or planned and the output that is actually being ob-

tained. Thus problems would be discrepancies (actual versus expected) in organizational performance, group functioning, and individual behavior or affective reactions. These data tell us that problems exist, but they do not specify what the causes are.

Where data are available, it is frequently useful to also identify the costs associated with the problems, or the *penalties* that the organization incurs by not fixing the problem. Penalties might be actual costs (increased expenses, etc.) or opportunity costs, such as revenue that could be realized if the problem were not there.

5 Describe organizational components: The next step begins analysis to determine the causes of problems. Data are collected about the nature of each of the four major organizational components, including information about the component and its critical features in this organization.

6 Assess congruence (fits): Using the data collected in step 5 as well as applicable submodels or theories, an assessment is made of the positive or negative fit between each of the pairs of components.

7 Generate hypotheses about problem causes: Having described the components and assessed congruence, the next step is to link the congruence analysis with the problem identification (step 4). Given the analysis, which poor fits seem to be associated with or account for the output problems that have been identified? The patterns of congruence and incongruence which appear to cause the patterns of problems are determined.

8 *Identify action steps:* The final step in problem analysis is to identify possible action steps. These steps might range from specific changes to dealing with relatively obvious problem causes to additional data collection to test the hypotheses developed concerning relatively more complex problems and causes.

In addition to these eight steps, some further steps need to be kept in mind. Once possible actions are identified, problem solving also involves making predictions about the consequences of those actions, choosing particular action steps, implementing the action steps, and evaluating the impact of those actions. In each case, it is, of course, important to have a general diagnostic framework to monitor the effects of actions.

The congruence model and this problem-analysis process outline are tools for structuring and dealing with the complex reality of organizations. Given the indeterminate nature of social systems, there is no one best way of handling a particular situation. The model and the process do, however, facilitate possible action. If these tools have merit, it is up to the manager to use them along with his or her intuitive sense (based on experience) to make the appropriate set of diagnostic, evaluative, and action decisions over time.

FUTURE DIRECTIONS

The model that we have presented here reflects a particular way of thinking about organizations. If that perspective has merit, then it may make sense to think about the possible extensions of the model as a tool for use in thinking about more complex problems or in structuring more complex situations. A number of directions for further thought, research, and theory development are as follows:

1 *Organizational change:* The issue of organizational change has received a good deal of attention from managers and academics alike. The question is how to implement organizational changes effective-

ly. Much talk has centered on the lack of a general model of organizational change. In one sense, however, it is hard to think about a general model of organizational change in the absence of a general model of organizations. The congruence perspective outlined here may provide some guidance and direction toward the development of a more integrated perspective on the processes of organizational change. Initial work in that area (Nadler, 1981) is encouraging in terms of the applicability of the congruence model to the change issue.

2 *Organizational development over time:* There has been a growing realization that organizations grow and develop over time, that they face different types of crises, evolve through different stages, and develop along some predictable lines (see, for example, Greiner, 1972; Galbraith & Nathanson, 1978). A model of organizations such as the one presented here might be a tool for developing a typology of growth patterns by indicating the different configurations of task, individual, organizational arrangements, and informal organizations that might be most appropriate for organizations in different environments and at different stages of development.

3 *Organizational pathology:* Organizational problem solving ultimately requires some sense of what types of problems may be encountered and of the kinds or patterns of causes one might expect. It is reasonable to assume that most problems that organizations encounter are not wholly unique but, rather, are predictable and expectable. The often-heard view that "our problems are unique" reflects in part the fact that there is no framework of organizational pathology. The question is, Are there certain basic "illlnesses" which organizations suffer? Can a framework of organizational pathology, similar to the physician's framework of medical pathology, be developed? The lack of a pathology framework in turn reflects the lack of a basic functional model of organization. Again, development of a congruence perspective might be able to provide a common language to use for the identification of general pathological patterns of organizational functioning.

4 *Organizational solution types:* Closely linked to the problem of pathology is the problem of treatment, intervention, or solutions to organizational problems. Again, there is a lack of a general framework to consider the nature of organizational interventions. In this case too, the congruence model could have value as a means for conceptualizing and ultimately describing the different intervention options available in response to problems (see one attempt at this in Nadler & Tichy, 1980).

SUMMARY

This paper has presented a general approach for thinking about organizational functioning and a process for using a model to analyze organizational problems. This particular model is one way of thinking about organizations. It clearly is not the only model, nor can we claim definitively that it is the best model. It is one tool, however, that appears to be useful for structuring the complexity of organizational life and for helping managers in creating, maintaining, and developing effective organizations.

REFERENCES

Aldrich, H. E., & Pfeffer, J. Environments of organizations. *Annual Review of Sociology,* 1976, **2,** 79–105.

Argyris, C., & Schon, D. A. *Theory in practice.* San Francisco: Jossey-Bass, 1974.

Bauer. R. A. Detection and anticipation of impact: The nature of the task. In R. A. Bauer (Ed.), *Social indicators,* pp. 1–67. Boston: M.I.T. Press, 1966.

Buckley, W. *Sociology and modern systems theory.* Englewood Cliffs, N.J.: Prentice-Hall, 1967.

Dunnette. M. D. *Handbook of industrial and organizational psychology.* Chicago: Rand-McNally, 1976.

Galbraith, J. R. *Designing complex organizations.* Reading. Mass.: Addison-Wesley, 1973.

———. *Organization design.* Reading, Mass.: Addison-Wesley, 1977.

———, & Nathanson, D. A. *Strategy implementation: The role of structure and process.* St. Paul, Minn.: West, 1978.

Goodman, P. S., & Pennings, J. M. *New perspectives on organizational effectiveness.* San Francisco: Jossey-Bass, 1977.

Greiner, L. E. Evolution and revolution as organizations grow. *Harvard Business Review,* 1972.

Hackman, J. R., & Oldham, G. A. *Work redesign.* Reading, Mass.: Addison-Wesley, 1979.

Hofer, C. W., & Schendel, D. *Strategy formulation: Analytical concepts.* St. Paul, Minn.: West, 1978.

Homans, G. C. *The human group.* New York: Harcourt Brace Jovanovich, 1950.

Katz, D., & Kahn, R. L. *The social psychology of organizations,* New York: Wiley, 1966. 2d ed., 1978.

Katz, R. L. *Cases and concepts in corporate strategy.* Englewood Cliffs, N.J.: Prentice-Hall, 1970.

Lawler, E. E. *Motivation in work organizations.* Belmont, Calif.: Wadsworth, 1973.

Lawrence, P. R., & Lorsch, J. W. *Developing organizations: Diagnosis and action.* Reading, Mass.: Addison-Wesley, 1969.

Leavitt, H. J. Applied organization change in industry. In J. G. March (Ed.), *Handbook of organizations,* pp. 1144–1170. Chicago: Rand-McNally, 1965.

Levinson. H. *Organizational diagnosis.* Cambridge, Mass.: Harvard, 1972.

———. *Psychological man.* Cambridge, Mass.: Levinson Institute, 1976.

Litwin, G. H., & Stringer, R. A. *Motivation and organizational climate.* Boston: Harvard University Graduate School of Business Administration, 1968.

Lorsch, J. W., & Sheldon, A. The individual in the organization: A systems view. In J. W. Lorsch and P. R. Lawrence (Eds.), *Managing group and intergroup relations.* Homewood, Ill.: Irwin-Dorsey, 1972.

Nadler, D. A. An integrative theory of organizational change. *Journal of Applied Behavioral Science,* 1981 (in press).

———, & Tichy, N. M. The limitations of traditional intervention technology in health care organizations. In N. Margulies & J. A. Adams, *Organization development in health care organizations.* Reading, Mass.: Addison-Wesley, 1980.

———, Hackman, J. R., & Lawler, E. E. *Managing organizational behavior.* Boston: Little, Brown, 1979.

Salancik, G. R., & Pfeffer, J. *The external control of organizations.* New York: Wiley, 1978.

Schein, E. H. *Organizational psychology.* Englewood Cliffs, N.J.: Prentice-Hall, 1970.

Seiler, J. A. *Systems analysis in organizational behavior.* Homewood, Ill.: Irwin-Dorsey, 1967.

Steers, R. M. *Organizational effectiveness: A behavioral view.* Pacific Palisades, Calif.: Goodyear, 1977.

Thompson, J. D. *Organizations in action.* New York: McGraw-Hill, 1967.

Tushman, M. L. A political approach to organizations: A review and rationale. *Academy of Management Review,* 1977, **2,** 206–216.

Van de Ven, A., & Ferry, D. *Organizational assessment.* New York: Wiley Interscience, 1980.

von Bertalanffy, L. *General systems theory: Foundations, development applications* (Rev. ed.). New York: Braziller, 1968.

Vroom, V. H. *Work and motivation.* New York: Wiley, 1964.

Weick, K. E. *The social psychology of organizing.* Reading, Mass.: Addison-Wesley, 1969.

Wiener, N. *The human use of human beings: Cybernetics and society.* Boston: Houghton Mifflin, 1950.

READING 7

WHAT IS THE RIGHT ORGANIZATION STRUCTURE?

by

Robert Duncan

Reprinted by permission of the publisher, from Organization Dynamics, Winter 1979, pp. 59-79. © 1979 by AMACOM, a division of American Management Associations.

Decision tree analysis, says Duncan, spells out the process the manager can and should use in selecting the right structure to "fit" the demands of the environment, as well as the specific steps he or she can take to make the appropriate structure work.

What Is the Right Organization Structure?
Decision Tree Analysis Provides the Answer

Robert Duncan

Organization design is a central problem for managers. What is the "best" structure for the organization? What are the criteria for selecting the "best" structure? What signals indicate that the organization's existing structure may not be appropriate to its tasks and its environment? This article discusses the purposes of organization structure and presents a decision tree analysis approach to help managers pick the right organization structure.

THE OBJECTIVES OF ORGANIZATIONAL DESIGN

What is organization structure and what is it supposed to accomplish? Organization structure is more than boxes on an chart; it is a pattern of interactions and coordination that links the technology, tasks, and human components of the organization to ensure that the organization accomplishes it purpose.

An organization's structure has es-

Organizational Dynamics, *Winter 1979.* © *1979, AMACOM, a division of American Management Associations. All rights reserved. 0090-2616/79/0016-0059/$02.00/0*

sentially two objectives: First, it facilitates the flow of information within the organization in order to reduce the uncertainty in decision making. The design of the organization should facilitate the collection of the information managers need for decision making. When managers experience a high degree of uncertainty—that is, when their information needs are great—the structure of the organization should not be so rigid as to inhibit managers from seeking new sources of information or developing new procedures or methods for doing their jobs. For example, in developing a new product, a manufacturing department may need to seek direct feedback from customers on how the new product is being accepted; the need to react quickly to customer response makes waiting for this information to come through normal marketing and sales channels unacceptable.

The second objective of organization design is to achieve effective coordination–integration. The structure of the organization should integrate organizational behavior across the parts of the organization so it is coordinated. This is particularly important when the units in the organization are interdependent. As James Thompson had indicated, the level of interdependence can vary. In *pooled interdependence* the parts of the organization are independent and are linked together only in contributing something to the same overall organization. In many conglomerates, the divisions are really separate organizations linked only in that they contribute profits to the overall organization. Simple rules—procedures—can be developed to specify what the various units have to do. In *sequential interdependence*, however, there is an ordering of activities, that is, one organizational unit has to perform its function before the next unit can per-

form its. For example, in an automobile plant manufacturing has to produce the automobiles before quality control can inspect them. Now such organizations have to develop plans to coordinate activities; quality control needs to know when and how many cars to expect for inspection.

Reciprocal interdependence is the most complex type of organizational interdependence. Reciprocal interdependence is present when the output of Unit A become the inputs of Unit B and the outputs of B cycle back to become the inputs of Unit A. The relationship between the operations and maintenance in an airline is a good example of this type of interdependence. Operations produces "sick" airplanes that need repair by maintenance. Maintenance repairs these planes and the repaired planes become inputs to the operations division to be reassigned to routes. When reciprocal interdependence between organization units is present, a more complex type of coordination is required. This is coordination by feedback. Airline operations and maintenance must communicate with one another so each one will know when the planes will be coming to them so they can carry out their respective functions.

Organizational design, then, is the allocation of resources and people to a specified mission or purpose and the structuring of these resources to achieve the mission. Ideally, the organization is designed to fit its environment and to provide the information and coordination needed.

It is useful to think of organization structure from an information-processing view. The key characteristic of organizational structure is that it links the elements of the organization by providing the channels of communication through which information flows. My research has indicated that when

Robert B. (Bob) Duncan *received his Ph.D. from Yale University in 1970 and his M.A. (1966) and A.B. (1964) from Indiana University. He joined the faculty of the Graduate School of Management, Northwestern University, in 1970 and is currently professor and chairman of the organization behavior department. At Northwestern he teaches courses on the management of organizational change and organizational design. His research is concerned with implementing changes and innovation in organizations and examining processes of organizational design and strategy formulation. He has studied these processes in a variety of settings including business, police, education, and health organizations. He is the author of numerous journal articles, as well as two books,* Innovations and Organizations *with G. Zaltman and J. Holbeck (Wiley-Interscience, 1973) and* Strategies for Planned Change *with G. Zaltman (Wiley-Interscience, 1977). He serves on the editorial boards of the* Academy of Management Journal *and* Management Science. *Dr. Duncan also acts frequently as a consultant on organizational change, organizational design, team building, and as a speaker in management development programs for business, public, educational, and health organizations.*

organizational structure is formalized and centralized, information flows are restricted and, as a consequence, the organization is not able to gather and process the informa-

tion it needs when faced with uncertainty. For example, when an organization's structure is highly centralized, decisions are made at the top and information tends to be filtered as it moves up the chain of command. When a decision involves a great deal of uncertainty, it is unlikely therefore that the few individuals at the top of the organization will have the information they require to make the best decision. So decentralization, that is, having more subordinates participate in the decision-making process, may generate the information needed to help reduce the uncertainty and thereby facilitate a better decision.

ALTERNATIVE ORGANIZATIONAL DESIGNS

The key question for the manager concerned with organization design is what are the different structures available to choose from. Contingency theories of organization have shown that there is no one best structure. However, organization theorists have been less clear in elaborating the decision process managers can follow in deciding which structure to implement.

In discussing organization design, organization theorists describe structure differently from the way managers responsible for organization design do. Organizational theorists describe structure as more or less formalized, centralized, specialized, or hierarchical. However, managers tend to think of organizational structure in terms of two general types, the *functional* and the *decentralized*. Most organizations today are either functional or decentralized or some modification or combination of these two general types. Therefore, if we are to develop a heuristic for helping managers make decisions about organization structure, we need to think of structures as functional or decen-

Figure 1

ENVIRONMENTAL COMPONENTS LIST

Internal Environment	External Environment
Organizational personnel component	Customer component
–Educational and technological background and skills	–Distributors of product or service
–Previous technological and managerial skill	–Actual users of product or service
–Individual member's involvement and commitment to attaining system's goals	Suppliers component
–Interpersonal behavior styles	–New materials suppliers
–Availability of manpower for utilization within the system	–Equipment suppliers
Organizational functional and staff units component	–Product parts suppliers
–Technological characteristics of organizational units	–Labor supply
–Interdependence of organizational units in carrying out their objectives	Competitor component
–Intraunit conflict among organizational functional and staff units	–Competitors for suppliers
–Intraunit conflict among organizational functional and staff units	–Competitors for customers
Organizational level component	Sociopolitical component
–Organizational objectives and goals	–Government regulatory control over the industry
–Integrative process integrating individuals and groups into contributing maximally to attaining organizational goals	–Public political attitude toward industry and its particular product
–Nature of the organization's product service	–Relationship with trade unions with jurisdiction in the organization
	Technological component
	–Meeting new technological requirements of own industry and related industries in production of product or service
	–Improving and developing new products by implementing new technological advances in the industry

tralized and not in terms of the more abstract dimensions of formalization, centralization, and so on, that organizational theorists tend to use.

ORGANIZATIONAL ENVIRONMENT AND DESIGN: A CRITICAL INTERACTION

In deciding on what kind of organization structure to use, managers need to first understand the characteristics of the environment they are in and the demands this environment makes on the organization in terms of information and coordination. Once the environment is understood, the manager can proceed with the design process.

The first step in designing an orga-nization structure, therefore, is to identify the organization's environment. The task environment constitutes that part of the environment defined by managers as relevant or potentially relevant for organizational decision making. Figure 1 presents a list of environmental components managers might encounter. Clearly, no one organization would encounter all these components in decision making, but this is the master list from which organizational decision makers would identify the appropriate task environments. For example, a manager in a manufacturing division could "define an environment consisting of certain personnel, certain staff units and suppliers, and perhaps certain technological components. The usefulness of the list in Figure 1 is that it provides a guide for deci-

Figure 2

CLASSIFICATION OF ORGANIZATIONAL ENVIRONMENTS

	Simple	Complex
Static	*low perceived uncertainty* Small number of factors and components in the environment Factors and components are somewhat Factors and components remain basically the same and are not changing *Example*: Soft drink industry 1	2 *moderately low perceived uncertainty* Large number of factors and components in the environment Factors and components are not similar to one another Factors and components remain basically the same *Example*: Food products
Dynamic	3 *moderately high perceived uncertainty* Small number of factors and components in the environment Factors and components are somewhat similar to one another Factors and components of the environment are in continual process of change *Example*: Fast food industry	4 *high perceived uncertainty* Large number of factors and components in the environment Factors and components are not similar to one another Factors and components of environment are in a continual process of change *Examples*: Commercial airline industry Telephone communications (AT&T)

sion makers, alerting them to the elements the environment they might consider in decision making.

Once managers have defined the task environment, the next step is to understand the state of that environment. What are its key characteristics? In describing organizational environments, we emphasize two dimensions: simple–complex and static–dynamic.

The simple–complex dimension of the environment focuses on whether the factors in the environment considered for decision making are few in number and similar or many in number and different. An example of a *simple* unit would be a lower-level production unit whose decisions are affected only by the parts department and materials department, on which it is dependent for supplies, and the marketing department, on which it is dependent for output. An example of a *complex* environment would be a programming and planning department. This group must consider a wide varity of environmental factors when making a decision. It may focus on the marketing and materials department, on customers, on suppliers, and so on. Thus this organizational unit has a much more heterogeneous group of environmental factors to deal with in decision making—its environment is more complex than that of the production unit.

The static–dynamic dimension of the environment is concerned with whether the factors of the environment remain the same over time or change. A *static* environment, for example, might be a production unit that has to deal with a marketing department whose requests for output remain the same and a materials department that is able

Figure 3

CHARACTERISTICS OF THE FUNCTIONAL ORGANIZATION

Organizational Functions	*Accomplished in Functional Organization*
Goals	Functional subgoal emphasis (projects lag)
Influence	Functional heads
Promotion	By special function
Budgeting	By function or department
Rewards	For special capability

Strengths	*Weaknesses*
1. Best in *stable* environment	1. Slow response time
2. Colleagueship ("home") for technical specialists	2. Bottlenecks caused by sequential tasks
3. Supports in-depth skill development	3. Decisions pile at top
4. Specialists freed from administrative/coordinating work	4. If multiproduct, product priority conflict
5. Simple decision/communication network excellent in small, limited-output organizations	5. Poor interunit coordination
	6. Stability paid for in less innovation
	7. Restricted view of whole

to supply a steady rate of inputs to the production unit. However, if the marketing department were continually changing its requests and the materials department were inconsistent in its ability to supply parts, the production unit would be operating in a more *dynamic* environment.

Figure 2 provides a four-way classification of organizational environments and some examples of organizations in each of these environments. Complex–dynamic (Cell 4) environments are probably the most characteristic type today. These environments involve rapid change and create high uncertainty for managers. The proper organizational structure is critical in such environments if managers are to have the information necessary for decision making. Also, as organizations move into this turbulent environment, it may be necessary for them to modify their structures. For example, AT&T has moved from a functional organization to a decentralized structure organized around different markets to enable it to cope with more competition in the telephone market

and in communications. This change in structure was in response to the need for more information and for a quicker response time to competitive moves.

STRATEGIES FOR ORGANIZATIONAL DESIGN

Once the organization's environment has been diagnosed, what type of structure the organization should have becomes the key question.

Simple design strategy

When the organization's environment is relatively simple, that is, there are not many factors to consider in decision making, and stable, that is, neither the make-up of the environment nor the demands made by environmental components are changing, the information and coordination needs for the organization are low. In such circumstances, a *functional organization structure* is most appropriate.

74

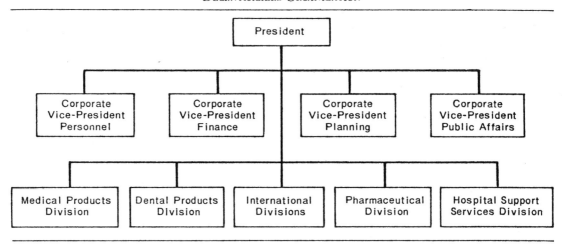

Figure 4

DECENTRALIZED ORGANIZATION

A key characteristic of the functional organization is specialization by functional areas. Figure 3 presents a summary of this structure's strengths and weaknesses. The key strengths of the functional organization are that it supports in-depth skill development and a simple decision-communication network. However, when disputes or uncertainty arises among managers about a decision, they get pushed up the hierarchy to be resolved. A primary weakness of the functional organization, therefore, is that when the organization's environment becomes more dynamic and uncertainty tends to increase, many decisions move to the top of the organization. Lower-level managers do not have the information required for decision making so they push decisions upward. Top-level managers become overloaded and are thus slow to respond to the environment.

Organizational design dilemma

The organizational designer faces a dilemma in such situations. Designs can be instituted that *reduce* the amount of information required for decision making. Decentralization is the principal strategy indicated. Or organizations can develop more lateral relations to *increase* the amount of information available for decision making.

A decentralized organization is possible whenever an organization's tasks are self-contained. Decentralized organizations are typically designed around products, projects, or markets. The decentralized healthcare organization in Figure 4 is organized around product areas (Medical and Dental) and market area (International). Each division has all the resources needed to perform its particular task. For example, Medical Products (Figure 4) has its own functional organization consisting of production, marketing, and R&D to carry out its mission. The information needed by Medical Products Division's managers is reduced because they have organized around a set of common medical products, and they don't have to worry about dental, pharmaceutical, or hospital support services or products.

Figure 5

CHARACTERISTICS OF THE DECENTRALIZED ORGANIZATION

Organizational Functions	Accomplished in Decentralized Organization
Goals	Special product emphasis (technologies lag)
Influence	
Promotion	Product, project heads
Budgeting	By product management
Rewards	By product, project, program
	For integrative capability

Strengths	Weaknesses
1. Suited to fast change	1. Innovation/growth restricted to existing project areas
2. High product, project, or program visibility	2. Tough to allocate pooled resources (i.e., computer, lab)
3. Full-time task orientation (ie., dollars, schedules, profits)	3. Shared functions hard to coordinate (i.e., purchasing)
4. Task responsibility, contact points clear to customers or clients	4. Deterioration of in-depth competence —hard to attract technical specialists
5. Processes multiple tasks in parallel, easy to cross functional lines	5. Possible internal task conflicts, priority conflicts
	6. May neglect high level of integration required in organization

In the decentralized organization, managers only have to worry about their own products or services; they have the resources to carry out these activities, and they don't have to compete for shared resources or schedule shared resources. There is also a full-time commitment to a particular product line. The decentralized structure is particularly effective when the organization's environment is very complex, that is, there are a large number of factors to be considered in decision making, and the environment can be segmented or broken down into product or market areas around which the organization can structure itself. For example, the health products organization (Figure 4) probably started out as a functional organization. However, as its product line increased, it undoubtedly became more difficult for one manufacturing unit to have the expertise to produce such a wide range of products efficiently and to handle the diversity of information needed to do it. It would also be difficult for one marketing unit to market such a diverse group of products; different kinds of information and skills would be required to sell the different products. Segmenting this complex environment into product areas facilitates increased specialization. As a result, divisional managers need less information than if they had to deal with all the products and services of the corporation.

Figure 5 summarizes the characteristics and the strengths and weaknesses of the decentralized organization. Decentralized organizations face several problems. For example, it is sometimes difficult to decide what resources are to be pooled in a corporate staff to be used to service the entire organization. If the divisions are very different from one another in terms of products, customers, technology, and so on, however, it becomes very difficult to staff a corporate services unit with the diverse knowledge needed to be able to help the divisions. A restricted approach to innovation is another problem decentralized organizations may encounter. Because each division is organized around a particular product or geographic area, each manager's attention is focused on his or her special area. As a result, their innovations focus on their particular specialties. Managers don't have the diverse information needed to produce radical innovations.

One major liability of decentralized organizations is their relative inability to provide integration–coordination among the divisions, even when their interdependence increases. When divisions are relatively autonomous and have only pooled interdependence, there is not much need for coordination. However, when uncertainty increases and the divisions have to work together because of increased either sequential or reciprocal interdependence between the units, decentralized organizations have no formal mechanisms to coordinate and resolve the increased needs for information.

Since today's organizational environments are becoming more complex and interpendent, large decentralized corporations are finding that the need to integrate has increased for at least five reasons:

1. The increased level of regulation organizations face requires more and more coordination across divisions to be sure that all regulatory requirements are being met. For example, crackdowns by the SEC on illegal foreign payments and the increased liabilities of boards of directors have required organizations to have better control systems and information sources to enable their headquarters staff groups to know what's going on in the divisions. Affirmative action requirements have required that divisions share information on how they are doing and where possible pools of affirmative action candidates may be found.

2. Organizational environments are changing, and this can lead to a requirement of more coordination across divisions. New customer demands may require what were previously autonomous divisions to coordinate their activities. For example, if the International Group in the health products company mentioned earlier faces a demand to develop some new products for overseas, it may be necessary to provide a means by which the Medical Products and Pharmaceutical Divisions can work in a coordinated and integrated way with International to develop these new products.

3. Technological changes are placing more emphasis on increased interaction among divisions. More and more, computer systems and R&D services are being shared, thus compelling the divisions to interact more with one another.

4. The cost of making "wrong" strategic decisions is increasing in terms of both sunk costs and losses because of failure to get market share. Since such "wrong" decisions sometimes result from a lack of contact between divisions, it emphasizes the need to have more coordination across divisions and more sharing of information. For example, AT&T has just recently begun to market telephone and support equipment to counter the competition of other suppliers of this equipment that have entered the market. To do this AT&T has organized around markets. It has also increased the opportunities for interaction among these market managers so they can share information, build on one another's expertise and competence, and ensure required coordination.

5. Scarce resources—for example, capital and raw materials—will require more interaction among divisions to set overall priorities. Is a university, for example, going to emphasize its undergraduate arts program or its professional schools? By setting up task forces of the deans of the schools, the university might be able to identify opportunities for new innovative programs that could benefit the entire organization. New programs in management of the arts—museums, orchestras, and so on—could draw on the expertise of the arts department and the business school and would not require a lot of new venture capital.

For a number of reasons, then, there is a need for increased coordination among divisions in decentralized organizations. Given the decentralized organization's weakness, organizational designers need to implement the second general design strategy, increasing the information flow to reduce uncertainty and facilitate coordination.

Lateral relations: Increasing information available for decision making

Lateral relations is really a process that is overlaid on an existing functional or decentralized structure. Lateral relations as a process moves decision making down to where the problem is in the organization. It differs from decentralization in that no self-contained tasks are created.

Jay Galbraith has identified various types of lateral relations. *Direct contact*, for example, can be used by managers of diverse groups as a mechanism to coordinate their different activities. With direct contact, managers can meet informally to discuss their common problems. *Liaison roles* are a formal communication link between two units. Engineering liaison with the manufacturing department is an excellent example of the liaison role. The engineer serving in the liaison role may be located in the production organization as a way of coordinating engineering and production activities.

When coordination between units becomes more complex, an *integrator role* may be established. Paul Lawrence and Jay Lorsch have indicated that the integrator role is particularly useful when organizational units that must be coordinated are differentiated from one another in terms of their structure, subgoals, time, orientation, and so on. In such situations, there is the possibility of conflict between the various units. For example, production, marketing, and R&D units in an organization may be highly differentiated from one another. Marketing, for example, is primarily concerned with having products to sell that are responsive to customer needs. R&D, on the other hand, may be concerned with developing innovative products that shape customer needs. Production, for its part, may want products to remain unchanged so that manufacturing setups don't have to be modified. Obviously there are differences among the three units in terms of their subgoals. The integrator role is instituted to coordinate and moderate such diverse orientations. The integrator could be a materials manager or a group executive whose additional function would be to coordinate and integrate the diverse units in ways that meet the organization's common objectives.

To be effective as an *integrator*, a

manager needs to have certain characteristics. First, he needs wide contacts in the organization so that he possesses the relevant information about the different units he is attempting to integrate. Second, the integrator needs to understand and share, at least to a degree, the goals and orientations of the different groups. He cannot be seen as being a partisan of one particular group's perspective. Third, the integrator has to be rather broadly trained technically, so that he can talk the language of the different groups. By being able to demonstrate that he has some expertise in each area, he will be viewed as more credible by each group and will also be better able to facilitate information exchange between the units. The integrator can in effect become an interpreter of each group's position to the others. Fourth, the groups that the integrator is working with must trust him. Again, the integrator is trying to facilitate information flow and cooperation between the groups and thus the groups must believe that he is working toward a solution acceptable to all the groups. Fifth, the integrator needs to exert influence on the basis of his expertise rather than through formal power. The integrator can provide information and identify alternative courses of action for the different units as they attempt to coordinate their activities. The more he can get them to agree on solutions and courses of action rather than having to use his formal power, the more committed they will be to implementing the solution. Last, the integrator's conflict resolution skills are important. Because differentiation between the units exists, conflict and disagreement are inevitable. It is important, therefore, that confrontation is used as the conflict resolution style. By confrontation we mean that parties to the conflict identify the causes of conflict and are committed to adopting a problem-solving approach to finding a mu-

tually acceptable solution to the conflict. The parties must also be committed, of course, to work to implement that solution.

When coordination involves working with six or seven different units, then task forces or teams can be established. Task forces involve a group of managers working together on the coordination problems of their diverse groups. For example, in a manufacturing organization, the marketing, production, R&D, finance, and engineering managers may meet twice a week (or more often when required) to discuss problems of coordination that they may be having that require their cooperation to solve. In this use a task force is a problem-solving group formed to facilitate coordination.

The matrix type of structure is the most complex form of lateral relations. The matrix is typically a formal structure in the organization; it is not a structure that is often added temporarily to an existing functional or decentralized structure. As Lawrence, Kolodny, and Davis have indicated in their article "The Human Side of the Matrix" (*Organizational Dynamics*, Summer 1977), there are certain key characteristics of a matrix structure. The most salient is that there is dual authority, that is, both the heads of the functions and the matrix manager have authority over those working in the matrix unit.

The matrix was initially developed in the aerospace industry where the organization had to be responsive to products/

markets as well as technology. Because the matrix focuses on a specific product or market, it can generate the information and concentrate the resources needed to respond to changes in that product or market rapidly. The matrix is now being used in a variety of business, public, and health organizations. Figure 6 provides a summary of the characteristics and strengths and weaknesses of the matrix form of organization.

The matrix structure is particularly useful when an organization wants to focus resources on producing a particular product or service. The use of the matrix in the aerospace industry, for example, allowed these organizations to build manufacturing units to product particular airplanes, thus allowing in-depth attention and specialization of skills.

Matrix organizations, however, are complicated to manage. Because both project managers and traditional functional area managers are involved in matrix organizations, personnel in the matrix have two bosses, and there is an inherent potential for conflict under such circumstances. As a result, the matrix form of lateral relations should only be used in those situations where an organization faces a unique problem in a particular market area or in the technological requirements of a product. When the information and technological requirements are such that a full-time focus on the market or product is needed, a matrix organization can be helpful. Citibank, for example, has used a matrix structure in its international activity to concentrate on geographic areas. Boeing Commercial Airplane has used the matrix to focus resources on a particular product.

Lateral relations require a certain organizational design and special interpersonal skills if this process for reducing uncertainty by increasing the information avail-

able for improving coordination is going to be effective. From a design perspective, four factors are required:

1. The organization's reward structure must support and reward cooperative problem solving that leads to coordination and integration. Will a manager's performance appraisal, for example, reflect his or her participation in efforts to achieve coordination and integration? If the organization's reward system does not recognize joint problem-solving efforts, then lateral relations will not be effective.

2. In assigning managers to participate in some form of lateral relations, it is important that they have responsibility for implementation. Line managers should be involved since they understand the problems more intimately than staff personnel and, more importantly, they are concerned about implementation. Staff members can be used, but line managers should be dominant since this will lead to more commitment on their part to implementing solutions that come out of lateral relations problem-solving efforts.

3. Participants must have the authority to commit their units to action. Managers who are participating in an effort to resolve problems of coordination must be able to indicate what particular action their units might take in trying to improve coordination. For example, in the manufacturing company task force example mentioned earlier, the marketing manager should be able to commit his group to increasing the lead time for providing information to production on deadlines for delivering new products to customers.

4. Lateral processes must be integrated into the vertical information flow. In the concern for increasing information exchange *across* the units in the organization there must be no loss of concern for vertical

Figure 6

CHARACTERISTICS OF THE MATRIX ORGANIZATION

Organizational Functions	Accomplished in Matrix Organization
Goals	Emphasis on product/market
Influence	Matrix manager and functional heads
Promotion	By function or into matrix manager job
Budgeting	By matrix organization project
Rewards	By special functional skills and performance in matrix

Strengths	Weaknesses
1. Full-time focus of personnel on project of matrix	1. Costly to maintain personnel pool to staff matrix
2. Matrix manager is coordinator of functions for single project	2. Participants experience dual authority of matrix manager and functional area managers
3. Reduces information requirements as focus is on single product/market	3. Little interchange with functional groups outside the matrix so there may be duplication of effort, "reinvention of the wheel"
4. Masses specialized technical skills to the product/market	4. Participants in matrix need to have good interpersonal skills in order for it to work

information exchange so that the top levels in the organization are aware of coordination efforts.

Certain skills are also required on the part of participants for lateral relations to work:

1. Individuals must deal with conflict effectively, in the sense of identifying the sources of conflict and then engaging in problem solving to reach a mutually acceptable solution to the conflict situation.

2. Participants need good interpersonal skills. They must be able to communicate effectively with one another and avoid making other participants defensive. The more they can learn to communicate with others in a descriptive, nonevaluative manner, the more open the communication process will be.

3. Participants in lateral relations need to understand that influence and power should be based on expertise rather than formal power. Because of the problem-solving nature of lateral relations, an individual's power and influence will change based on the particular problem at hand and the individual's ability to provide key information to solve the problem. At various times different members will have more influence because of their particular expertise.

Lateral relations, then, is a process that is overlaid onto the existing functional or decentralized organization structure. Lateral relations requires various skills, so it is imperative that an organization never adopts this approach without training the people involved. Before implementing lateral relations, team building might be used to develop the interpersonal skills of the participating managers. These managers might spend time

Figure 7

Organizational Design Decision Tree Heuristic

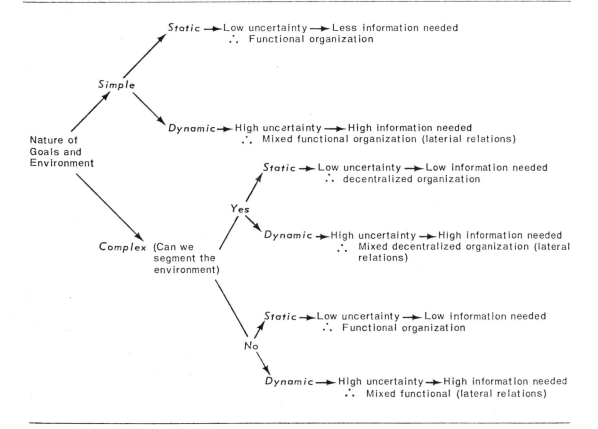

Static ➙ Low uncertainty ➙ Less information needed
∴ Functional organization

Simple

Dynamic ➙ High uncertainty ➙ High information needed
∴ Mixed functional organization (lateral relations)

Nature of
Goals and
Environment

Static ➙ Low uncertainty ➙ Low information needed
∴ decentralized organization

Yes

Dynamic ➙ High uncertainty ➙ High information needed
∴ Mixed decentralized organization (lateral relations)

Complex (Can we
segment the
environment)

Static ➙ Low uncertainty ➙ Low information needed
∴ Functional organization

No

Dynamic ➙ High uncertainty ➙ High information needed
∴ Mixed functional (lateral relations)

learning how to operate more effectively in groups, how to improve communication skills, and how to deal with conflict in a positive way so that it does not become disruptive to the organization.

The organizational design decision tree

We have discussed the different kinds of organization structure that managers can implement. We are now prepared to identify the decision-making process the manager can use in selecting the appropriate structure to "fit" the demands of the environment. Figure 7 presents a decision tree analysis for selecting either the functional or decentralized organization structure. This decision analysis also indicates when the existing functional or decentralized organization structure should be supplemented with some form of lateral relations in the form of a task force or team or a matrix. In general, an organization should use one of the simpler forms of lateral relations rather than the more complex and expensive matrix. In using this decision tree, there are a number of questions that the designer needs to ask.

The first question is whether the organization's environment is *simple*, that is, there are few factors to consider in the environment, or *complex*, that is, there are a number of different environmental factors to be considered in decision making. If the environment is defined as *simple*, the next question focuses on whether the environmental factors are *static*, that is, remain the same over time, or are *dynamic*, that is, change over time. If we define the environment as static, there is likely to be little uncertainty associated with decision making. In turn, information requirements for decision making are low. In this simple–static environment, the functional organization is most efficient. It can most quickly gather and process the information required to deal with this type of environment.

At this point the question might be raised, are there any organizational environments that are in fact both simple and static or is this a misperception on the part of the managers that oversimplifies the environment? There may be environments like this, but the key is that these environments may change, that is, they may become more dynamic as the marketplace changes, as resources become scarce, or the organization's domain is challenged. For example, the motor home/recreational vehicle industry was very successful in the early 1970s. Its market was relatively homogeneous (simple) and there was a constantly high demand (static) for its products. Then the oil embargo of 1973 hit, and the environment suddenly became dynamic. The industry had a very difficult time changing because it had done no contingency planning about "what would happen if" demand shifted, resources became scarce, and so on. The important point is that an organization's environment may be simple and static today but change tomorrow. Managers should continually scan the environment and be sensitive to the fact that things can change and contingency planning may be useful.

"Then the oil embargo of 1973 hit, and the previously homogeneous, static environment suddenly became dynamic. The motor home recreational vehicle industry had a very difficult time changing because it had done no contingency planning about 'what would happen if' demand shifted, resources became scarce, and so on."

Figure 8
FUNCTIONAL ORGANIZATION WITH TASK FORCE

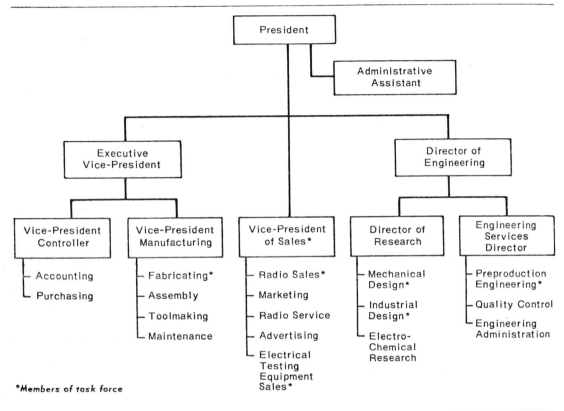

*Members of task force

If this simple environment is defined as dynamic, with some components in the environment changing, some uncertainty may be experienced by decision makers. Thus information needs will be greater than when the environment was static. Therefore, in this simple–dynamic environment the mixed functional organization with lateral relations is likely to be the most effective in gathering and processing the information required for decision making. Because the organization's environment is simple, the creation of self-contained units would not be efficient. It is more economical to have central functional areas responsible for all products and markets as these products and markets are relatively similar to one another. However, when uncertainty arises and there is need for more information, some form of lateral relations can be added, to the existing functional organization.

Figure 8 shows the functional organization of a manufacturing organization. The organization suddenly may face a problem with its principal product. Competitors may have developed an attractive replacement. As a result of this unique problem, the president of the firm may set up a task force chaired by the vice-president of sales to develop new products. The task force consists

Figure 9

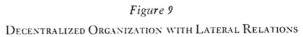

DECENTRALIZED ORGANIZATION WITH LATERAL RELATIONS

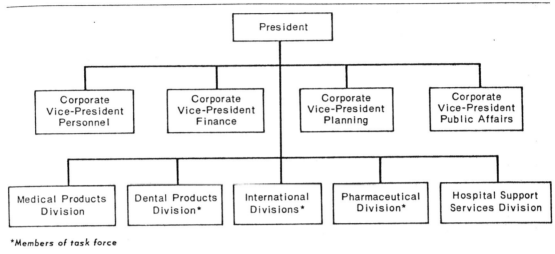

*Members of task force

of members from manufacturing, sales, research, and engineering services. Its function, obviously, will be to develop and evaluate suggestions for new products.

If the organization's environment is defined by the managers as complex, that is, there are a large number of factors and components that need to be considered in decision making, the next next question to ask is, can the organization *segment* its environment into geographic areas, market, or product areas? If the environment is defined as segmentable, then the next question focuses on whether the environment is static or dynamic. If the environment is defined as static, there is going to be low uncertainty and thus information needs for decision making are not going to be high. Thus, in the complex–segmentable–static environment, the decentralized organization is most appropriate, and the health products organization discussed earlier is a good example of this. The organization can break the environment apart in the sense that it can organize around prod-

ucts or markets, for example, and thus information, resources, and so forth, are only required to produce and market these more homogeneous outputs of the organization.

In the complex–segmentable–dynamic environment there is a change in the components of the environment and the demands they are making on the organization, or in fact the organization has to now consider different factors in the environment that it had not previously considered in decision making. Uncertainty and coordination needs may be higher. The result is that decision makers need more information to reduce uncertainty and provide information to facilitate coordination. The mixed decentralized organization with lateral relations is the appropriate structure here.

Figure 9 presents the design of a multidivision decentralized health products organization. Some form of lateral relations may be added to this structure to help generate more information. For example, the International Division may be attempting to develop new products but may be encountering problems, with the result that the entire organization, stimulated by the president's concern, may be experiencing uncertainty about how to proceed. In such a situation, a task force of the manager of the International Group and the Dental Group and the Pharmaceutical Group might work together in developing ideas for new products in the International Division. The lateral relations mechanism of the task force facilitates information exchange *across* the organization to reduce uncertainty and increase coordination of the efforts of the divisions that should be mutually supportive. By working together, in the task force, the division managers will be exchanging information and will be gaining a better understanding of their common problems and how they need to work and coordinate with one another in order to solve these problems.

If the organization's complex environment is defined by managers as nonsegmentable, the functional organization will be appropriate because it is not possible to break the environment up into geographic or product/service areas.

In effect, there simply might be too much interdependence among environmental components, or the technology of the organization may be so interlinked, that it is not possible to create self-contained units organized around components of the environment.

A hospital is a good example of this organization type. The environment is clearly complex. There are numerous and diverse environmental components that have to be considered in decision making (for example, patients, regulatory groups, medical societies, third-party payers, and suppliers). In the complex–nonsegmentable–static environment, environmental components are rather constant in their demands. Thus here the functional organization is most appropriate.

However, the functional organization, through its very specific rules, procedures, and channels of communication, will likely be too slow in generating the required information. Therefore, some form of lateral relations may be added to the functional organization. Figure 10 presents an example of an aerospace functional organization that uses a matrix structure for its airplane and missile products divisions. The matrix struc-

"While using the appropriate structure may have some direct impact on the organization's ability to attain its goals, its biggest impact will be on the adaptability of the organization and the role behavior of its managers."

Figure 10

FUNCTIONAL ORGANIZATION WITH MATRIX

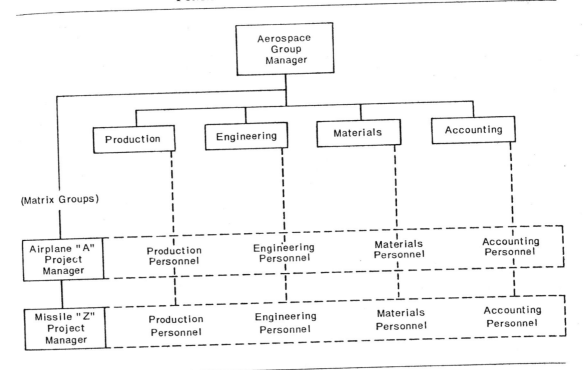

SYMPTOMS OF INAPPROPRIATE ORGANIZATIONAL STRUCTURE

ture provides in-depth concentration of personnel and resources on these different product areas, each of which has its own very unique information and technological requirements.

The key question at this point is "So what?" What are the costs to an organization if it is using the wrong structure, given its product/service and the environment in which it operates? In order to be effective, an organization needs to attain its goals and objectives, it needs to adapt to the environment, and last, it should be designed in such a way that its

managers experience low role conflict and ambiguity.

Therefore, there are certain kinds of information the manager responsible for organizational design should be sensitive to in monitoring whether the appropriate structure is being used. While using the appropriate structure may have some direct impact on the organization's ability to attain its goals, its biggest impact will probably be on the adaptability of the organization and the role behavior of its managers.

Certain kinds of symptoms regarding ineffective adaptability may occur. For example:

• Organizational decision makers may not be able to anticipate problems before they occur. There may be a tendency in the organization to wait until problems occur and then react to them because the organization simply does not have enough information to develop contingency plans.

• Decision makers may err in trying to predict trends in their decision environment. Without proper coordination across divisions, the organization may lose control over the relationship between its internal functioning and its environment.

• The organization may not be able to get key information for decision making to the right place for effective decision making. For example, division managers from different product groups may have information that quality and liability standards on their respective products are unrealistically high. However, because of decentralization and lack of effective coordination through some form of lateral relations, this information may not get to the staff groups in the organization that are responsible for setting corporate policy in this area.

• The organization, having identified a problem vis-à-vis its environment, may simply not be able to take corrective action quickly enough.

Symptoms of poor fit between structure and environment may also show at the level of the individual in terms of some increase in either role conflict or role ambiguity. It is important, therefore, that the organization monitor the level of role conflict and role ambiguity among its managers and the resulting stress they experience so the system has a baseline for comparison. If there is a significant increase from this baseline in conflict and ambiguity and stress, then the organization may consider that the increase is a symptom of an organizational design problem. For example:

• Individuals may be experiencing increased role conflict. This may occur when the organization is implementing a functional organization in a dynamic environment. The environment may be changing and the individuals may be required to make quick responses to this changing environment. Having to wait for new policy changes to come down the hierarchy may delay the organization from responding appropriately. Decision makers at the top of the organization will also suffer from role conflict when the environment is changing rapidly. In the functional organization, when new situations occur they are referred to higher levels of the organization for decision and action. The result is that top-level decision makers become overloaded and the organization's response to the environment slows down. In a dynamic environment, the functional organization constrains the decision-making adaptation process.

• Individuals in the organization also may experience increased role ambiguity—they may be unclear as to what is expected of them in their roles. For example, role ambiguity is likely to occur when the decentralized organization is implemented without some effective use of lateral relations. Individuals may feel they don't have the information needed for decision making. Divisional managers may not know what the corporate staff's policy is on various issues, and corporate staff may have lost touch with the divisions.

These are the kinds of information managers should be aware of as indicators of dysfunctional organization design. These data can be collected in organizational diagnosis surveys that we have developed so that a more systemic monitoring of structure exists just as we monitor organizational climate. As fine tuning the organization's design to its environment becomes more critical, organizations will begin to monitor their organizational design more systematically.

Summary

What are the advantages to managers in using the design decision tree? There appear to be several:

1. It provides a *broad framework* for identifying the key factors a manager should think about in considering an organizational design. For example: What is our environment? What different structural options do we have?

2. It forces the manager to *diagnose* the decision environment. What is our environment like? How stable is it? How complex is it? Is it possible to reduce complexity by segmenting the environment into product or geographical subgroups?

3. It causes managers to think about *how much interdependence* there is among segments of the organization. How dependent on one another are different parts of the organization in terms of technology, services, support, help in getting their tasks completed? The decision points in the heuristic forces managers to questions themselves about what other parts of the organization they need to coordinate their activities with, and then to think about how to do it.

4. Once the organization is in either a functional or decentralized structure, the decision tree points out what can be done to meet *the increased needs for information* through the use of lateral relations. Lateral relations provide a mechanism for supplementing the existing structure to facilitate dealing with the organization's increased needs for information and coordination.

Managers in a variety of organizations have commented that the decision tree gives them ". . . a handle for thinking about organizational design so we can tinker with it, fine tune it and make it work better. We don't have to be coerced by structure. We now have a better feel for when certain structures should be used and for the specific steps we can take to make a given structure work."

Selected Bibliography

For a general background on organization theory as it applies to design, see James Thompson's *Organizations in Action* (McGraw-Hill, 1967) and Paul Lawrence and Jay Lorsch's *Organizations and Environment* (Irwin, 1967). For a specific treatment of organizational design see Jay Galbraith's *Organizational Design* (Addison-Wesley, 1977) and (with Dan Nathanson) *Strategy Implementation: The Role of Struc-ture and Process* (West Publishing, 1978). The Autumn 1977 *Organizational Dynamics* issue was devoted principally to design. Two articles are particularly helpful—Jay Lorsch's "Organizational Design: A Situational Perspective" pp. 2–14 and Jeffrey Pfeffer and Gerald Salancik's "Organizational Design: The Case for a Coalitional Model of Organizations." pp. 15–29 For a focus on the learning process regarding design see Robert Duncan and Andrew Weiss's "Organizational Learning: Implications for Organizational Design" in Barry Staw's (ed.), *Research*

READING 8

ORGANIZATIONAL STRATEGY AND BEHAVIOR

by

D.A. Nadler, J.R. Hackman & E.E. Lawler, III

Chapter 13

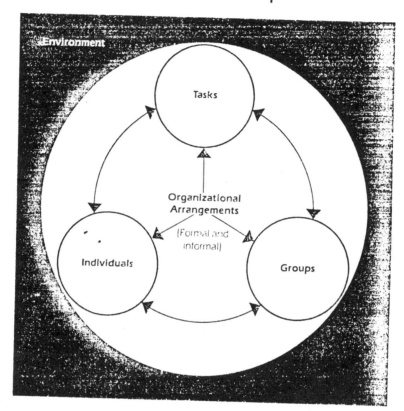

Organizational Strategy and Behavior

The Neighborhood Health Center was formed in the late 1960s to provide comprehensive outpatient care to the residents of one section of a large eastern city. With heavy funding from the federal government (through the Office of Economic Opportunity) the center was designed to provide care for the poor that went far beyond that provided in hospital clinics. The group of physicians who originally formed the center had a set of values that placed an emphasis on preventive medicine, patient education, and the provision of services by a variety of health practitioners, not just the physician. As the center began to grow and prosper, an organization design was developed to help implement the goal of comprehensive care. Health care teams were created which included physicians, nurse practitioners, family health workers, medical assistants and dentists.

Each patient was assigned to a team so that patients received care with continuity; the different practitioners working with an individual or a family worked with each other to help treat cases. At the same time, practitioners were grouped by function (nurses, family health workers, physicians, and so on) into departments. The result was a matrix design with functional departments on one side of the structure and interdisciplinary health care teams on the other. By the mid-1970s the center had grown to about 300 employees and had an annual operating budget of about $8 million.

By the late 1970s, however, a number of changes had occurred in the environment of the center, which forced management to reevaluate the mission and structure of the organization. First, the direct federal funding for support of the center began to decline annually. The goal of the federal government was that the center would become self-supporting. Reduced direct funding made the center dependent on third party payments (payment from sources other than the patient, such as Blue Cross, Medicaid, Medicare). These sources only provided reimbursement for physician contacts with patients, with no payment for other health practitioners. The remaining federal money was channeled through a community advisory board that was established to serve as a board of directors for the center. Finally, the area of the city in which the center was located began to experience high rates of housing abandonment, with a large and continuing drop in the population in the service area.

In response to these changes, cutbacks in service were made, layoffs were instituted, while the center attempted to continue providing the same type of service as best it could. Finally, the top management group began to realize that if it continued on its current course, the center would be out of business before long. Management began to explore actively some alternative actions that would enable the center to continue to provide comprehensive service within a changed environment. Alternatives such as setting up satellite centers in more populated areas and finding special funding for nonphysician based activities were considered.

THE NEIGHBORHOOD HEALTH CENTER is a graphic example of how an organization may have to make significant changes if it is to continue to exist as environmental conditions change. The case underscores the need to consider the nature of the environment and how the organization relates to that environment as critical factors in understanding organizational behavior. Until this point, our focus has been on the organization and its components. Relatively little attention has been given to what lies beyond the boundaries of the organization — namely, the larger environment. In fact, the environment is extremely important.

In the first chapter, we argued for thinking about organizations as open social systems (Katz and Kahn, 1966). This open-systems view takes account of the fact that organizations continually conduct transactions with different parts of the environment. The health center, for example, conducts transactions with its clients or patients; it also has to deal with financial institutions, regulatory bodies, community organizations, professional societies, and so on. If the organization is to survive, it must develop approaches to deal with these many elements of its environment. If the health center were to continue to provide the same kind of service, with the same kind of team structure, to the same service area, in the face of declining population and changing funding formulas, it could not last for long.

It, therefore, becomes clear that environmental relations are important for understanding and managing patterns of organizational behavior. Environmental relations and organizational behavior are related in several ways. First, the nature of environmental relations and how they are managed determines many of the patterns of organizational behavior. Depending on the way in which the health center decides to cope with its changing environment, very different types of organizational behavior will be required. Moving to satellites will require different types of individual performance, team functioning, and organizational design. On the other hand, patterns of organizational behavior may influence the nature of environmental relations. The effectiveness of the top management work team, for example, critically affects what kinds of decisions are made about environmental relations. Similarly, the types of coalitions and cliques that exist and the patterns of conflict management and resolution determine the way in which key decisions are made and implemented. Thus, environmental relations and organizational behavior influence one another.

One way of thinking about the interactions between the organization and the environment is to consider the various *strategies* that organizations develop for relating with the rest of the world. In this chapter, we will employ a strategic perspective, and the emphasis will be on understanding how strategy influences organizational behavior and vice versa. First, we will define the general concepts of strategy. Second, we will examine the ways in which strategy develops in organizations. Third, we will discuss some of the specific components of strategy, and finally, we will consider the relationship between strategy and organizational behavior.

Throughout this discussion, the emphasis will be on recognizing strategy and understanding its implications for managing organizational behavior. We will not consider in detail how to formulate and evaluate strategy, as these issues are considered in depth elsewhere (see, for example, Hofer and Schendel, 1978; Newman and Logan, 1976; Andrews, 1971).

What Is Organizational Strategy?

RELATING TO
THE ENVIRONMENT

In its simplest and most basic form, strategy is the approach organizations take to managing the relationship between them and their environments (Ansoff, 1969). While we speak of organizations operating within an environment, in actuality the environment is made up of many groups, individuals, organizations, and other institutions. Figure 13.1 illustrates some of the key elements in the environment of most organizations. Clearly, an organization must relate to its employees both as individuals and through the groups that may represent their interests, such

Figure 13.1 *Critical Elements of the Organization's Environment*

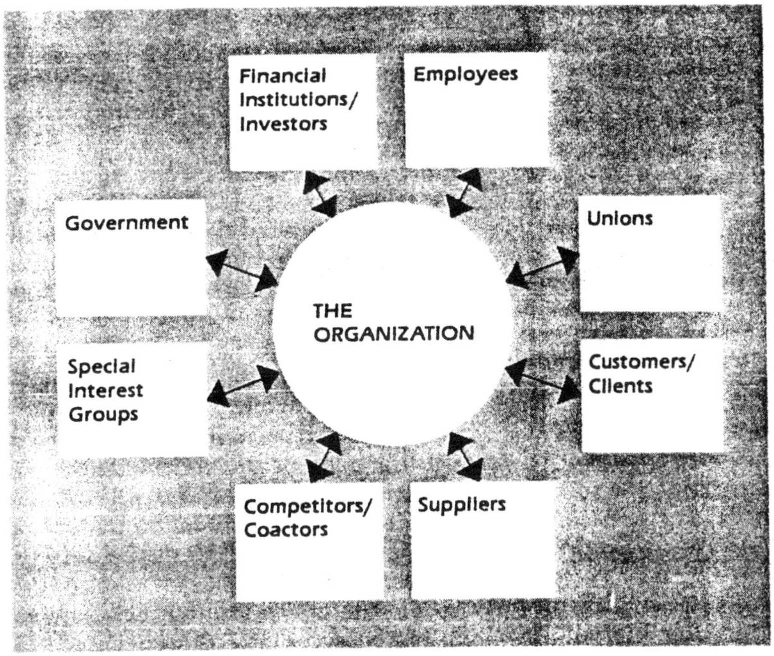

as unions. Organizations have customers or clients with which they must interact. Further, organizations depend on other organizations to supply the needed materials, information, energy, and so on, necessary to produce a product or service. Within the environment, other organizations are also acting. Some act as competitors, while others act as either allies or coactors. Special interest groups have their own constituencies, such as professional groups, lobbies, environmental groups, and others. Various levels of government have great impact through taxation, regulation, and government spending. Lastly, in some way organizations relate to financial institutions and, in some cases, to individual financial investors.

We can illustrate some of these relationships by recalling the health center. The center must find individuals who can be hired as physicians, dentists, nurses, family health workers, and others. It has contractual relations with a labor union, which represents the employees other than dentists, doctors, and nurses. It has a client/patient population to which it provides services, and it relies on a variety of different suppliers for materials ranging from stethoscopes to electric power. Within this section of the city, there are what is known as "medicaid mills" (small physicians' offices aimed at providing minimum service to medicaid patients), which compete with the center as well as other health care organizations which provide complementary types of care. Within the community, political groups make demands on the center; some of these factions are represented on the center board. In addition, groups such as the local medical board and third-party payment agencies have both a direct and indirect effect on the center. The government plays a major role through regulation of service, funding procedures, and other methods. Finally, the management of the organization's financial assets requires interaction with banks in the area.

In summary, organizations face a domain or a set of relationships with institutions that exist in their environment, many of which are critical for the organization's survival (Evan, 1966; Thompson, 1967; Starbuck, 1976). Together, the components of the environment put *constraints* on organizational action and make *demands* on the organization (Katz, 1970); but, at the same time, the environment provides *opportunities* (Andrews, 1971) for the organization to make use of its own unique or distinctive resources and competencies.

USING A SET OF RESOURCES

Organizations face environments with sets of resources at their disposal. Every organization has a special combination of competencies, assets, and experiences, that it can put to use in meeting environmental demands, working within constraints, and taking advantage of opportunities. These resources can vary in nature and value. Referring again to the health center, it has its own set of resources. Clearly, it has individuals with skills, experience, and a commitment to a concept of providing health care. It also has physical assets such as buildings. medical equipment, and the like. It has a number of less tangible resources, such as the image it has in the community with health planners and with funding agencies.

Organizations can make very different use of their resources. Resources can be concentrated in one specific area (such as one product. one market, or one technology) or spread over a variety of areas of activity. Through patterns of use, resources can be depleted or can be strengthened and increased. Thus, a crucial question is what is called *resource allocation* (Bower, 1970) or *strategic choice* (Child, 1972, 1973): the way in which the organization decides to allocate its existing resources among alternative projects, programs, products, or courses of action. Again, the health care center's possible decision to open satellite centers and to invest dollars and energy in the project is a decision to allocate resources in a different manner than they were in the past.

STRATEGY AS THE ENVIRONMENT–RESOURCES MATCH

Now that we have established a view of organizations as functioning within environments and working with a set of available resources, we can define strategy in more detail. To begin with, strategy is the process by which the organization attempts to match its use of resources effectively to the demands, constraints, and opportunities in the environment (Hofer, 1976). This matching of the organization's resources to the environment is essentially a determination by the organization about what its role will be within that environment. As Andrews (1971) states, strategy is the "pattern of purposes and policies defining the company and its business."[1]

More specifically, beyond deciding "what business we're in," the formulation of strategy involves identifying the things that an organization needs to do in order to compete successfully. Consequently, strategy is also "the determination of the basic long-term goals and objectives of the enterprise, and the adoption of courses of action and allocation of resources necessary for carrying out these goals" (Chandler, 1962). Making decisions about strategy involves the identification of goals for the organization, the allocation of resources to achieve those goals, and thus. the determination of the specific *tasks* that the organization needs to accomplish or perform.

Putting together the views and definitions of strategy, we can devise a framework or model for thinking about how strategy is formed and how it relates to organizational behavior (see Figure 13.2). Organizations scan their environments to identify con-

---

[1] Much of the strategy literature has been developed from observations of private sector organizations. Thus, the terms *business policy* or *corporate strategy* are used. The concepts are, of course, applicable to public and not-for-profit organizations.

Figure 13.2 *A Basic Strategy Model*

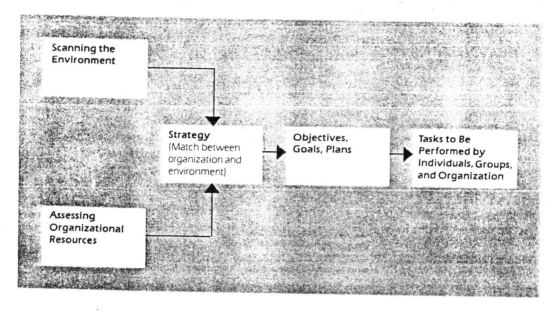

straints, demands, and opportunities. This scanning is sometimes very detailed and systematic (Aguillar, 1967). At the same time, the organization assesses its own resources and the way in which those resources are utilized. Out of this dual examination, a match between the organization's resources and an environment (present or future) is identified, and decisions are made about the allocation of resources needed to obtain that match. That set of decisions is the course of a strategy. From these decisions flows a set of objectives, goals, and plans that represent how the organization will attempt to implement the strategy. By implication, these objectives, goals, and plans define a set of tasks that must be performed.

In a broad sense, then, strategy is the determination of *what* the organization needs to do. As a result of developing a strategy, it becomes clear which of the tasks that individuals, groups, and the total organization could perform are the most critical. Having identified such tasks, the organizational issues concern *how* those tasks will be done. Thus, strategy and organization interact and combine to determine how effective the organization will be (see Figure 13.3). For an organization to be effective, it needs to have both an appropriate strategy and the means to implement that strategy (that is, performing critical tasks) through the use of individuals, groups, and organization design. As we will see, strategy has implications for how an organization is designed, and organizational behavior has implications for

What Is Organizational Strategy /

Figure 13.3 *The Relationship between Strategy and Organization*

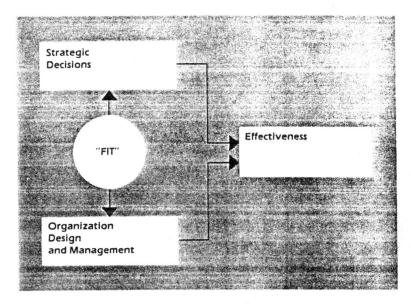

what kind of strategies develop. Strategy, organizational design, and management need to be consistent (Galbraith and Nathanson, 1978).

While the model of strategy development shown in Figure 13.2 does reflect a general view of strategy, it has two major drawbacks. First, the model implies that strategy emerges from a preplanned and rational process of environmental scanning, organizational assessment, and strategy formulation by the organization. In truth, the process by which strategies emerge is frequently much more complex and haphazard than this. Second, strategy has been talked about in relatively vague and abstract terms. To understand what strategy is and how it influences organizational behavior, a clearer and more detailed understanding is needed of how strategy is formulated and of the components of strategy.

Methods of Strategy Formulation

How does strategy actually develop in organizations? Specifically, how do organizations go about scanning the environment, assessing resources, and forecasting a pattern of resource allocation that will create a match between environment and resources? The model of strategy development presented in Figure

13.2 implies that strategic decisions are made in a sequential and rational basis and that the systematic determination of strategy precedes the implementation of those strategies by the organization.

In truth, there are a number of ways in which strategy is formulated in organizations. Three general approaches that have been observed are the rational planning approach, the political processes approach, and the adaptive approach.

RATIONAL PLANNING APPROACH

This most traditional approach conceives of strategy formulation as a process of rational and sequential thought that leads to the development of plans which are then executed. The environment is systematically scanned, the organization's resources are assessed, and decisions are made among alternative courses of action and their long-range implications. This rational process may be carried out in at least two ways. One way is by having top management serve as the strategic planners, either as individuals or in working groups. A second method is to use some form of planning staff, either through a planning department or group. This group, sometimes with the aid of outside consultants, develops environmental forecasts, explores several strategic options, and makes recommendations for top management decisions.

The health center, at first glance, provides an example of the beginning of the rational planning approach to strategy. Faced with problems in the environment, the top management group has begun to meet regularly to analyze the environment and to explore strategic options such as the creation of satellite centers, the search for new funding sources for nonphysician care, and the like. Were this approach to be carried through, the group might create a set of long-range plans with specific objectives (for example, four satellites handling 30 percent of the patient load to be in place by the end of three years). Each year, the plan might be reexamined by this group and changes made in light of new developments in the environment and the relative success to date in implementing the existing plan.

POLITICAL PROCESSES APPROACH

Recently, the observation has been made that the rational planning approach does not adequately describe how decisions actually are made or how strategic planning is conducted within many organizations. A more accurate view might be one that takes account of the various political processes that occur within organizations and how these processes affect the development of strategies (Allison, 1971; MacMillan, 1978).

If we think of organizations as being made up of cliques, coalitions, and networks, as proposed in Chapter 12, then it is only natural that these aspects of the emergent or informal organization will come to play when strategic decisions are being made. Strategic decisions often involve issues of personal or group values, since such decisions may alter the sense of what constitutes the organization's mission, function, or goals. Groups may attempt to influence such decisions so that the organization will move in a direction consistent with their values. Thus, strategy is not necessarily the result of rational planning (although it may frequently have those trappings); rather, often it is the outcome of competition, conflict, coalition formation, and bargaining (such as those discussed in Chapter 12) among numerous interest groups within the organization (see, for example, studies by Bower, 1970; Aharoni, 1966).

The health center case provides an illustration of political processes and strategy formulation. While on the surface the center's top management appears to be starting a process of rational planning of strategy, various political factors have influenced strategy in the past and no doubt will continue to influence how strategy evolves in the future. In the top management group, a number of people represent the supporting practitioners, such as family health workers or nurse practitioners. These groups form a coalition highly committed to the team-care approach and would rather see the organization go out of business than give up the team-care approach. On the other hand, a number of physicians in the management group are much less committed to the team concept and would prefer to see the center survive, even if some of the work of nonphysicians had to be greatly deemphasized. In the middle is a group composed of several top managers who are not physicians and whose views fall somewhere in between the two other factions. All three are important for continued functioning of the center and all three have different bases of power.

The strategy that eventually emerges from top management, probably, will be the result of negotiation, bargaining, and compromise among the three key power groups. The strategy may thus be very different than what would emerge if we assumed that this group was to be completely rational and objective in its analysis and decision making, or if we assumed that all of the group members shared a set of common goals for the organization.

ADAPTIVE
PROCESSES
APPROACH

In many instances, strategy simply seems to emerge over time. In the extreme, nobody is explicitly formulating strategy, so it is formed as a result of a stream of decisions, none of which are oriented toward or based on a larger strategic perspective. This approach is what some have called "muddling through" (Lindblom, 1959). Strategy is never consciously or explicitly formulated, but as a result of sets of implicitly strategic decisions, strategies are indeed created. They may be effective or ineffective strategies, but they are still strategies.

During the early 1970s, the health center used an adaptive or muddling-through approach. No one in top management ever gave much thought to long-range trends in the environment and their implications for the center. No long-run plans to cope with environmental changes were formed; rather, sets of decisions were made in response to crises that occurred. As funding decreased and no other sources of revenue appeared, staff were cut and services-curtailed. These were indeed strategic decisions, but they were made in response to a short-run crisis with little attention to long-range questions such as, If we continue to cut services in response to decreasing funding and demand, at what point will we be out of business? In some cases, such an approach may be effective. In this instance it was not because the changes in the environment were too severe and harmful to enable the center to maintain adequate environmental relations.

An Expanded View of Strategy Formulation

To some extent, organizations tend to make use of all three approaches to strategy formulation. If one examined strategic decisions for any organization, one would find that a combination of rational planning, political processes, and muddling-through was used. The difference among organizations lies in which of the approaches is used most extensively and for which types of decisions. In reality, some strategies are explicitly and rationally developed but do not ever become implemented because of political processes. Some strategies never are explicitly formulated, but somehow do become implemented. In some cases, no planning is done, but a set of decisions are labeled as a strategy after the fact.

One approach to untangling the types of strategies is to use a recently proposed typology of strategies (Mintzberg, 1976). It expands on our discussion so far because it considers both strategy formulation and implementation. In it the explicit and formally preplanned strategies are called *intended strategies*. In the health care case, the founders had an explicit strategy for providing a certain kind of unique medical care to the specific market. This is an example of an intended strategy.

A strategy that emerges from the stream of decisions made and implemented in actuality is called a *realized strategy*. In the early years of the health center, the originally intended strategy was achieved and thus was a realized strategy. In other cases, strategies that are planned are not achieved for various reasons; such strategies can be called *unrealized strategies*. Finally, where an adaptive or muddling-through approach is used, there is no explicit strategy and no formal planning, but after the fact, it is possible to look at the set of decisions that were made and label them as a strategy. For example, in the health center case, during the mid-1970s, the center did not have a definite plan or strategy, but looking back at the organization, the individual short-term decisions added up to a strategy of contraction of resources and services in response to the environment. A strategy that is not explicitly developed but that can be labeled after the fact is called a *retroactive strategy*.

Building on this broader view of strategy development and formulation, it is possible to expand the model presented earlier in Figure 13.2. A number of factors are potential components of the strategy-formulation process. As mentioned earlier, scanning the environment and assessing organizational resources are important elements. In addition, the individual values of key decision makers and the political processes that exist in the organization are also important in influencing the type of strategy that evolves.

In any organization, some combination of these factors will influence how strategy is developed, whether or not the process is rational, political, or adaptive. What results is a set of decisions. These may be an intended strategy that is explicit or a set of decisions with no explicit strategic component, but which will later be seen as a retroactive strategy. As an outcome of these decisions, critical tasks are identified for the organization to perform. Depending on how the organization is designed, how groups function, and how individuals behave, different patterns of organizational functioning will result. These, in turn, influence the components of strategy formulation and may lead to changes in strategy, particularly depending on whether original strategies (intended or not) are either realized or unrealized. Figure 13.4 presents this view of strategy formation.

The Components of Strategy

So far, strategy has been described as a set of decisions about the organization vis-à-vis its environment. This is consistent with the views of a number of strategy theorists (Mintzberg, 1976), that a strategy is, in reality, a stream of decisions. The question that still remains, however, is, Decisions about what?

A number of theorists have attempted to identify the critical components of a strategy (see Hofer, 1976). One approach is that used by Katz (1970) which views strategy as a set of decisions by which an organization moves from a current posture or set of environmental relations to a desired future posture, by deploying resources according to a plan. Specifically, he distinguishes three types of decisions which fall under the heading of strategy (see Table 13.1).

The first type of decision are those concerning the *scope* of the organization. Decisions about scope concern the type of environment in which the organization will operate and what will be the distinctive characteristics of that organization in that environment. It involves the identification of the specific competitive

Figure 13.4 *An Expanded Strategy Determination Model*

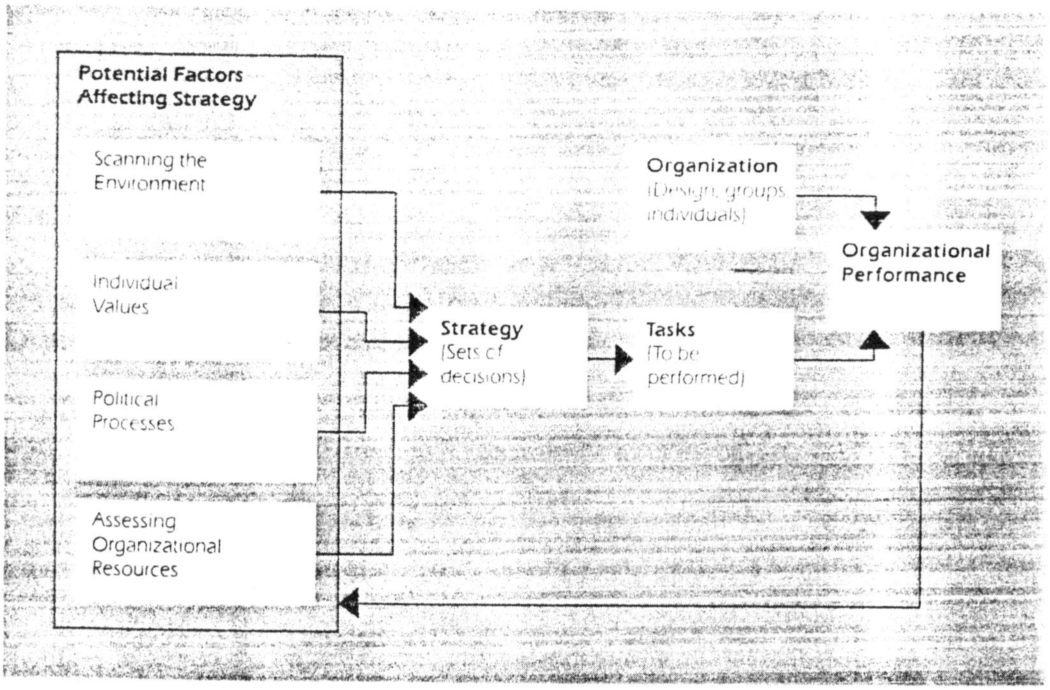

advantage or distinctive competence of the organization. The health center, for example, began by identifying a geographical area that needed service and by defining team care as the competitive advantage that it offered over other providers of health care. The decision was also made within the larger context of federal funding policies; team care that involved community residents in the health care team as family health workers made the center an attractive project for the government to fund during the 1960s. The strategic issue facing the center in the late 1970s was how to change the scope of its strategy in order to remain effective in a changed environment.

The second type of decision concerns the development of *objectives* that reflect performance characteristics needed if scope of strategy is to be realized. This might translate into specific goals such as rate of growth, market share, capital structure, and so on. For example, the objectives of the health center might be the number of patients served, satellites in service, additional inflow of funds, and the like.

The third type of decision concerns *resource allocation* within the organization so that objectives can be reached. Decisions about expense budgets, facilities, human resources planning,

Table 13.1 *Basic Components of an Organizational Strategy*

1. Scope	Decisions about the *markets* and *customers* to be served, the types and characteristics of *products*, and the *competitive basis.*
2. Objectives	Decisions about desired *performance characteristics* or goals related to the scope, such as rate of growth, market share, profitability, and so on.
3. Resource allocation	Decisions about the *allocation* of *organization resources* such as funds, facilities, personnel, management attention, and such among the organization's different activities.

Adapted from Katz, 1970.

and such are all examples of resource allocation decisions. If the health center decides to expand its scope by enlarging the geographical area served and sees that done through achieving the objectives of establishing new satellite centers, then a set of decisions about funding the satellites, management time allocated to the satellite development, resources devoted to political relations in the new communities all need to be made. It is important to note that resource allocation means more than actions within the boundaries of the organization. Frequently, an organization may attempt to actively change the environment in some way; for example, through lobbying or joining together with other organizations in coalitions (MacMillan, 1978). In these cases, organizational resources (management time, money, and reputation) are also being allocated in support of a strategy.

In summary, a strategy is a set of decisions concerning the scope of the organization's activities, objectives to be reached if the scope is to be realized, and resource allocations to be made in order to achieve objectives. These decisions involve action both inside and outside the boundaries of the organization.

Implications for Organizational Behavior

The aim of our examination of strategy has been to gain an understanding of what strategy is so that the relationship between strategy and the management of organizational behavior can be better understood. For some time, many models of organizational behavior have ignored the role of the environment and the role of strategy as an influence on patterns of behavior. The existence of strategy and the fact that managers make strategic decisions, impacts on organizational behavior in a number of ways.

1. *Strategic decisions determine organizational tasks.* As a result of strategic decisions about scope, objectives, and resource allocation, the critical tasks that an organization needs to perform are defined. Strategic decisions also spell out the critical dimensions of organizational tasks (for example, providing comprehensive health care as opposed to minimal health care). Going back to the organizational framework presented in Chapter 1 and used throughout each chapter of this book, tasks are a central concern in understanding patterns of organizational behavior. Ultimately, it is the job of the manager to get individuals and groups to perform tasks effectively. The attention given to reward systems, staffing, job design, group design, and organization design occurs in order to accomplish tasks. The organizational designer must consider the question of "designing to do what?" The recognition of the existence of strategy helps, in that strategy defines the "what" that is critical.

The implication is that managers at all levels need to become aware of what organizational strategy is. Efforts to solve problems and improve organizational effectiveness through job redesign, group design, or organization design, for example, need to be done within the context of total organizational strategy as well as the specific portions of that strategy implemented by individual organizational units.

2. *Strategic decisions influence organizational design.* The choices of scope, objectives, and resource allocations are especially influential in organizational design (as discussed in Chapters 10, 11, and 12). Research indicates that the effectiveness of organizational designs depends on which strategies are chosen (Aldrich and Pfeffer, 1976). Ideally, there should be consistency or "fit" between the demands and requirements of a strategy and the characteristics of an organizational design (Galbraith and Nathanson, 1978).

An example of the potential effect of strategy on organizational design can be seen in the health center. Clearly, the organizational structure that has been devised to manage the health center at one location during a period of contraction will need to be altered if the center undertakes a strategy of expansion through the implementation of satellites. As the organization changes its scope, different kinds of individual performance will be needed, new groups will need to be designed and managed, and new organizational groupings will need to be created, along with new and more appropriate mechanisms for coordination and control. A change in strategy can create the need for profound changes in organizational design. Conversely, to consider organizational design without also heeding potential changes in strategy can lead to problems, as changes may be made to create an organization that is consistent with a strategy no longer operational.

3. *Strategic decisions influence and are influenced by or-*

ganizational power questions. Organizational strategy is directly related to questions of power, politics, and conflict (MacMillan, 1978). First, strategic choices and the relations that exist within the environment have implications for the distribution of power internally among different cliques, coalitions, and groups (Hickson et al., 1971; Aldrich and Pfeffer, 1976). Depending on the nature of the environment and the demands of strategy, disparate groups can vary in their relative power in the organization. For example, in the health center, the dependence on federal funding based on physician-contact hours with patients may increase the power of physicians relative to other groups in the facility. The physicians as a group control a critical resource (that is, reimbursable contact hours with patients) and, therefore, are more critical to the survival of the center. Similarly, those administrators who are adept at finding and obtaining federal funding that is not tied to physician contact may be more powerful than administrators who are less able to bring funds into the center. As a result of strategic issues and choices, therefore, groups will become more or less powerful in the organization.

The relationship between strategy and power is somewhat circular. As groups become more powerful, they may also be able to influence the determination of strategy to a greater extent. We mentioned earlier that strategy develops not only through rational and preplanned processes, but also as the result of political processes between individuals, groups, or cliques. Strategic choices influence power relationships internally, and these relationships frequently influence subsequent strategic choices.

4. *Organizational effectiveness is jointly determined by strategic and organizational design decisions.* It should be apparent by now that decisions about strategy and decisions about organizational design (at the individual, group, and system level) are very much interdependent and combine *jointly* to determine how effective an organization will be. A potentially successful strategy may fail if the organizational structure is poorly designed, if groups function ineffectively, or if individuals are not motivated. Likewise, an organization may not be effective even though it has motivated workers and productive groups, if that organization is attempting to implement an inappropriate strategy. In the most general terms, organizational effectiveness is a reflection of both strategic and organizational design decisions.

Summary

Organizations are open systems; thus, organizational behavior cannot be considered in a vacuum. To survive, any organization must adapt to changes in its environment, and this process of adapting what the organization does and how it does it, to compensate for (or anticipate) changes in the environment, is the process of strategy development. Strategy defines what the organization does and, therefore, provides an important factor in understanding organizational behavior by defining what the purpose of the organization will be.

Suggested Readings

Andrews, K. R. *The Concept of Corporate Strategy.* Homewood, Ill.: Dow-Jones Irwin, 1971.

Galbraith, J. R., and Nathanson, D. A. *Strategy Implementation: The Role of Structure and Process.* St. Paul, Minn.: West Publishing, 1978.

Hofer, C. W., and Schendel, D. *Strategy Formulation: Analytical Concepts.* St. Paul, Minn.: West Publishing, 1978.

MacMillan, I. C. *Strategy Formulation: Political Concepts.* St. Paul, Minn.: West Publishing, 1978.

Miles, R. E., and Snow, E. E. *Organizational Strategy, Structure, and Process.* New York: McGraw-Hill, 1978.

THE MANAGER'S JOB: FOLKLORE AND FACT

by

H. Mintzberg

The manager's job: folklore and fact

Henry Mintzberg

The classical view says that the manager organizes, coordinates, plans, and controls; the facts suggest otherwise

Just what does the manager do? For years the manager, the heart of the organization, has been assumed to be like an orchestra leader, controlling the various parts of his organization with the ease and precision of a Seiji Ozawa. However, when one looks at the few studies that have been done—covering managerial positions from the president of the United States to street gang leaders—the facts show that managers are not reflective, regulated workers, informed by their massive MIS systems, scientific, and professional. The evidence suggests that they play a complex, intertwined combination of interpersonal, informational, and decisional roles. The author's message is that if managers want to be more effective, they must recognize what their job really is and then use the resources at hand to support rather than hamper their own nature. Understanding their jobs as well as understanding themselves takes both introspection and objectivity on the managers' part. At the end of the article the author includes a set of self-study questions to help provide that insight.

Mr. Mintzberg is associate professor in the Faculty of Management at McGill University, Montreal, Canada. He is currently a visiting professor at Centre d'étude et de Recherche sur les organisations et la gestion (I.A.E.) in Aix-en-Provence, France. Some of the material in this article is condensed from the author's book *The Nature of Managerial Work*, published by Harper & Row.

If you ask a manager what he does, he will most likely tell you that he plans, organizes, coordinates, and controls. Then watch what he does. Don't be surprised if you can't relate what you see to these four words.

When he is called and told that one of his factories has just burned down, and he advises the caller to see whether temporary arrangements can be made to supply customers through a foreign subsidiary, is he planning, organizing, coordinating, or controlling? How about when he presents a gold watch to a retiring employee? Or when he attends a conference to meet people in the trade? Or on returning from that conference, when he tells one of his employees about an interesting product idea he picked up there?

The fact is that these four words, which have dominated management vocabulary since the French industrialist Henri Fayol first introduced them in 1916, tell us little about what managers actually do. At best, they indicate some vague objectives managers have when they work.

The field of management, so devoted to progress and change, has for more than half a century not seriously addressed *the* basic question: What do managers do? Without a proper answer, how can we teach management? How can we design planning or information systems for managers? How can we improve the practice of management at all?

Editors' note: Footnotes are listed on page 61.

Our ignorance of the nature of managerial work shows up in various ways in the modern organization—in the boast by the successful manager that he never spent a single day in a management training program; in the turnover of corporate planners who never quite understood what it was the manager wanted; in the computer consoles gathering dust in the back room because the managers never used the fancy on-line MIS some analyst thought they needed. Perhaps most important, our ignorance shows up in the inability of our large public organizations to come to grips with some of their most serious policy problems.

Somehow, in the rush to automate production, to use management science in the functional areas of marketing and finance, and to apply the skills of the behavioral scientist to the problem of worker motivation, the manager—that person in charge of the organization or one of its subunits—has been forgotten.

My intention in this article is simple: to break the reader away from Fayol's words and introduce him to a more supportable, and what I believe to be a more useful, description of managerial work. This description derives from my review and synthesis of the available research on how various managers have spent their time.

In some studies, managers were observed intensively ("shadowed" is the term some of them used); in a number of others, they kept detailed diaries of their activities; in a few studies, their records were analyzed. All kinds of managers were studied—foremen, factory supervisors, staff managers, field sales managers, hospital administrators, presidents of companies and nations, and even street gang leaders. These "managers" worked in the United States, Canada, Sweden, and Great Britain. In the ruled insert on page 53 is a brief review of the major studies that I found most useful in developing this description, including my own study of five American chief executive officers.

A synthesis of these findings paints an interesting picture, one as different from Fayol's classical view as a cubist abstract is from a Renaissance painting. In a sense, this picture will be obvious to anyone who has ever spent a day in a manager's office, either in front of the desk or behind it. Yet, at the same time, this picture may turn out to be revolutionary, in that it throws into doubt so much of the folklore that we have accepted about the manager's work.

I first discuss some of this folklore and contrast it with some of the discoveries of systematic research—the hard facts about how managers spend their time. Then I synthesize these research findings in a description of ten roles that seem to describe the essential content of all managers' jobs. In a concluding section, I discuss a number of implications of this synthesis for those trying to achieve more effective management, both in classrooms and in the business world.

Some folklore and facts about managerial work

There are four myths about the manager's job that do not bear up under careful scrutiny of the facts.

1

Folklore: The manager is a reflective, systematic planner. The evidence on this issue is overwhelming, but not a shred of it supports this statement.

Fact: Study after study has shown that managers work at an unrelenting pace, that their activities are characterized by brevity, variety, and discontinuity, and that they are strongly oriented to action and dislike reflective activities. Consider this evidence:

☐
Half the activities engaged in by the five chief executives of my study lasted less than nine minutes, and only 10% exceeded one hour.[1] A study of 56 U.S. foremen found that they averaged 583 activities per eight-hour shift, an average of 1 every 48 seconds.[2] The work pace for both chief executives and foremen was unrelenting. The chief executives met a steady stream of callers and mail from the moment they arrived in the morning until they left in the evening. Coffee breaks and lunches were inevitably work related, and ever-present subordinates seemed to usurp any free moment.
☐
A diary study of 160 British middle and top managers found that they worked for a half hour or more without interruption only about once every two days.[3]
☐
Of the verbal contacts of the chief executives in my study, 93% were arranged on an ad hoc basis. Only 1% of the executives' time was spent in open-ended

observational tours. Only 1 out of 368 verbal contacts was unrelated to a specific issue and could be called general planning. Another researcher finds that "in *not one single case* did a manager report the obtaining of important external information from a general conversation or other undirected personal communication."[4]

□

No study has found important patterns in the way managers schedule their time. They seem to jump from issue to issue, continually responding to the needs of the moment.

Is this the planner that the classical view describes? Hardly. How, then, can we explain this behavior? The manager is simply responding to the pressures of his job. I found that my chief executives terminated many of their own activities, often leaving meetings before the end, and interrupted their desk work to call in subordinates. One president not only placed his desk so that he could look down a long hallway but also left his door open when he was alone—an invitation for subordinates to come in and interrupt him.

Clearly, these managers wanted to encourage the flow of current information. But more significantly, they seemed to be conditioned by their own work loads. They appreciated the opportunity cost of their own time, and they were continually aware of their ever-present obligations—mail to be answered, callers to attend to, and so on. It seems that no matter what he is doing, the manager is plagued by the possibilities of what he might do and what he must do.

When the manager must plan, he seems to do so implicitly in the context of daily actions, not in some abstract process reserved for two weeks in the organization's mountain retreat. The plans of the chief executives I studied seemed to exist only in their heads—as flexible, but often specific, intentions. The traditional literature notwithstanding, the job of managing does not breed reflective planners; the manager is a real-time responder to stimuli, an individual who is conditioned by his job to prefer live to delayed action.

2

Folklore: The effective manager has no regular duties to perform. Managers are constantly being told to spend more time planning and delegating, and less time seeing customers and engaging in negotia-

tions. These are not, after all, the true tasks of the manager. To use the popular analogy, the good manager, like the good conductor, carefully orchestrates everything in advance, then sits back to enjoy the fruits of his labor, responding occasionally to an unforeseeable exception.

But here again the pleasant abstraction just does not seem to hold up. We had better take a closer look at those activities managers feel compelled to engage in before we arbitrarily define them away.

Fact: In addition to handling exceptions, managerial work involves performing a number of regular duties, including ritual and ceremony, negotiations, and processing of soft information that links the organization with its environment. Consider some evidence from the research studies:

□

A study of the work of the presidents of small companies found that they engaged in routine activities because their companies could not afford staff specialists and were so thin on operating personnel that a single absence often required the president to substitute.[5]

□

One study of field sales managers and another of chief executives suggest that it is a natural part of both jobs to see important customers, assuming the managers wish to keep those customers.[6]

□

Someone, only half in jest, once described the manager as that person who sees visitors so that everyone else can get his work done. In my study, I found that certain ceremonial duties—meeting visiting dignitaries, giving out gold watches, presiding at Christmas dinners—were an intrinsic part of the chief executive's job.

□

Studies of managers' information flow suggest that managers play a key role in securing "soft" external information (much of it available only to them because of their status) and in passing it along to their subordinates.

3

Folklore: The senior manager needs aggregated information, which a formal management information system best provides. Not too long ago, the words *total information system* were everywhere in the management literature. In keeping with the classical view of the manager as that individual perched on the apex of a regulated, hierarchical system, the literature's manager was to receive all his important information from a giant, comprehensive MIS.

But lately, as it has become increasingly evident that these giant MIS systems are not working—that managers are simply not using them—the enthusiasm has waned. A look at how managers actually process information makes the reason quite clear. Managers have five media at their command—documents, telephone calls, scheduled and unscheduled meetings, and observational tours.

Fact: Managers strongly favor the verbal media—namely, telephone calls and meetings. The evidence comes from every single study of managerial work. Consider the following:

□

In two British studies, managers spent an average of 66% and 80% of their time in verbal (oral) communication.[7] In my study of five American chief executives, the figure was 78%.

□

These five chief executives treated mail processing as a burden to be dispensed with. One came in Saturday morning to process 142 pieces of mail in just over three hours, to "get rid of all the stuff." This same manager looked at the first piece of "hard" mail he had received all week, a standard cost report, and put it aside with the comment, "I never look at this."

□

These same five chief executives responded immediately to 2 of the 40 routine reports they received during the five weeks of my study and to four items in the 104 periodicals. They skimmed most of these periodicals in seconds, almost ritualistically. In all, these chief executives of good-sized organizations initiated on their own—that is, not in response to something else—a grand total of 25 pieces of mail during the 25 days I observed them.

An analysis of the mail the executives received reveals an interesting picture—only 13% was of specific and immediate use. So now we have another piece in the puzzle: not much of the mail provides live, current information—the action of a competitor, the mood of a government legislator, or the rating of last night's television show. Yet this is the information that drove the managers, interrupting their meetings and rescheduling their workdays.

Consider another interesting finding. Managers seem to cherish "soft" information, especially gossip,

hearsay, and speculation. Why? The reason is its timeliness; today's gossip may be tomorrow's fact. The manager who is not accessible for the telephone call informing him that his biggest customer was seen golfing with his main competitor may read about a dramatic drop in sales in the next quarterly report. But then it's too late.

To assess the value of historical, aggregated, "hard" MIS information, consider two of the manager's prime uses for his information—to identify problems and opportunities[8] and to build his own mental models of the things around him (e.g., how his organization's budget system works, how his customers buy his product, how changes in the economy affect his organization, and so on). Every bit of evidence suggests that the manager identifies decision situations and builds models not with the aggregated abstractions an MIS provides, but with specific tidbits of data.

Consider the words of Richard Neustadt, who studied the information-collecting habits of Presidents Roosevelt, Truman, and Eisenhower:

"It is not information of a general sort that helps a President see personal stakes; not summaries, not surveys, not the *bland amalgams*. Rather ... it is the odds and ends of *tangible detail* that pieced together in his mind illuminate the underside of issues put before him. To help himself he must reach out as widely as he can for every scrap of fact, opinion, gossip, bearing on his interests and relationships as President. He must become his own director of his own central intelligence."[9]

The manager's emphasis on the verbal media raises two important points:

First, verbal information is stored in the brains of people. Only when people write this information down can it be stored in the files of the organization—whether in metal cabinets or on magnetic tape—and managers apparently do not write down much of what they hear. Thus the strategic data bank of the organization is not in the memory of its computers but in the minds of its managers.

Second, the manager's extensive use of verbal media helps to explain why he is reluctant to delegate tasks. When we note that most of the manager's important information comes in verbal form and is stored in his head, we can well appreciate his reluctance. It is not as if he can hand a dossier over to

Research on managerial work

Considering its central importance to every aspect of management, there has been surprisingly little research on the manager's work, and virtually no systematic building of knowledge from one group of studies to another. In seeking to describe managerial work, I conducted my own research and also scanned the literature widely to integrate the findings of studies from many diverse sources with my own. These studies focused on two very different aspects of managerial work. Some were concerned with the characteristics of the work—how long managers work, where, at what pace and with what interruptions, with whom they work, and through what media they communicate. Other studies were more concerned with the essential content of the work—what activities the managers actually carry out, and why. Thus, after a meeting, one researcher might note that the manager spent 45 minutes with three government officials in their Washington office, while another might record that he presented his company's stand on some proposed legislation in order to change a regulation.

A few of the studies of managerial work are widely known, but most have remained buried as single journal articles or isolated books. Among the more important ones I cite (with full references in the footnotes) are the following:

□ Sune Carlson developed the diary method to study the work characteristics of nine Swedish managing directors. Each kept a detailed log of his activities. Carlson's results are reported in his book *Executive Behavior*. A number of British researchers, notably Rosemary Stewart, have subsequently used Carlson's method. In *Managers and Their Jobs*, she describes the study of 160 top and middle managers of British companies during four weeks, with particular attention to the differences in their work.

□ Leonard Sayles's book *Managerial Behavior* is another important reference. Using a method he refers to as "anthropological," Sayles studied the work content of middle- and lower-level managers in a large U.S. corporation. Sayles moved freely in the company, collecting whatever information struck him as important.

□ Perhaps the best-known source is *Presidential Power*, in which Richard Neustadt analyzes the power and managerial behavior of Presidents Roosevelt, Truman, and Eisenhower. Neustadt used secondary sources—documents and interviews with other parties—to generate his data.

□ Robert H. Guest, in *Personnel*, reports on a study of the foreman's working day. Fifty-six U.S. foremen were observed and each of their activities recorded during one eight-hour shift.

□ Richard C. Hodgson, Daniel J. Levinson, and Abraham Zaleznik studied a team of three top executives of a U.S. hospital. From that study they wrote *The Executive Role Constellation*. These researchers addressed in particular the way in which work and socioemotional roles were divided among the three managers.

□ William F. Whyte, from his study of a street gang during the Depression, wrote *Street Corner Society*. His findings about the gang's leadership, which George C. Homans analyzed in *The Human Group*, suggest some interesting similarities of job content between street gang leaders and corporate managers.

My own study involved five American CEOs of middle- to large-sized organizations—a consulting firm, a technology company, a hospital, a consumer goods company, and a school system. Using a method called "structural observation," during one intensive week of observation for each executive I recorded various aspects of every piece of mail and every verbal contact. My method was designed to capture data on both work characteristics and job content. In all, I analyzed 890 pieces of incoming and outgoing mail and 368 verbal contacts.

someone; he must take the time to "dump memory" —to tell that someone all he knows about the subject. But this could take so long that the manager may find it easier to do the task himself. Thus the manager is damned by his own information system to a "dilemma of delegation"—to do too much himself or to delegate to his subordinates with inadequate briefing.

4

Folklore: Management is, or at least is quickly becoming, a science and a profession. By almost any definitions of *science* and *profession*, this statement is false. Brief observation of any manager will quickly lay to rest the notion that managers practice a science. A science involves the enaction of systematic, analytically determined procedures or programs. If we do not even know what procedures managers use, how can we prescribe them by scientific analysis? And how can we call management a profession if we cannot specify what managers are to learn? For after all, a profession involves "knowledge of some department of learning or science" (*Random House Dictionary*).[10]

Fact: The managers' programs—to schedule time, process information, make decisions, and so on—remain locked deep inside their brains. Thus, to describe these programs, we rely on words like *judgment* and *intuition*, seldom stopping to realize that they are merely labels for our ignorance.

I was struck during my study by the fact that the executives I was observing—all very competent by any standard—are fundamentally indistinguishable from their counterparts of a hundred years ago (or a thousand years ago, for that matter). The information they need differs, but they seek it in the same way—by word of mouth. Their decisions concern modern technology, but the procedures they use to make them are the same as the procedures of the nineteenth-century manager. Even the computer, so important for the specialized work of the organization, has apparently had no influence on the work procedures of general managers. In fact, the manager is in a kind of loop, with increasingly heavy work pressures but no aid forthcoming from management science.

Considering the facts about managerial work, we can see that the manager's job is enormously complicated and difficult. The manager is overburdened with obligations; yet he cannot easily delegate his tasks. As a result, he is driven to overwork and is forced to do many tasks superficially. Brevity, fragmentation, and verbal communication characterize his work. Yet these are the very characteristics of managerial work that have impeded scientific attempts to improve it. As a result, the management scientist has concentrated his efforts on the specialized functions of the organization, where he could more easily analyze the procedures and quantify the relevant information.[11]

But the pressures of the manager's job are becoming worse. Where before he needed only to respond to owners and directors, now he finds that subordinates with democratic norms continually reduce his freedom to issue unexplained orders, and a growing number of outside influences (consumer groups, government agencies, and so on) expect his attention. And the manager has had nowhere to turn for help. The first step in providing the manager with some help is to find out what his job really is.

Back to a basic description of managerial work

Now let us try to put some of the pieces of this puzzle together. Earlier, I defined the manager as that person in charge of an organization or one of its subunits. Besides chief executive officers, this definition would include vice presidents, bishops,

foremen, hockey coaches, and prime ministers. Can all of these people have anything in common? Indeed they can. For an important starting point, all are vested with formal authority over an organizational unit. From formal authority comes status, which leads to various interpersonal relations, and from these comes access to information. Information, in turn, enables the manager to make decisions and strategies for his unit.

The manager's job can be described in terms of various "roles," or organized sets of behaviors identified with a position. My description, shown in *Exhibit I*, comprises ten roles. As we shall see, formal authority gives rise to the three interpersonal roles, which in turn give rise to the three informational roles; these two sets of roles enable the manager to play the four decisional roles.

Interpersonal roles

Three of the manager's roles arise directly from his formal authority and involve basic interpersonal relationships.

1

First is the *figurehead* role. By virtue of his position as head of an organizational unit, every manager must perform some duties of a ceremonial nature. The president greets the touring dignitaries, the foreman attends the wedding of a lathe operator, and the sales manager takes an important customer to lunch.

The chief executives of my study spent 12% of their contact time on ceremonial duties; 17% of their incoming mail dealt with acknowledgments and requests related to their status. For example, a letter to a company president requested free merchandise for a crippled schoolchild; diplomas were put on the desk of the school superintendent for his signature.

Duties that involve interpersonal roles may sometimes be routine, involving little serious communication and no important decision making. Nevertheless, they are important to the smooth functioning of an organization and cannot be ignored by the manager.

2

Because he is in charge of an organizational unit, the manager is responsible for the work of the people of that unit. His actions in this regard constitute the

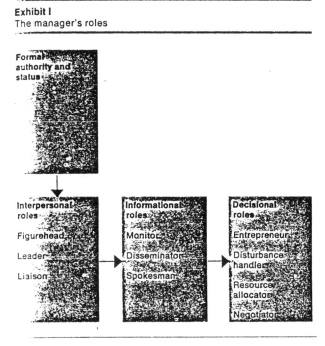

Exhibit I
The manager's roles

leader role. Some of these actions involve leadership directly—for example, in most organizations the manager is normally responsible for hiring and training his own staff.

In addition, there is the indirect exercise of the leader role. Every manager must motivate and encourage his employees, somehow reconciling their individual needs with the goals of the organization. In virtually every contact the manager has with his employees, subordinates seeking leadership clues probe his actions: "Does he approve?" "How would he like the report to turn out?" "Is he more interested in market share than high profits?"

The influence of the manager is most clearly seen in the leader role. Formal authority vests him with great potential power; leadership determines in large part how much of it he will realize.

3
The literature of management has always recognized the leader role, particularly those aspects of it related to motivation. In comparison, until recently it has hardly mentioned the *liaison* role, in which the manager makes contacts outside his vertical chain of command. This is remarkable in light of the finding of virtually every study of managerial

work that managers spend as much time with peers and other people outside their units as they do with their own subordinates—and, surprisingly, very little time with their own superiors.

In Rosemary Stewart's diary study, the 160 British middle and top managers spent 47% of their time with peers, 41% of their time with people outside their unit, and only 12% of their time with their superiors. For Robert H. Guest's study of U.S. foremen, the figures were 44%, 46%, and 10%. The chief executives of my study averaged 44% of their contact time with people outside their organizations, 48% with subordinates, and 7% with directors and trustees.

The contacts the five CEOs made were with an incredibly wide range of people: subordinates; clients, business associates, and suppliers; and peers—managers of similar organizations, government and trade organization officials, fellow directors on outside boards, and independents with no relevant organizational affiliations. The chief executives' time with and mail from these groups is shown in *Exhibit II* on page 57. Guest's study of foremen shows, likewise, that their contacts were numerous and wide ranging, seldom involving fewer than 25 individuals, and often more than 50.

As we shall see shortly, the manager cultivates such contacts largely to find information. In effect, the liaison role is devoted to building up the manager's own external information system—informal, private, verbal, but, nevertheless, effective.

Informational roles

By virtue of his interpersonal contacts, both with his subordinates and with his network of contacts, the manager emerges as the nerve center of his organizational unit. He may not know everything, but he typically knows more than any member of his staff.

Studies have shown this relationship to hold for all managers, from street gang leaders to U.S. presidents. In *The Human Group*, George C. Homans explains how, because they were at the center of the information flow in their own gangs and were also in close touch with other gang leaders, street gang leaders were better informed than any of their followers.[12] And Richard Neustadt describes the following account from his study of Franklin D. Roosevelt:

"The essence of Roosevelt's technique for information-gathering was competition. 'He would call you in,' one of his aides once told me, 'and he'd ask you to get the story on some complicated business, and you'd come back after a couple of days of hard labor and present the juicy morsel you'd uncovered under a stone somewhere, and *then* you'd find out he knew all about it, along with something else you *didn't* know. Where he got this information from he wouldn't mention, usually, but after he had done this to you once or twice you got damn careful about *your* information.' "[13]

We can see where Roosevelt "got this information" when we consider the relationship between the interpersonal and informational roles. As leader, the manager has formal and easy access to every member of his staff. Hence, as noted earlier, he tends to know more about his own unit than anyone else does. In addition, his liaison contacts expose the manager to external information to which his subordinates often lack access. Many of these contacts are with other managers of equal status, who are themselves nerve centers in their own organization. In this way, the manager develops a powerful data base of information.

The processing of information is a key part of the manager's job. In my study, the chief executives spent 40% of their contact time on activities devoted exclusively to the transmission of information; 70% of their incoming mail was purely informational (as opposed to requests for action). The manager does not leave meetings or hang up the telephone in order to get back to work. In large part, communication *is* his work. Three roles describe these informational aspects of managerial work.

1

As *monitor*, the manager perpetually scans his environment for information, interrogates his liaison contacts and his subordinates, and receives unsolicited information, much of it as a result of the network of personal contacts he has developed. Remember that a good part of the information the manager collects in his monitor role arrives in verbal form, often as gossip, hearsay, and speculation. By virtue of his contacts, the manager has a natural advantage in collecting this soft information for his organization.

2

He must share and distribute much of this information. Information he gleans from outside personal contacts may be needed within his organization. In his *disseminator* role, the manager passes some of his privileged information directly to his subordinates, who would otherwise have no access to it. When his subordinates lack easy contact with one another, the manager will sometimes pass information from one to another.

3

In his *spokesman* role, the manager sends some of his information to people outside his unit—a president makes a speech to lobby for an organization cause, or a foreman suggests a product modification to a supplier. In addition, as part of his role as spokesman, every manager must inform and satisfy the influential people who control his organizational unit. For the foreman, this may simply involve keeping the plant manager informed about the flow of work through the shop.

The president of a large corporation, however, may spend a great amount of his time dealing with a host of influences. Directors and shareholders must be advised about financial performance; consumer groups must be assured that the organization is fulfilling its social responsibilities; and government officials must be satisfied that the organization is abiding by the law.

Decisional roles

Information is not, of course, an end in itself; it is the basic input to decision making. One thing is clear in the study of managerial work: the manager plays the major role in his unit's decision-making system. As its formal authority, only he can commit the unit to important new courses of action; and as its nerve center, only he has full and current information to make the set of decisions that determines the unit's strategy. Four roles describe the manager as decision-maker.

1

As *entrepreneur*, the manager seeks to improve his unit, to adapt it to changing conditions in the environment. In his monitor role, the president is constantly on the lookout for new ideas. When a good one appears, he initiates a development project that he may supervise himself or delegate to an employee (perhaps with the stipulation that he must approve the final proposal).

There are two interesting features about these development projects at the chief executive level.

Exhibit II
The chief executives' contacts

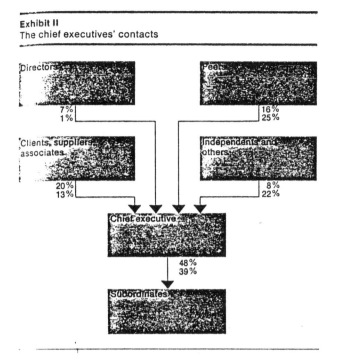

Note: The top figure indicates the proportion of total contact time spent with each group and the bottom figure, the proportion of mail from each group.

First, these projects do not involve single decisions or even unified clusters of decisions. Rather, they emerge as a series of small decisions and actions sequenced over time. Apparently, the chief executive prolongs each project so that he can fit it bit by bit into his busy, disjointed schedule and so that he can gradually come to comprehend the issue, if it is a complex one.

Second, the chief executives I studied supervised as many as 50 of these projects at the same time. Some projects entailed new products or processes; others involved public relations campaigns, improvement of the cash position, reorganization of a weak department, resolution of a morale problem in a foreign division, integration of computer operations, various acquisitions at different stages of development, and so on.

The chief executive appears to maintain a kind of inventory of the development projects that he himself supervises—projects that are at various stages of development, some active and some in limbo. Like a juggler, he keeps a number of projects in the air; periodically, one comes down, is given a new burst of energy, and is sent back into orbit. At various intervals, he put new projects on-stream and discards old ones.

2

While the entrepreneur role describes the manager as the voluntary initiator of change, the *disturbance handler* role depicts the manager involuntarily responding to pressures. Here change is beyond the manager's control. He must act because the pressures of the situation are too severe to be ignored: strike looms, a major customer has gone bankrupt, or a supplier reneges on his contract.

It has been fashionable, I noted earlier, to compare the manager to an orchestra conductor, just as Peter F. Drucker wrote in *The Practice of Management:*

"The manager has the task of creating a true whole that is larger than the sum of its parts, a productive entity that turns out more than the sum of the resources put into it. One analogy is the conductor of a symphony orchestra, through whose effort, vision and leadership individual instrumental parts that are so much noise by themselves become the living whole of music. But the conductor has the composer's score; he is only interpreter. The manager is both composer and conductor." [14]

Now consider the words of Leonard R. Sayles, who has carried out systematic research on the manager's job:

"[The manager] is like a symphony orchestra conductor, endeavouring to maintain a melodious performance in which the contributions of the various instruments are coordinated and sequenced, patterned and paced, while the orchestra members are having various personal difficulties, stage hands are moving music stands, alternating excessive heat and cold are creating audience and instrument problems, and the sponsor of the concert is insisting on irrational changes in the program." [15]

In effect, every manager must spend a good part of his time responding to high-pressure disturbances. No organization can be so well run, so standardized, that it has considered every contingency in the uncertain environment in advance. Disturbances arise not only because poor managers ignore situations until they reach crisis proportions, but also because good managers cannot possibly anticipate all the consequences of the actions they take.

3

The third decisional role is that of *resource allocator.* To the manager falls the responsibility of deciding

Self-study questions for managers

1
Where do I get my information, and how? Can I make greater use of my contacts to get information? Can other people do some of my scanning for me? In what areas is my knowledge weakest, and how can I get others to provide me with the information I need? Do I have powerful enough mental models of those things I must understand within the organization and in its environment?

2
What information do I disseminate in my organization? How important is it that my subordinates get my information? Do I keep too much information to myself because dissemination of it is time-consuming or inconvenient? How can I get more information to others so they can make better decisions?

3
Do I balance information collecting with action taking? Do I tend to act before information is in? Or do I wait so long for all the information that opportunities pass me by and I become a bottleneck in my organization?

4
What pace of change am I asking my organization to tolerate? Is this change balanced so that our operations are neither excessively static nor overly disrupted? Have we sufficiently analyzed the impact of this change on the future of our organization?

5
Am I sufficiently well informed to pass judgment on the proposals that my subordinates make? Is it possible to leave final authorization for more of the proposals with subordinates? Do we have problems of coordination because subordinates in fact now make too many of these decisions independently?

6
What is my vision of direction for this organization? Are these plans primarily in my own mind in loose form? Should I make them explicit in order to guide the decisions of others in the organization better? Or do I need flexibility to change them at will?

7
How do my subordinates react to my managerial style? Am I sufficiently sensitive to the powerful influence my actions have on them? Do I fully understand their reactions to my actions? Do I find an appropriate balance between encouragement and pressure? Do I stifle their initiative?

8
What kind of external relationships do I maintain, and how? Do I spend too much of my time maintaining these relationships? Are there certain types of people whom I should get to know better?

9
Is there any system to my time scheduling, or am I just reacting to the pressures of the moment? Do I find the appropriate mix of activities, or do I tend to concentrate on one particular function or one type of problem just because I find it interesting? Am I more efficient with particular kinds of work at special times of the day or week? Does my schedule reflect this? Can someone else (in addition to my secretary) take responsibility for much of my scheduling and do it more systematically?

10
Do I overwork? What effect does my work load have on my efficiency? Should I force myself to take breaks or to reduce the pace of my activity?

11
Am I too superficial in what I do? Can I really shift moods as quickly and frequently as my work patterns require? Should I attempt to decrease the amount of fragmentation and interruption in my work?

12
Do I orient myself too much toward current, tangible activities? Am I a slave to the action and excitement of my work, so that I am no longer able to concentrate on issues? Do key problems receive the attention they deserve? Should I spend more time reading and probing deeply into certain issues? Could I be more reflective? Should I be?

13
Do I use the different media appropriately? Do I know how to make the most of written communication? Do I rely excessively on face-to-face communication, thereby putting all but a few of my subordinates at an informational disadvantage? Do I schedule enough of my meetings on a regular basis? Do I spend enough time touring my organization to observe activity at first hand? Am I too detached from the heart of my organization's activities, seeing things only in an abstract way?

14
How do I blend my personal rights and duties? Do my obligations consume all my time? How can I free myself sufficiently from obligations to ensure that I am taking this organization where I want it to go? How can I turn my obligations to my advantage?

---

who will get what in his organizational unit. Perhaps the most important resource the manager allocates is his own time. Access to the manager constitutes exposure to the unit's nerve center and decision-maker. The manager is also charged with designing his unit's structure, that pattern of formal relationships that determines how work is to be divided and coordinated.

Also, in his role as resource allocator, the manager authorizes the important decisions of his unit before they are implemented. By retaining this power, the manager can ensure that decisions are interrelated; all must pass through a single brain. To fragment this power is to encourage discontinuous decision making and a disjointed strategy.

There are a number of interesting features about the manager's authorizing others' decisions. First, despite the widespread use of capital budgeting procedures—a means of authorizing various capital expenditures at one time—executives in my study made a great many authorization decisions on an ad hoc basis. Apparently, many projects cannot wait or simply do not have the quantifiable costs and benefits that capital budgeting requires.

Second, I found that the chief executives faced incredibly complex choices. They had to consider the impact of each decision on other decisions and on the organization's strategy. They had to ensure that the decision would be acceptable to those who influence the organization, as well as ensure that resources would not be overextended. They had to understand the various costs and benefits as well as the feasibility of the proposal. They also had to consider questions of timing. All this was necessary for the simple approval of someone else's proposal. At the same time, however, delay could lose time, while quick approval could be ill considered and quick rejection might discourage the subordinate who had spent months developing a pet project.

One common solution to approving projects is to pick the man instead of the proposal. That is, the manager authorizes those projects presented to him by people whose judgment he trusts. But he cannot always use this simple dodge.

4

The final decisional role is that of *negotiator*. Studies of managerial work at all levels indicate that managers spend considerable time in negotiations: the president of the football team is called in to work out a contract with the holdout superstar; the corporation president leads his company's contingent to negotiate a new strike issue; the foreman argues a grievance problem to its conclusion with the shop steward. As Leonard Sayles puts it, negotiations are a "way of life" for the sophisticated manager.

These negotiations are duties of the manager's job; perhaps routine, they are not to be shirked. They are an integral part of his job, for only he has the authority to commit organizational resources in "real time," and only he has the nerve center information that important negotiations require.

The integrated job

It should be clear by now that the ten roles I have been describing are not easily separable. In the terminology of the psychologist, they form a gestalt, an integrated whole. No role can be pulled out of the framework and the job be left intact. For example, a manager without liaison contacts lacks

external information. As a result, he can neither disseminate the information his employees need nor make decisions that adequately reflect external conditions. (In fact, this is a problem for the new person in a managerial position, since he cannot make effective decisions until he has built up his network of contacts.)

Here lies a clue to the problems of team management.[16] Two or three people cannot share a single managerial position unless they can act as one entity. This means that they cannot divide up the ten roles unless they can very carefully reintegrate them. The real difficulty lies with the informational roles. Unless there can be full sharing of managerial information—and, as I pointed out earlier, it is primarily verbal—team management breaks down. A single managerial job cannot be arbitrarily split, for example, into internal and external roles, for information from both sources must be brought to bear on the same decisions.

To say that the ten roles form a gestalt is not to say that all managers give equal attention to each role. In fact, I found in my review of the various research studies that

... sales managers seem to spend relatively more of their time in the interpersonal roles, presumably a reflection of the extrovert nature of the marketing activity;

... production managers give relatively more attention to the decisional roles, presumably a reflection of their concern with efficient work flow;

... staff managers spend the most time in the informational roles, since they are experts who manage departments that advise other parts of the organization.

Nevertheless, in all cases the interpersonal, informational, and decisional roles remain inseparable.

Toward more effective management

What are the messages for management in this description? I believe, first and foremost, that this description of managerial work should prove more important to managers than any prescription they might derive from it. That is to say, *the manager's effectiveness is significantly influenced by his insight into his own work.* His performance depends on how well he understands and responds to the pressures and dilemmas of the job. Thus managers who can be introspective about their work are likely to be effective at their jobs. The ruled insert on page 58 offers 14 groups of self-study questions for managers. Some may sound rhetorical; none is meant to be. Even though the questions cannot be answered simply, the manager should address them.

Let us take a look at three specific areas of concern. For the most part, the managerial logjams—the dilemma of delegation, the data base centralized in one brain, the problems of working with the management scientist—revolve around the verbal nature of the manager's information. There are great dangers in centralizing the organization's data bank in the minds of its managers. When they leave, they take their memory with them. And when subordinates are out of convenient verbal reach of the manager, they are at an informational disadvantage.

1

The manager is challenged to find systematic ways to share his privileged information. A regular debriefing session with key subordinates, a weekly memory dump on the dictating machine, the maintaining of a diary of important information for limited circulation, or other similar methods may ease the logjam of work considerably. Time spent disseminating this information will be more then regained when decisions must be made. Of course, some will raise the question of confidentiality. But managers would do well to weigh the risks of exposing privileged information against having subordinates who can make effective decisions.

If there is a single theme that runs through this article, it is that the pressures of his job drive the manager to be superficial in his actions—to overload himself with work, encourage interruption, respond quickly to every stimulus, seek the tangible and avoid the abstract, make decisions in small increments, and do everything abruptly.

2

Here again, the manager is challenged to deal consciously with the pressures of superficiality by giving serious attention to the issues that require it, by stepping back from his tangible bits of information in order to see a broad picture, and by making use of analytical inputs. Although effective managers have to be adept at responding quickly to numerous and varying problems, the danger in managerial work is that they will respond to every issue equally (and that means abruptly) and that they will never work the tangible bits and pieces of informational input into a comprehensive picture of their world.

As I noted earlier, the manager uses these bits of information to build models of his world. But the manager can also avail himself of the models of the specialists. Economists describe the functioning of markets, operations researchers simulate financial flow processes, and behavioral scientists explain the needs and goals of people. The best of these models can be searched out and learned.

In dealing with complex issues, the senior manager has much to gain from a close relationship with the management scientists of his own organization. They have something important that he lacks—time to probe complex issues. An effective working relationship hinges on the resolution of what a colleague and I have called "the planning dilemma." [17] Managers have the information and the authority; analysts have the time and the technology. A successful working relationship between the two will be effected when the manager learns to share his information and the analyst learns to adapt to the manager's needs. For the analyst, adaptation means worrying less about the elegance of the method and more about its speed and flexibility.

It seems to me that analysts can help the top manager especially to schedule his time, feed in analytical information, monitor projects under his supervision, develop models to aid in making choices, design contingency plans for disturbances that can be anticipated, and conduct "quick-and-dirty" analysis for those that cannot. But there can be no cooperation if the analysts are out of the mainstream of the manager's information flow.

3

The manager is challenged to gain control of his own time by turning obligations to his advantage and by turning those things he wishes to do into obligations. The chief executives of my study initiated only 32% of their own contacts (and another 5% by mutual agreement). And yet to a considerable extent they seemed to control their time. There were two key factors that enabled them to do so.

First, the manager has to spend so much time discharging obligations that if he were to view them as just that, he would leave no mark on his organization. The unsuccessful manager blames failure on the obligations; the effective manager turns his obligations to his own advantage. A speech is a chance to lobby for a cause; a meeting is a chance to reorganize a weak department; a visit to an important customer is a chance to extract trade information.

Second, the manager frees some of his time to do those things that he—perhaps no one else—thinks important by turning them into obligations. Free time is made, not found, in the manager's job; it is forced into the schedule. Hoping to leave some time open for contemplation or general planning is tantamount to hoping that the pressures of the job will go away. The manager who wants to innovate initiates a project and obligates others to report back to him; the manager who needs certain environmental information establishes channels that will automatically keep him informed; the manager who has to tour facilities commits himself publicly.

The educator's job

Finally, a word about the training of managers. Our management schools have done an admirable job of training the organization's specialists—management scientists, marketing researchers, accountants, and organizational development specialists. But for the most part they have not trained managers.[18]

Management schools will begin the serious training of managers when skill training takes a serious place next to cognitive learning. Cognitive learning is detached and informational, like reading a book or listening to a lecture. No doubt much important cognitive material must be assimilated by the manager-to-be. But cognitive learning no more makes a manager than it does a swimmer. The latter will drown the first time he jumps into the water if his coach never takes him out of the lecture hall, gets him wet, and gives him feedback on his performance.

In other words, we are taught a skill through practice plus feedback, whether in a real or a simulated situation. Our management schools need to identify the skills managers use, select students who show potential in these skills, put the students into situations where these skills can be practiced, and then give them systematic feedback on their performance.

My description of managerial work suggests a number of important managerial skills—developing peer relationships, carrying out negotiations, motivating subordinates, resolving conflicts, establishing infor-

mation networks and subsequently disseminating information, making decisions in conditions of extreme ambiguity, and allocating resources. Above all, the manager needs to be introspective about his work so that he may continue to learn on the job.

Many of the manager's skills can, in fact, be practiced, using techniques that range from role playing to videotaping real meetings. And our management schools can enhance the entrepreneurial skills by designing programs that encourage sensible risk taking and innovation.

No job is more vital to our society than that of the manager. It is the manager who determines whether our social institutions serve us well or whether they squander our talents and resources. It is time to strip away the folklore about managerial work, and time to study it realistically so that we can begin the difficult task of making significant improvements in its performance.

1. All the data from my study can be found in Henry Mintzberg, The Nature of Managerial Work (New York: Harper & Row, 1973).

2. Robert H. Guest, "Of Time and the Foreman," Personnel, May 1956, p. 478.

3. Rosemary Stewart, Managers and Their Jobs (London: Macmillan, 1967); see also Sune Carlson, Executive Behaviour (Stockholm: Strömbergs, 1951), the first of the diary studies.

4. Francis J. Aguilar, Scanning the Business Environment (New York: Macmillan, 1967), p. 102.

5. Unpublished study by Irving Choran, reported in Mintzberg, The Nature of Managerial Work.

6. Robert T. Davis, Performance and Development of Field Sales Managers (Boston: Division of Research, Harvard Business School, 1957); George H. Copeman, The Role of the Managing Director (London: Business Publications, 1963).

7. Stewart, Managers and Their Jobs; Tom Burns, "The Directions of Activity and Communication in a Departmental Executive Group," Human Relations 7, no. 1 (1954): 73.

8. H. Edward Wrapp, "Good Managers Don't Make Policy Decisions," HBR September-October 1967, p. 91; Wrapp refers to this as spotting opportunities and relationships in the stream of operating problems and decisions; in his article Wrapp raises a number of excellent points related to this analysis.

9. Richard E. Neustadt, Presidential Power (New York: John Wiley, 1960), pp. 153-154; italics added.

10. For a more thorough, though rather different, discussion of this issue, see Kenneth R. Andrews, "Toward Professionalism in Business Management," HBR March-April 1969, p. 49.

11. C. Jackson Grayson, Jr., in "Management Science and Business Practice," HBR July-August 1973, p. 41, explains in similar terms why, as chairman of the Price Commission, he did not use those very techniques that he himself promoted in his earlier career as a management scientist.

12. George C. Homans, The Human Group (New York: Harcourt, Brace & World, 1950), based on the study by William F. Whyte entitled Street Corner Society, rev. ed. (Chicago: University of Chicago Press, 1955).

13. Neustadt, Presidential Power, p. 157.

14. Peter F. Drucker, The Practice of Management (New York: Harper & Row, 1954), pp. 341-342.

15. Leonard R. Sayles, Managerial Behavior (New York: McGraw-Hill, 1964), p. 162.

16. See Richard C. Hodgson, Daniel J. Levinson, and Abraham Zaleznik, The Executive Role Constellation (Boston: Division of Research, Harvard Business School, 1965), for a discussion of the sharing of roles.

17. James S. Hekimian and Henry Mintzberg, "The Planning Dilemma," The Management Review, May 1968, p. 4.

18. See J. Sterling Livingston, "Myth of the Well-Educated Manager," HBR January-February 1971, p. 79.

READING 10

MANAGERS AND LEADERS: ARE THEY DIFFERENT?

by

A. Zaleznick

Managers and leaders: Are they different?

Abraham Zaleznik

A bureaucratic society which breeds managers may stifle young leaders who need mentors and emotional interchange to develop

Most societies, and that includes business organizations, are caught between two conflicting needs: one, for managers to maintain the balance of operations, and one for leaders to create new approaches and imagine new areas to explore. One might well ask why there is a conflict. Cannot both managers and leaders exist in the same society, or even better, cannot one person be both a manager and a leader? The author of this article does not say that is impossible but suggests that because leaders and managers are basically different types of people, the conditions favorable to the growth of one may be inimical to the other. Exploring the world views of managers and leaders, the author illustrates, using Alfred P. Sloan and Edwin Land among others as examples, that managers and leaders have different attitudes toward their goals, careers, relations with others, and themselves. And tracing their different lines of development, the author shows how leaders are of a psychologically different type than managers; their development depends on their forming a one-to-one relationship with a mentor.

Abraham Zaleznik is the Cahners-Rabb Professor of Social Psychology of Management at the Harvard Business School. He is also a psychoanalyst and an active member, American Psychoanalytic Association. This is Dr. Zaleznik's fifth article for HBR, the last one being "Power and Politics in Organizational Life," which appeared in the May-June 1970 issue. The present article is based on a working paper prepared for Time Inc.'s conference on leadership, held in Washington in September, 1976.

Illustration by Hans-Georg Rauch

What is the ideal way to develop leadership? Every society provides its own answer to this question, and each, in groping for answers, defines its deepest concerns about the purposes, distributions, and uses of power. Business has contributed its answer to the leadership question by evolving a new breed called the manager. Simultaneously, business has established a new power ethic that favors collective over individual leadership, the cult of the group over that of personality. While ensuring the competence, control, and the balance of power relations among groups with the potential for rivalry, managerial leadership unfortunately does not necessarily ensure imagination, creativity, or ethical behavior in guiding the destinies of corporate enterprises.

Leadership inevitably requires using power to influence the thoughts and actions of other people. Power in the hands of an individual entails human risks: first, the risk of equating power with the ability to get immediate results; second, the risk of ignoring the many different ways people can legitimately accumulate power; and third, the risk of losing self-control in the desire for power. The need to hedge these risks accounts in part for the development of collective leadership and the managerial ethic. Consequently, an inherent conservatism dominates the culture of large organizations. In *The Second American Revolution*, John D. Rockefeller, 3rd. describes the conservatism of organizations:

"An organization is a system, with a logic of its own, and all the weight of tradition and inertia. The deck is stacked in favor of the tried and proven way of doing things and against the taking of risks and striking out in new directions."[1]

Out of this conservatism and inertia organizations provide succession to power through the development of managers rather than individual leaders. And the irony of the managerial ethic is that it fosters a bureaucratic culture in business, supposedly the last bastion protecting us from the encroachments and controls of bureaucracy in government and education. Perhaps the risks associated with power in the hands of an individual may be necessary ones for business to take if organizations are to break free of their inertia and bureaucratic conservatism.

Manager vs. leader personality

Theodore Levitt has described the essential features of a managerial culture with its emphasis on rationality and control:

"Management consists of the rational assessment of a situation and the systematic selection of goals and purposes (what is to be done?); the systematic development of strategies to achieve these goals; the marshalling of the required resources; the rational design, organization, direction, and control of the activities required to attain the selected purposes; and, finally, the motivating and rewarding of people to do the work."[2]

In other words, whether his or her energies are directed toward goals, resources, organization structures, or people, a manager is a problem solver. The manager asks himself, "What problems have to be solved, and what are the best ways to achieve results so that people will continue to contribute to this organization?" In this conception, leadership is a practical effort to direct affairs; and to fulfill his task, a manager requires that many people operate at different levels of status and responsibility. Our democratic society is, in fact, unique in having solved the problem of providing well-trained managers for business. The same solution stands ready to be applied to government, education, health care, and other institutions. It takes neither genius nor

heroism to be a manager, but rather persistence, tough-mindedness, hard work, intelligence, analytical ability and, perhaps most important, tolerance and good will.

Another conception, however, attaches almost mystical beliefs to what leadership is and assumes that only great people are worthy of the drama of power and politics. Here, leadership is a psychodrama in which, as a precondition for control of a political structure, a lonely person must gain control of him or herself. Such an expectation of leadership contrasts sharply with the mundane, practical, and yet important conception that leadership is really managing work that other people do.

Two questions come to mind. Is this mystique of leadership merely a holdover from our collective childhood of dependency and our longing for good and heroic parents? Or, is there a basic truth lurking behind the need for leaders that no matter how competent managers are, their leadership stagnates because of their limitations in visualizing purposes and generating value in work? Without this imaginative capacity and the ability to communicate, managers, driven by their narrow purposes, perpetuate group conflicts instead of reforming them into broader desires and goals.

If indeed problems demand greatness, then, judging by past performance, the selection and development of leaders leave a great deal to chance. There are no known ways to train "great" leaders. Furthermore, beyond what we leave to chance, there is a deeper issue in the relationship between the need for competent managers and the longing for great leaders.

What it takes to ensure the supply of people who will assume practical responsibility may inhibit the development of great leaders. Conversely, the presence of great leaders may undermine the development of managers who become very anxious in the relative disorder that leaders seem to generate. The antagonism in aim (to have many competent managers as well as great leaders) often remains obscure in stable and well-developed societies. But the antagonism surfaces during periods of stress and change, as it did in the Western countries during both the Great Depression and World War II. The tension also appears in the struggle for power between the-

1. John D. Rockefeller, 3rd., The Second American Revolution (New York: Harper-Row, 1973), p. 72.

2. Theodore Levitt, "Management and the Post Industrial Society," The Public Interest, Summer 1976, p. 73.

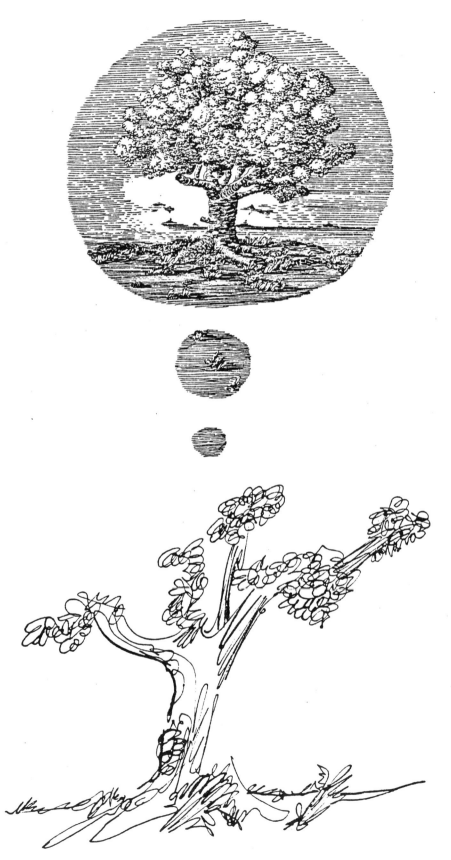

orists and professional managers in revolutionary societies.

It is easy enough to dismiss the dilemma I pose (of training managers while we may need new leaders, or leaders at the expense of managers) by saying that the need is for people who can be *both* managers and leaders. The truth of the matter as I see it, however, is that just as a managerial culture is different from the entrepreneurial culture that develops when leaders appear in organizations, managers and leaders are very different kinds of people. They differ in motivation, personal history, and in how they think and act.

A technologically oriented and economically successful society tends to depreciate the need for great leaders. Such societies hold a deep and abiding faith in rational methods of solving problems, including problems of value, economics, and justice. Once rational methods of solving problems are broken down into elements, organized, and taught as skills, then society's faith in technique over personal qualities in leadership remains the guiding conception for a democratic society contemplating its leadership requirements. But there are times when tinkering and trial and error prove inadequate to the emerging problems of selecting goals, allocating resources, and distributing wealth and opportunity. During such times, the democratic society needs to find leaders who use themselves as the instruments of learning and acting, instead of managers who use their accumulation of collective experience to get where they are going.

The most impressive spokesman, as well as exemplar of the managerial viewpoint, was Alfred P. Sloan, Jr. who, along with Pierre du Pont, designed the modern corporate structure. Reflecting on what makes one management successful while another fails, Sloan suggested that "good management rests on a reconciliation of centralization and decentralization, or 'decentralization with coordinated control' ".[3]

Sloan's conception of management, as well as his practice, developed by trial and error, and by the accumulation of experience. Sloan wrote:

"There is no hard and fast rule for sorting out the various responsibilities and the best way to assign them. The balance which is struck . . . varies according to what is being decided, the circumstances of the time, past experience, and the temperaments and skills of the executive involved."[4]

In other words, in much the same way that the inventors of the late nineteenth century tried, failed, and fitted until they hit on a product or method, managers who innovate in developing organizations are "tinkerers." They do not have a grand design or experience the intuitive flash of insight that, borrowing from modern science, we have come to call the "breakthrough."

Managers and leaders differ fundamentally in their world views. The dimensions for assessing these differences include managers' and leaders' orientations toward their goals, their work, their human relations, and their selves.

Attitudes toward goals

Managers tend to adopt impersonal, if not passive, attitudes toward goals. Managerial goals arise out of necessities rather than desires, and, therefore, are deeply embedded in the history and culture of the organization.

Frederic G. Donner, chairman and chief executive officer of General Motors from 1958 to 1967, expressed this impersonal and passive attitude toward goals in defining GM's position on product development:

". . . To meet the challenge of the marketplace, we must recognize changes in customer needs and desires far enough ahead to have the right products in the right places at the right time and in the right quantity.

"We must balance trends in preference against the many compromises that are necessary to make a final product that is both reliable and good looking, that performs well and that sells at a competitive price in the necessary volume. We must design, not just the cars we would like to build, but more importantly, the cars that our customers want to buy."[5]

Nowhere in this formulation of how a product comes into being is there a notion that consumer tastes and preferences arise in part as a result of what manufacturers do. In reality, through product design, advertising, and promotion, consumers learn to like what they then say they need. Few would argue that people who enjoy taking snapshots *need* a camera that also develops pictures. But in response to novelty, convenience, a shorter inte between acting (taking the snap) and gaining pleasure (seeing the shot), the Polaroid camera succeeded in the marketplace. But it is inconceivable that Edwin Land responded to impressions of consumer need. Instead, he translated a technology (polarization of light) into a product, which proliferated and stimulated consumers' desires.

The example of Polaroid and Land suggests how leaders think about goals. They are active instead of reactive, shaping ideas instead of responding to them. Leaders adopt a personal and active attitude toward goals. The influence a leader exerts in altering moods, evoking images and expectations, and in establishing specific desires and objectives determines the direction a business takes. The net result of this influence is to change the way people think about what is desirable, possible, and necessary.

Conceptions of work

What do managers and leaders do? What is the nature of their respective work?

Leaders and managers differ in their conceptions Managers tend to view work as an enabling process involving some combination of people and ideas interacting to establish strategies and make decisions. Managers help the process along by a range of skills, including calculating the interests in opposition, staging and timing the surfacing of controversial issues, and reducing tensions. In this enabling process, managers appear flexible in the use of tactics: they negotiate and bargain, on the one hand, and use rewards and punishments, and other forms of coercion, on the other. Machiavelli wrote for managers and not necessarily for leaders.

Alfred Sloan illustrated how this enabling process works in situations of conflict. The time was the early 1920s when the Ford Motor Co. still dominated the automobile industry using, as did General Motors, the conventional water-cooled engine. With the full backing of Pierre du Pont, Charles Kettering dedicated himself to the design of an air-cooled engine, which, if successful, would have been a great technical and market coup for GM. Kettering believed in his product, but the manufacturing division heads at GM remained skeptical and later op-

3 Alfred P. Sloan, Jr., *My Years with General Motors* (New York: Doubleday & Co. 1964), p. 429.

4 Ibid., p. 429.

5 Ibid. p. 440.

6 Ibid. p. 91.

posed the new design on two grounds: first, that it was technically unreliable, and second, that the corporation was putting all its eggs in one basket by investing in a new product instead of attending to the current marketing situation.

In the summer of 1923 after a series of false starts and after its decision to recall the copper-cooled Chevrolets from dealers and customers, GM management reorganized and finally scrapped the project. When it dawned on Kettering that the company had rejected the engine, he was deeply discouraged and wrote to Sloan that without the "organized resistance" against the project it would succeed and that unless the project were saved, he would leave the company.

Alfred Sloan was all too aware of the fact that Kettering was unhappy and indeed intended to leave General Motors. Sloan was also aware of the fact that, while the manufacturing divisions strongly opposed the new engine, Pierre du Pont supported Kettering. Furthermore, Sloan had himself gone on record in a letter to Kettering less than two years earlier expressing full confidence in him. The problem Sloan now had was to make his decision stick, keep Kettering in the organization (he was much too valuable to lose), avoid alienating du Pont, and encourage the division heads to move speedily in developing product lines using conventional water-cooled engines.

The actions that Sloan took in the face of this conflict reveal much about how managers work. First, he tried to reassure Kettering by presenting the problem in a very ambiguous fashion, suggesting that he and the Executive Committee sided with Kettering, but that it would not be practical to force the divisions to do what they were opposed to. He presented the problem as being a question of the people, not the product. Second, he proposed to reorganize around the problem by consolidating all functions in a new division that would be responsible for the design, production, and marketing of the new car. This solution, however, appeared as ambiguous as his efforts to placate and keep Kettering in General Motors. Sloan wrote: "My plan was to create an independent pilot operation under the sole jurisdiction of Mr. Kettering, a kind of copper-cooled-car division. Mr. Kettering would designate his own chief engineer and his production staff to solve the technical problems of manufacture." [6]

While Sloan did not discuss the practical value of this solution, which included saddling an inventor

127

with management responsibility, he in effect used this plan to limit his conflict with Pierre du Pont.

In effect, the managerial solution that Sloan arranged and pressed for adoption limited the options available to others. The structural solution narrowed choices, even limiting emotional reactions to the point where the key people could do nothing but go along, and even allowed Sloan to say in his memorandum to du Pont, "We have discussed the matter with Mr. Kettering at some length this morning and he agrees with us absolutely on every point we made. He appears to receive the suggestion enthusiastically and has every confidence that it can be put across along these lines." [7]

Having placated people who opposed his views by developing a structural solution that appeared to give something but in reality only limited options, Sloan could then authorize the car division's general manager, with whom he basically agreed, to move quickly in designing water-cooled cars for the immediate market demand.

Years later Sloan wrote, evidently with tongue in cheek, "The cooper-cooled car never came up again in a big way. It just died out, I don't know why." [8]

In order to get people to accept solutions to problems, managers need to coordinate and balance continually. Interestingly enough, this managerial work has much in common with what diplomats and mediators do, with Henry Kissinger apparently an outstanding practitioner. The manager aims at shifting balances of power toward solutions acceptable as a compromise among conflicting values.

What about leaders, what do they do? Where managers act to limit choices, leaders work in the opposite direction, to develop fresh approaches to long-standing problems and to open issues for new options. Stanley and Inge Hoffmann, the political scientists, liken the leader's work to that of the artist. But unlike most artists, the leader himself is an integral part of the aesthetic product. One cannot look at a leader's art without looking at the artist. On Charles de Gaulle as a political artist, they wrote: "And each of his major political acts, however tortuous the means or the details, has been whole, indivisible and unmistakably his own, like an artistic act." [9]

The closest one can get to a product apart from the artist is the ideas that occupy, indeed at times obsess, the leader's mental life. To be effective, however, the leader needs to project his ideas into images that excite people, and only then develop choices that give the projected images substance. Consequently, leaders create excitement in work.

John F. Kennedy's brief presidency shows both the strengths and weaknesses connected with the excitement leaders generate in their work. In his inaugural address he said, "Let every nation know, whether it wishes us well or ill, that we shall pay any price, bear any burden, meet any hardship, support any friend, oppose any foe, in order to assure the survival and the success of liberty."

This much-quoted statement forced people to react beyond immediate concerns and to identify with Kennedy and with important shared ideals. But upon closer scrutiny the statement must be seen as absurd because it promises a position which if in fact adopted, as in the Viet Nam War, could produce disastrous results. Yet unless expectations are aroused and mobilized, with all the dangers of frustration inherent in heightened desire, new thinking and new choice can never come to light.

Leaders work from high-risk positions, indeed often are temperamentally disposed to seek out risk and danger, especially where opportunity and reward appear high. From my observations, why one individual seeks risks while another approaches problems conservatively depends more on his or her personality and less on conscious choice. For some, especially those who become managers, the instinct for survival dominates their need for risk, and their ability to tolerate mundane, practical work assists their survival. The same cannot be said for leaders who sometimes react to mundane work as to an affliction.

Relations with others

Managers prefer to work with people; they avoid solitary activity because it makes them anxious. Several years ago, I directed studies on the psychological aspects of career. The need to seek out others with whom to work and collaborate seemed to stand out as important characterstics of managers. When asked, for example, to write imaginative stories in response to a picture showing a single figure (a boy contemplating a violin, or a man silhouetted in a state of reflection), managers populated their stories with people. The following is an example of a manager's imaginative story about the young boy contemplating a violin:

"Mom and Dad insisted that junior take music lessons so that someday he can become a concert musician. His instrument was ordered and had just arrived. Junior is weighing the alternatives of playing football with the other kids or playing with the squeak box. He can't understand how his parents could think a violin is better than a touchdown.

"After four months of practicing the violin, junior has had more than enough, Daddy is going out of his mind, and Mommy is willing to give in reluctantly to the men's wishes. Football season is now over, but a good third baseman will take the field next spring." [10]

This story illustrates two themes that clarify managerial attitudes toward human relations. The first, as I have suggested, is to seek out activity with other people (i.e. the football team), and the second is to maintain a low level of emotional involvement in these relationships. The low emotional involvement appears in the writer's use of conventional metaphors, even clichés, and in the depiction of the ready transformation of potential conflict into harmonious decisions. In this case, Junior, Mommy, and Daddy agree to give up the violin for manly sports.

These two themes may seem paradoxical, but their coexistence supports what a manager does, including reconciling differences, seeking compromises, and establishing a balance of power. A further idea demonstrated by how the manager wrote the story is that managers may lack empathy, or the capacity to sense intuitively the thoughts and feelings of others. To illustrate attempts to be empathic, here is another story written to the same stimulus picture by someone considered by his peers to be a leader:

"This little boy has the appearance of being a sincere artist, one who is deeply affected by the violin, and has an intense desire to master the instrument.

"He seems to have just completed his normal practice session and appears to be somewhat crestfallen at his inability to produce the sounds which he is sure lie within the violin.

7. Ibid. p. 91.
8. Ibid. p. 93.
9. Stanley and Inge Hoffmann, "The Will for Grandeur: de Gaulle as Political Artist," *Daedalus*, Summer 1968, p. 849.
10. Abraham Zaleznik, Gene W. Dalton, and Louis B. Barnes, *Orientation and Conflict in Career*, (Boston: Division of Research, Harvard Business School, 1970), p. 316.
11. Ibid. p. 294.

"He appears to be in the process of making a vow to himself to expend the necessary time and effort to play this instrument until he satisfies himself that he is able to bring forth the qualities of music which he feels within himself.

"With this type of determination and carry through, this boy became one of the great violinists of his day." [11]

Empathy is not simply a matter of paying attention to other people. It is also the capacity to take in emotional signals and to make them mean something in a relationship with an individual. People who describe another person as "deeply affected" with "intense desire," as capable of feeling "crestfallen" and as one who can "vow to himself," would seem to have an inner perceptiveness that they can use in their relationships with others.

Managers relate to people according to the role they play in a sequence of events or in a decision-making *process*, while leaders, who are concerned with ideas, relate in more intuitive and empathetic ways. The manager's orientation to people, as actors in a sequence of events, deflects his or her attention away from the substance of people's concerns and toward their roles in a process. The distinction is simply between a manager's attention to *how* things get done and a leader's to *what* the events and decisions mean to participants.

In recent years, managers have taken over from game theory the notion that decision-making events can be one of two types: the win-lose situation (or zero-sum game) or the win-win situation in which everybody in the action comes out ahead. As part of the process of reconciling differences among people and maintaining balances of power, managers strive to convert win-lose into win-win situations.

As an illustration, take the decision of how to allocate capital resources among operating divisions in a large, decentralized organization. On the face of it, the dollars available for distribution are limited at any given time. Presumably, therefore, the more one division gets, the less is available for other divisions.

Managers tend to view this situation (as it affects human relations) as a conversion issue: how to make what seems like a win-lose problem into a win-win problem. Several solutions to this situation come to mind. First, the manager focuses others' attention on procedure and not on substance. Here the actors become engrossed in the bigger problem of *how* to make decisions, not *what* decisions to make. Once committed to the bigger problem, the actors have to support the outcome since they were involved in formulating decision rules. Because the actors believe in the rules they formulated, they will accept present losses in the expectation that next time they will win.

Second, the manager communicates to his subordinates indirectly, using "signals" instead of "messages." A signal has a number of possible implicit positions in it while a message clearly states a position. Signals are inconclusive and subject to reinterpretation should people become upset and angry, while messages involve the direct consequence that some people will indeed not like what they hear. The nature of messages heightens emotional response, and, as I have indicated, emotionally makes managers anxious. With signals, the question of who wins and who loses often becomes obscured.

Third, the manager plays for time. Managers seem to recognize that with the passage of time and the delay of major decisions, compromises emerge that take the sting out of win-lose situations; and the original "game" will be superseded by additional ones. Therefore, compromises may mean that one wins and loses simultaneously, depending on which of the games one evaluates.

There are undoubtedly many other tactical moves managers use to change human situations from win-lose to win-win. But the point to be made is that such tactics focus on the decision-making process itself and interest managers rather than leaders. The interest in tactics involves costs as well as benefits, including making organizations fatter in bureaucratic and political intrigue and leaner in direct, hard activity and warm human relationships. Consequently, one often hears subordinates characterize managers as inscrutable, detached, and manipulative. These adjectives arise from the subordinates' perception that they are linked together in a process whose purpose, beyond simply making decisions, is to maintain a controlled as well as rational and equitable structure. These adjectives suggest that managers need order in the face of the potential chaos that many fear in human relationships.

In contrast, one often hears leaders referred to in adjectives rich in emotional content. Leaders attract strong feelings of identity and difference, or of love and hate. Human relations in leader-dominated

structures often appear turbulent, intense, and at times even disorganzied. Such an atmosphere intensifies individual motivation and often produces unanticipated outcomes. Does this intense motivation lead to innovation and high performance, or does it represent wasted energy?

Senses of self

In *The Varieties of Religious Experience*, William James describes two basic personality types, "once-born" and "twice-born." [12] People of the former personality type are those for whom adjustments to life have been straightforward and whose lives have been more or less a peaceful flow from the moment of their births. The twice-borns, on the other hand, have not had an easy time of it. Their lives are marked by a continual struggle to attain some sense of order. Unlike the once-borns they cannot take things for granted. According to James, these personalities have equally different world views. For a once-born personality, the sense of self, as a guide to conduct and attitude, derives from a feeling of being at home and in harmony with one's environment. For a twice-born, the sense of self derives from a feeling of profound separateness.

A sense of belonging or of being separate has a practical significance for the kinds of investments managers and leaders make in their careers. Managers see themselves as conservators and regulators of an existing order of affairs with which they personally identify and from which they gain rewards. Perpetuating and strengthening existing institutions enhances a manager's sense of self-worth: he or she is performing in a role that harmonizes with the ideals of duty and responsibility. William James had this harmony in mind—this sense of self as flowing easily to and from the outer world—in defining a once-born personality. If one feels oneself as a member of institutions, contributing to their well-being, then one fulfills a mission in life and feels rewarded for having measured up to ideals. This reward transcends material gains and answers the more fundamental desire for personal integrity which is achieved by identifying with existing institutions.

Leaders tend to be twice-born personalities, people who feel separate from their environment, including other people. They may work in organizations, but they never belong to them. Their sense of who they are does not depend upon memberships, work

12. William James, *Varieties of Religious Experience* (New York: Mentor Books, 1958).

roles, or other social indicators of identity. What seems to follow from this idea about separateness is some theoretical basis for explaining why certain individuals search out opportunities for change. The methods to bring about change may be technological, political, or ideological, but the object is the same: to profoundly alter human, economic, and political relationships.

Sociologists refer to the preparation individuals undergo to perform in roles as the socialization process. Where individuals experience themselves as an integral part of the social structure (their self-esteem gains strength through participation and conformity), social standards exert powerful effects in maintaining the individual's personal sense of continuity, even beyond the early years in the family. The line of development from the family to schools, then to career is cumulative and reinforcing. When the line of development is not reinforcing because of significant disruptions in relationships or other problems experienced in the family or other social institutions, the individual turns inward and struggles to establish self-esteem, identity, and order. Here the psychological dynamics center on the experience with loss and the efforts at recovery.

In considering the development of leadership, we have to examine two different courses of life history: (1) development through socialization, which prepares the individual to guide institutions and to maintain the existing balance of social relations; and (2) development through personal mastery, which impels an individual to struggle for psychological and social change. Society produces its managerial talent through the first line of development, while through the second leaders emerge.

Development of leadership

The development of every person begins in the family. Each person experiences the traumas associated with separating from his or her parents, as well as the pain that follows such frustration. In the same vein, all individuals face the difficulties of achieving self-regulation and self-control. But for some, perhaps a majority, the fortunes of childhood provide adequate gratifications and sufficient opportunities to find substitutes for rewards no longer

available. Such individuals, the "once-borns," make moderate identifications with parents and find a harmony between what they expect and what they are able to realize from life.

But suppose the pains of separation are amplified by a combination of parental demands and the individual's needs to the degree that a sense of isolation, of being special, and of wariness disrupts the bonds that attach children to parents and other authority figures? Under such conditions, and given a special aptitude, the origins of which remain mysterious, the person becomes deeply involved in his or her inner world at the expense of interest in the outer world. For such a person, self-esteem no longer depends solely upon positive attachments and real rewards. A form a self-reliance takes hold along with expectations of performance and achievement, and perhaps even the desire to do great works.

Such self-perceptions can come to nothing if the individual's talents are negligible. Even with strong talents, there are no guarantees that achievement will follow, let alone that the end result will be for good rather than evil. Other factors enter into development. For one thing, leaders are like artists and other gifted people who often struggle with neuroses; their ability to function varies considerably even over the short run, and some potential leaders may lose the struggle altogether. Also, beyond early childhood, the patterns of development that affect managers and leaders involve the selective influence of particular people. Just as they appear flexible and evenly distributed in the types of talents available for development, managers form moderate and widely distributed attachments. Leaders, on the other hand, establish, and also break off, intensive one-to-one relationships.

It is a common observation that people with great talents are often only indifferent students. No one, for example, could have predicted Einstein's great achievements on the basis of his mediocre record in school. The reason for mediocrity is obviously not the absence of ability. It may result, instead, from self-absorption and the inability to pay attention to the ordinary tasks at hand. The only sure way an individual can interrupt reverie-like preoccupation and self-absorption is to form a deep attachment to a great teacher or other benevolent person who understands and has the ability to communicate with the gifted individual.

Whether gifted individuals find what they need in one-to-one relationships depends on the availability of sensitive and intuitive mentors who have a vocation in cultivating talent. Fortunately, when the generations do meet and the self-selections occur, we learn more about how to develop leaders and how talented people of different generations influence each other.

While apparently destined for a mediocre career, people who form important one-to-one relationships are able to accelerate and intensify their development through an apprenticeship. The background for such apprenticeships, or the psychological readiness of an individual to benefit from an intensive relationship, depends upon some experience in life that forces the individual to turn inward. A case example will make this point clearer. This example comes from the life of Dwight David Eisenhower, and illustrates the transformation of a career from competent to outstanding.[13]

Dwight Eisenhower's early career in the Army foreshadowed very little about his future development. During World War I, while some of his West Point classmates were already experiencing the war firsthand in France, Eisenhower felt "embedded in the monotony and unsought safety of the Zone of the Interior . . . that was intolerable punishment."[14]

Shortly after World War I, Eisenhower, then a young officer somewhat pessimistic about his career chances, asked for a transfer to Panama to work under General Fox Connor, a senior officer whom Eisenhower admired. The army turned down Eisenhower's request. This setback was very much on Eisenhower's mind when Ikey, his first-born son, succumbed to influenza. By some sense of responsibility for its own, the army transferred Eisenhower to Panama, where he took up his duties under General Connor with the shadow of his lost son very much upon him.

In a relationship with the kind of father he would have wanted to be, Eisenhower reverted to being the son he lost. In this highly charged situation, Eisenhower began to learn from his mentor. General Connor offered, and Eisenhower gladly took, a magnificent tutorial on the military. The effects of this relationship on Eisenhower cannot be measured quantitatively, but, in Eisenhower's own reflections and the unfolding of his career, one cannot overestimate its significance in the reintegration of a person shattered by grief.

As Eisenhower wrote later about Connor, "Life with General Connor was a sort of graduate school in military affairs and the humanities, leavened by a man who was experienced in his knowledge of men and their conduct. I can never adequately express my gratitude to this one gentleman. . . . In a lifetime of association with great and good men, he is the one more or less invisible figure to whom I owe an incalculable debt."[15]

Some time after his tour of duty with General Connor, Eisenhower's breakthrough occurred. He received orders to attend the Command and General Staff School at Fort Leavenworth, one of the most competitive schools in the army. It was a coveted appointment, and Eisenhower took advantage of the opportunity. Unlike his performance in high school and West Point, his work at the Command School was excellent; he was graduated first in his class.

Psychological biographies of gifted people repeatedly demonstrate the important part a mentor plays in developing an individual. Andrew Carnegie owed much to his senior, Thomas A. Scott. As head of the Western Division of the Pennsylvania Railroad, Scott recognized talent and the desire to learn in the young telegrapher assigned to him. By giving Carnegie increasing responsibility and by providing him with the opportunity to learn through close personal observation, Scott added to Carnegie's self-confidence and sense of achievement. Because of his own personal strength and achievement, Scott did not fear Carnegie's aggressiveness. Rather, he gave it full play in encouraging Carnegie's initiative.

Mentors take risks with people. They bet initially on talent they perceive in younger people. Mentors also risk emotional involvement in working closely with their juniors. The risks do not always pay off, but the willingness to take them appears crucial in developing leaders.

Can organizations develop leaders?

The examples I have given of how leaders develop suggest the importance of personal influence and the one-to-one relationship. For organizations to encourage consciously the development of leaders compared with managers would mean developing one-to-one relationships between junior and senior executives and, more important, fostering a culture of individualism and possibly elitism. The elitism arises out of the desire to identify talent and other qualities suggestive of the ability to lead and not simply to manage.

The Jewel Companies Inc. enjoy a reputation for developing talented people. The chairman and chief executive officer, Donald S. Perkins, is perhaps a good example of a person brought along through the mentor approach. Franklin J. Lunding, who was Perkins's mentor, expressed the philosophy of taking risks with young people this way:

"Young people today want in on the action. They don't want to sit around for six months trimming lettuce." [16]

This statement runs counter to the culture that attaches primary importance to slow progression based on experience and proved competence. It is a high-risk philosophy, one that requires time for the attachment between senior and junior people to grow and be meaningful, and one that is bound to produce more failures than successes.

The elitism is an especially sensitive issue. At Jewel the MBA degree symbolized the elite. Lunding attracted Perkins to Jewel at a time when business school graduates had little interest in retailing in general, and food distribution in particular. Yet the elitism seemed to pay off: not only did Perkins become the president at age 37, but also under the leadership of young executives recruited into Jewel with the promise of opportunity for growth and advancement, Jewel managed to diversify into discount and drug chains and still remain strong in food retailing. By assigning each recruit to a vice president who acted as sponsor, Jewel evidently tried to build a structure around the mentor approach to developing leaders. To counteract the elitism implied in such an approach, the company also introduced an "equalizer" in what Perkins described as "the first assistant philosophy." Perkins stated:

"Being a good first assistant means that each management person thinks of himself not as the order-giving, domineering boss, but as the first assistant to those who 'report' to him in a more typical organizational sense. Thus we mentally turn our organizational charts upside-down and challenge ourselves to seek ways in which we can lead ... by helping ... by teaching ... by listening ... and by managing in the true democratic sense ... that is, with the consent of the managed. Thus the satisfactions of leadership come from helping others to get things done and changed—and not from getting credit for doing and changing things ourselves." [17]

While this statement would seem to be more egalitarian than elitist, it does reinforce a youth-oriented culture since it defines the senior officer's job as primarily helping the junior person.

A myth about how people learn and develop that seems to have taken hold in the American culture also dominates thinking in business. The myth is that people learn best from their peers. Supposedly, the threat of evaluation and even humiliation recedes in peer relations because of the tendency for mutual identification and the social restraints on authoritarian behavior among equals. Peer training in organizations occurs in various forms. The use, for example, of task forces made up of peers from several interested occupational groups (sales, production, research, and finance) supposedly removes the restraints of authority on the individual's willingness to assert and exchange ideas. As a result, so the theory goes, people interact more freely, listen more objectively to criticism and other points of view and, finally, learn from this healthy interchange.

Another application of peer training exists in some large corporations, such as Philips, N.V. in Holland, where organization structure is built on the principle of joint responsibility of two peers, one representing the commercial end of the business and the other the technical. Formally, both hold equal responsibility for geographic operations or product groups, as the case may be. As a practical matter, it may turn out that one or the other of the peers dominates the management. Nevertheless, the main interaction is between two or more equals.

The principal question I would raise about such arrangements is whether they perpetuate the managerial orientation, and preclude the formation of one-to-one relationships between senior people and potential leaders.

Aware of the possible stifling effects of peer relationships on aggressiveness and individual initiative,

13. This example is included in Abraham Zaleznik and Manfred F.R. Kets de Vries, *Power and the Corporate Mind* (Boston: Houghton Mifflin, 1975).

14. Dwight D. Eisenhower, *At Ease: Stories I Tell to Friends* (New York: Doubleday, 1967), p. 136.

15. Ibid. p. 187.

16. "Jewel Lets Young Men Make Mistakes," *Business Week*, January 17, 1970, p. 90.

17. "What Makes Jewel Shine so Bright," *Progressive Grocer*, September, 1973, p. 76.

another company, much smaller than Philips, utilizes joint responsibility of peers for operating units, with one important difference. The chief executive of this company encourages competition and rivalry among peers, ultimately appointing the one who comes out on top for increased responsibility. These hybrid arrangements produce some unintended consequences that can be disastrous. There is no easy way to limit rivalry. Instead, it permeates all levels of the operation and opens the way for the formation of cliques in an atmosphere of intrigue.

A large, integrated oil company has accepted the importance of developing leaders through the direct influence of senior on junior executives. One chairman and chief executive officer regularly selected one talented university graduate whom he appointed his special assistant, and with whom he would work closely for a year. At the end of the year, the junior executive would become available for assignment to one of the operating divisions, where he would be assigned to a responsible post rather than a training position. The mentor relationship had acquainted the junior executive firsthand with the use of power, and with the important antidotes to the power disease called *hubris*—performance and integrity.

Working in one-to-one relationships, where there is a formal and recognized difference in the power of the actors, takes a great deal of tolerance for emotional interchange. This interchange, inevitable in close working arrangements, probably accounts for the reluctance of many executives to become involved in such relationships. *Fortune* carried an interesting story on the departure of a key executive, John W. Hanley, from the top management of Procter & Gamble, for the chief executive officer position at Monsanto.[18] According to this account, the chief executive and chairman of P&G passed over Hanley for appointment to the presidency and named another executive vice president to this post instead.

The chairman evidently felt he could not work well with Hanley who, by his own acknowledgement, was aggressive, eager to experiment and change practices, and constantly challenged his superior. A chief executive officer naturally has the right to select people with whom he feels congenial. But I wonder whether a greater capacity on the part of senior officers to tolerate the competitive impulses and behavior of their subordinates might not be healthy for corporations. At least a greater tolerance for interchange would not favor the managerial team

18 "Jack Hanley Got There by Selling Harder," *Fortune*, November, 1976.

player at the expense of the individual who might become a leader.

I am constantly surprised at the frequency with which chief executives feel threatened by open challenges to their ideas, as though the source of their authority, rather than their specific ideas, were at issue. In one case a chief executive officer, who was troubled by the aggressiveness and sometimes outright rudeness of one of his talented vice presidents, used various indirect methods such as group meetings and hints from outside directors to avoid dealing with his subordinate. I advised the executive to deal head-on with what irritated him. I suggested that by direct, face-to-face confrontation, both he and his subordinate would learn to validate the distinction between the authority to be preserved and the issues to be debated.

To confront is also to tolerate aggressive interchange, and has the net effect of stripping away the veils of ambiguity and signaling so characteristic of managerial cultures, as well as encouraging the emotional relationship leaders need if they are to survive.

READING 11

A NEW STRATEGY FOR JOB ENRICHMENT

by

J.R. Hackman, G.R. Oldham, R. Janson & K. Purdy

From: California Management Review, 1975, 17(4), pp. 57-71.
Used by Permission.

J. Richard Hackman, Greg Oldham,
Robert Janson, and Kenneth Purdy

A New Strategy for Job Enrichment

Practitioners of job enrichment have been living through a time of excitement, even euphoria. Their craft has moved from the psychology and management journals to the front page and the Sunday supplement. Job enrichment, which began with the pioneering work of Herzberg and his associates, originally was intended as a means to increase the motivation and satisfaction of people at work—and to improve productivity in the bargain.[1-5] Now it is being acclaimed in the popular press as a cure for problems ranging from inflation to drug abuse.

Much current writing about job enrichment is enthusiastic, sometimes even messianic, about what it can accomplish. But the hard questions of exactly what should be done to improve jobs, and how, tend to be glossed over. Lately, because the harder questions have not been dealt with adequately, critical winds have begun to blow. Job enrichment has been described as yet another "management fad," as "nothing new," even as a fraud. And reports of job-enrichment failures are beginning to appear in management and psychology journals.

This article attempts to redress the excesses that have characterized some of the recent writings about job enrichment. As the technique increases in popularity as a management tool, top managers inevitably will find themselves making decisions about its use. The intent of this paper is to help both managers and behavioral scientists become better able to make those decisions on a solid basis of fact and data.

Succinctly stated, we present here a new strategy for going about the redesign of work. The strategy is based on three years of collaborative work and cross-fertilization among the authors—two of whom are academic researchers and two of whom are active practitioners in job enrichment. Our approach is new, but it has been tested in many organizations. It draws on the contributions of both management practice and psychological theory, but it is firmly in the middle ground between them. It builds on and complements previous work by Herzberg and others, but provides for the first time a set of tools for *diagnosing* existing jobs—and a map for translating the diagnostic results into specific action steps for change.

What we have, then, is the following:

1. A theory that specifies when people will get personally "turned on" to their work. The theory shows what kinds of jobs are most likely to generate excitement and commitment about work, and what kinds of employees it works best for.

2. A set of action steps for job enrichment based on the theory, which prescribe in concrete

SUMMER / 1975 / VOL. XVII / NO. 4

terms what to do to make jobs more motivating for the people who do them.

3. Evidence that the theory holds water and that it can be used to bring about measurable—and sometimes dramatic—improvements in employee work behavior, in job satisfaction, and in the financial performance of the organizational unit involved.

The Theory Behind the Strategy

What makes people get turned on to their work? For workers who are really prospering in their jobs, work is likely to be a lot like play. Consider, for example, a golfer at a driving range, practicing to get rid of a hook. His activity is *meaningful* to him; he has chosen to do it because he gets a "kick" from testing his skills by playing the game. He knows that he alone is *responsible* for what happens when he hits the ball. And he has *knowledge of the results* within a few seconds.

Behavioral scientists have found that the three "psychological states" experienced by the golfer in the above example also are critical in determining a person's motivation and satisfaction on the job.

● *Experienced meaningfulness:* The individual

J. Richard Hackman is Associate Professor of Administrative Sciences and of Psychology at Yale University. He is the author of numerous articles on organizational behavior and co-author of the recent book *Behavior in Organizations.*

Greg Oldham is Assistant Professor of Business Administration at the University of Illinois. His work has been published in several leading journals, and his current research interests include leadership, job design, and motivation.

Robert Janson is Vice-President of Roy W. Walters & Associates, a consulting firm specializing in applications of the behavioral sciences to the solution of organizational problems. He has contributed numerous articles to personnel and training journals, as well as to books on motivation and work design.

Kenneth Purdy is a senior associate with Roy W. Walters & Associates. He has written numerous articles on job design and the quality of work.

must perceive his work as worthwhile or important by some system of values he accepts.

● *Experienced responsibility:* He must believe that he personally is accountable for the outcomes of his efforts.

● *Knowledge of results:* He must be able to determine, on some fairly regular basis, whether or not the outcomes of his work are satisfactory.

When these three conditions are present, a person tends to feel very good about himself when he performs well. And those good feelings will prompt him to try to continue to do well—so he can continue to earn the positive feelings in the future. That is what is meant by "internal motivation"—being turned on to one's work because of the positive internal feelings that are generated by doing well, rather than being dependent on external factors (such as incentive pay or compliments from the boss) for the motivation to work effectively.

What if one of the three psychological states is missing? Motivation drops markedly. Suppose, for example, that our golfer has settled in at the driving range to practice for a couple of hours. Suddenly a fog drifts in over the range. He can no longer see if the ball starts to tail off to the left a hundred yards out. The satisfaction he got from hitting straight down the middle—and the motivation to try to correct something whenever he didn't—are both gone. If the fog stays, it's likely that he soon will be packing up his clubs.

The relationship between the three psychological states and on-the-job outcomes is illustrated in Figure 1. When all three are high, then in-

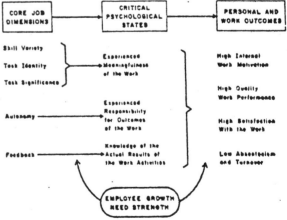

Figure 1. Relationships among core job dimensions, critical psychological states, and on-the-job outcomes.

ternal work motivation, job satisfaction, and work quality are high, and absenteeism and turnover are low.

What job characteristics make it happen? Recent research has identified five "core" characteristics of jobs that elicit the psychological states described above.[6-8] These five core job dimensions provide the key to objectively measuring jobs and to changing them so that they have high potential for motivating people who do them.

♦ Toward meaningful work. Three of the five core dimensions contribute to a job's meaningfulness for the worker:

1. Skill Variety—the degree to which a job requires the worker to perform activities that challenge his skills and abilities. When even a single skill is involved, there is at least a seed of potential meaningfulness. When several are involved, the job has the potential of appealing to more of the whole person, and also of avoiding the monotony of performing the same task repeatedly, no matter how much skill it may require.

2. Task Identity—the degree to which the job requires completion of a "whole" and identifiable piece of work—doing a job from beginning to end with a visible outcome. For example, it is clearly more meaningful to an employee to build complete toasters than to attach electrical cord after electrical cord, especially if he never sees a completed toaster. (Note that the whole job, in this example, probably would involve greater skill variety as well as task identity.)

3. Task Significance—the degree to which the job has a substantial and perceivable impact on the lives of other people, whether in the immediate organization or the world at large. The worker who tightens nuts on aircraft brake assemblies is more likely to perceive his work as significant than the worker who fills small boxes with paper clips—even though the skill levels involved may be comparable.

Each of these three job dimensions represents an important route to experienced meaningfulness. If the job is high in all three, the worker is quite likely to experience his job as very meaningful. It is not necessary, however, for a job to be very high in all three dimensions. If the job is low in

any one of them, there will be a drop in overall experienced meaningfulness. But even when two dimensions are low the worker may find the job meaningful if the third is high enough.

♦ Toward personal responsibility. A fourth core dimension leads a worker to experience increased responsibility in his job. This is *autonomy*, the degree to which the job gives the worker freedom, independence, and discretion in scheduling work and determining how he will carry it out. People in highly autonomous jobs know that they are personally responsible for successes and failures. To the extent that their autonomy is high, then, how the work goes will be felt to depend more on the individual's own efforts and initiatives·rather than on detailed instructions from the boss or from a manual of job procedures.

♦ Toward knowledge of results. The fifth and last core dimension is *feedback*. This is the degree to which a worker, in carrying out the work activities required by the job, gets information about the effectiveness of his efforts. Feedback is most powerful when it comes directly from the work itself—for example, when a worker has the responsibility for gauging and otherwise checking a component he has just finished, and learns in the process that he has lowered his reject rate by meeting specifications more consistently.

♦ The overall "motivating potential" of a job.

Figure 1 shows how the five core dimensions combine to affect the psychological states that are critical in determining whether or not an employee will be internally motivated to work effectively. Indeed, when using an instrument to be described later, it is possible to compute a "motivating potential score" (MPS) for any job. The MPS provides a single summary index of the degree to which the objective characteristics of the job will prompt high internal work motivation. Following the theory outlined above, a job high in motivating potential must be high in at least one (and hopefully more) of the three dimensions that lead to experienced meaningfulness and high in both autonomy and feedback as well. The MPS provides a quantitative index of the degree to which this is in fact the case (see Appendix for detailed formula). As will be seen later, the MPS can be very useful in diagnosing jobs and in assessing the effectiveness of job-enrichment activities.

Does the theory work for everybody? Unfortunately not. Not everyone is able to become internally motivated in his work, even when the motivating potential of a job is very high indeed.

Research has shown that the *psychological needs* of people are very important in determining who can (and who cannot) become internally motivated at work. Some people have strong needs for personal accomplishment, for learning and developing themselves beyond where they are now, for being stimulated and challenged, and so on. These people are high in "growth-need strength."

Figure 2 shows diagrammatically the proposition

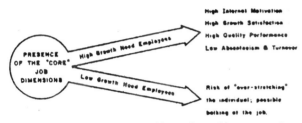

Figure 2. The moderating effect of employee growth-need strength.

that individual growth needs have the power to moderate the relationship between the characteristics of jobs and work outcomes. Many workers with high growth needs will turn on eagerly when they have jobs that are high in the core dimensions. Workers whose growth needs are not so strong may respond less eagerly—or, at first, even balk at being "pushed" or "stretched" too far.

Psychologists who emphasize human potential argue that everyone has within him at least a spark of the need to grow and develop personally. Steadily accumulating evidence shows, however, that unless that spark is pretty strong, chances are it will get snuffed out by one's experiences in typical organizations. So, a person who has worked for twenty years in stultifying jobs may find it difficult or impossible to become internally motivated overnight when given the opportunity.

We should be cautious, however, about creating rigid categories of people based on their measured growth-need strength at any particular time. It is true that we can predict from these measures who is likely to become internally motivated on a job and who will be less willing or able to do so. But what we do not know yet is whether or not the growth-need "spark" can be rekindled for those individuals who have had their growth needs dampened by years of growth-depressing experience in their organizations.

Since it is often the organization that is responsible for currently low levels of growth desires, we believe that the organization also should provide the individual with the chance to reverse that trend whenever possible, even if that means putting a person in a job where he may be "stretched" more than he wants to be. He can always move back later to the old job--and in the meantime the embers of his growth needs just might burst back into flame, to his surprise and pleasure, and for the good of the organization.

From Theory to Practice: A Technology for Job Enrichment

When job enrichment fails, it often fails because of inadequate *diagnosis* of the target job and employees' reactions to it. Often, for example, job enrichment is assumed by management to be a solution to "people problems" on the job and is implemented even though there has been no diagnostic activity to indicate that the root of the problem is in fact how the work is designed. At other times, some diagnosis is made—but it provides no concrete guidance about what specific aspects of the job require change. In either case, the success of job enrichment may wind up depending more on the quality of the intuition of the change agent--or his luck—than on a solid base of data about the people and the work.

In the paragraphs to follow, we outline a new technology for use in job enrichment which explicitly addresses the diagnostic as well as the action components of the change process. The technology has two parts: (1) a set of diagnostic tools that are useful in evaluating jobs and people's reactions to them prior to change—and in pinpointing exactly what aspects of specific jobs are most critical to a successful change attempt; and (2) a set of "implementing concepts" that provide concrete guidance for action steps in job enrichment. The implementing concepts are tied directly to the diagnostic tools; the output of the diagnostic activity specifies which action steps are likely to have the most impact in a particular situation.

The diagnostic tools. Central to the diagnostic procedure we propose is a package of instruments to be used by employees, supervisors, and outside observers in assessing the target job and employees' reactions to it.[9] These instruments gauge the following:

1. The objective characteristics of the jobs themselves, including both an overall indication of the "motivating potential" of the job as it exists (that is, the MPS score) and the score of the job on each of the five core dimensions described previously. Because knowing the strengths and weaknesses of the job is critical to any work-resdesign effort, assessments of the job are made by supervisors and outside observers as well as the employees themselves—and the final assessment of a job uses data from all three sources.

2. The current levels of motivation, satisfaction, and work performance of employees on the job. In addition to satisfaction with the work itself, measures are taken of how people feel about other aspects of the work setting, such as pay, supervision, and relationships with co-workers.

3. The level of growth-need strength of the employees. As indicated earlier, employees who have strong growth needs are more likely to be more responsive to job enrichment than employees with weak growth needs. Therefore, it is important to know at the outset just what kinds of satisfactions the people who do the job are (and are not) motivated to obtain from their work. This will make it possible to identify which persons are best to start changes with, and which may need help in adapting to the newly enriched job.

What, then, might be the actual steps one would take in carrying out a job diagnosis using these tools? Although the approach to any particular diagnosis depends upon the specifics of the particular work situation involved, the sequence of questions listed below is fairly typical.

● *Step 1. Are motivation and satisfaction central to the problem?* Sometimes organizations undertake job enrichment to improve the work motivation and satisfaction of employees when in fact the real problem with work performance lies elsewhere—for example, in a poorly designed production system, in an error-prone computer, and so on. The first step is to examine the scores of employees on the motivation and satisfaction portions of the diagnostic instrument. (The questionnaire taken by employees is called the Job Diagnostic Survey and will be referred to hereafter as the JDS.) If motivation and satisfaction are problematic, the change agent would continue to Step 2; if not, he would look to other aspects of the work situation to identify the real problem.

● *Step 2. Is the job low in motivating potential?* To answer this question, one would examine the motivating potential score of the target job and compare it to the MPS's of other jobs to determine whether or not *the job itself* is a probable cause of the motivational problems documented in Step 1. If the job turns out to be low on the MPS, one would continue to Step 3; if it scores high, attention should be given to other possible reasons for the motivational difficulties (such as the pay system, the nature of supervision, and so on).

● *Step 3. What specific aspects of the job are causing the difficulty?* This step involves examining the job on each of the five core dimensions to pinpoint the specific strengths and weaknesses of the job as it is currently structured. It is useful at this stage to construct a "profile" of the target job, to make visually apparent where improvements need to be made. An illustrative profile for two jobs (one "good" job and one job needing improvement) is shown in Figure 3.

Job A is an engineering maintenance job and is high on all of the core dimensions; the MPS of this job is a very high 260. (MPS scores can range from 1 to about 350; an "average" score would be about 125.) Job enrichment would not be recommended for this job; if employees working on the job were unproductive and unhappy, the reasons are likely to have little to do with the nature or design of the work itself.

Job B, on the other hand, has many problems.

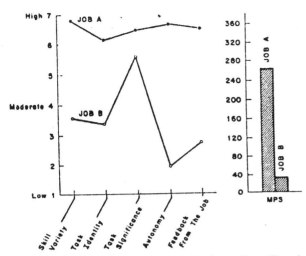

Figure 3. The JDS diagnostic profile for a "good" and a "bad" job.

This job involves the routine and repetitive processing of checks in the "back room" of a bank. The MPS is 30, which is quite low—and indeed, would be even lower if it were not for the moderately high task significance of the job. (Task significance is moderately high because the people are handling large amounts of other people's money, and therefore the quality of their efforts potentially has important consequences for their unseen clients.) The job provides the individuals with very little direct feedback about how effectively they are doing it; the employees have little autonomy in how they go about doing the job; and the job is moderately low in both skill variety and task identity.

For Job B, then, there is plenty of room for improvement—and many avenues to examine in planning job changes. For still other jobs, the avenues for change often turn out to be considerably more specific: for example, feedback and autonomy may be reasonably high, but one or more of the core dimensions that contribute to the experienced meaningfulness of the job (skill variety, task identity, and task significance) may be low. In such a case, attention would turn to ways to increase the standing of the job on these latter three dimensions.

● *Step 4. How "ready" are the employees for change?* Once it has been documented that there is need for improvement in the job--and the particularly troublesome aspects of the job have been identified--then it is time to begin to think about the specific action steps which will be

taken to enrich the job. An important factor in such planning is the level of growth needs of the employees, since employees high on growth needs usually respond more readily to job enrichment than do employees with little need for growth. The JDS provides a direct measure of the growth-need strength of the employees. This measure can be very helpful in planning how to introduce the changes to the people (for instance, cautiously versus dramatically), and in deciding who should be among the first group of employees to have their jobs changed.

In actual use of the diagnostic package, additional information is generated which supplements and expands the basic diagnostic questions outlined above. The point of the above discussion is merely to indicate the kinds of questions which we believe to be most important in diagnosing a job prior to changing it. We now turn to how the diagnostic conclusions are translated into specific job changes.

The implementing concepts. Five "implementing concepts" for job enrichment are identified and discussed below.[10] Each one is a specific action step aimed at improving both the quality of the working experience for the individual and his work productivity. They are: (1) forming natural work units; (2) combining tasks; (3) establishing client relationships; (4) vertical loading; (5) opening feedback channels.

The links between the implementing concepts and the core dimensions are shown in Figure 4—which illustrates our theory of job enrichment, ranging from the concrete action steps through the core dimensions and the psychological states to the actual personal and work outcomes.

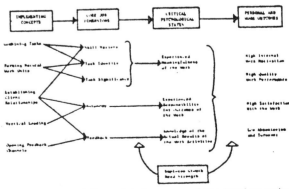

Figure 4. The full model: how use of the implementing concepts can lead to positive outcomes.

After completing the diagnosis of a job, a change agent would know which of the core dimensions were most in need of remedial attention. He could then turn to Figure 4 and select those implementing concepts that specifically deal with the most troublesome parts of the existing job. How this would take place in practice will be seen below.

♦ Forming natural work units. The notion of distributing work in some logical way may seem to be an obvious part of the design of any job. In many cases, however, the logic is one imposed by just about any consideration except job-holder satisfaction and motivation. Such considerations include technological dictates, level of worker training or experience, "efficiency" as defined by industrial engineering, and current workload. In many cases the cluster of tasks a worker faces during a typical day or week is natural to anyone *but* the worker.

For example, suppose that a typing pool (consisting of one supervisor and ten typists) handles all work for one division of a company. Jobs are delivered in rough draft or dictated form to the supervisor, who distributes them as evenly as possible among the typists. In such circumstances the individual letters, reports, and other tasks performed by a given typist in one day or week are randomly assigned. There is no basis for identifying with the work or the person or department for whom it is performed, or for placing any personal value upon it.

The principle underlying natural units of work, by contrast, is "ownership"—a worker's sense of continuing responsibility for an identifiable body of work. Two steps are involved in creating natural work units. The first is to identify the basic work items. In the typing pool, for example, the items might be "pages to be typed." The second step is to group the items in natural categories. For example, each typist might be assigned continuing responsibility for all jobs requested by one or several specific departments. The assignments should be made, of course, in such a way that workloads are about equal in the long run. (For example, one typist might end up with all the work from one busy department, while another handles jobs from several smaller units.)

At this point we can begin to see specifically how the job-design principles relate to the core dimensions (cf. Figure 4). The ownership fostered by natural units of work can make the difference between a feeling that work is meaningful and rewarding and the feeling that it is irrelevant and boring. As the diagram shows, natural units of work are directly related to two of the core dimensions: task identity and task significance.

A typist whose work is assigned naturally rather than randomly—say, by departments—has a much greater chance of performing a whole job to completion. Instead of typing one section of a large report, the individual is likely to type the whole thing, with knowledge of exactly what the product of the work is (task identity). Furthermore, over time the typist will develop a growing sense of how the work affects coworkers in the department serviced (task significance).

♦ Combining tasks. The very existence of a pool made up entirely of persons whose sole function is typing reflects a fractionalization of jobs that has been a basic precept of "scientific management." Most obvious in assembly-line work, fractionalization has been applied to non-manufacturing jobs as well. It is typically justified by efficiency, which is usually defined in terms of either low costs or some time-and-motion type of criteria.

It is hard to find fault with measuring efficiency ultimately in terms of cost-effectiveness. In doing so, however, a manager should be sure to consider *all* the costs involved. It is possible, for example, for highly fractionalized jobs to meet all the time-and-motion criteria of efficiency, but if the resulting job is so unrewarding that performing it day after day leads to high turnover, absenteeism, drugs and alcohol, and strikes, then productivity is really lower (and costs higher) than data on efficiency might indicate.

The principle of combining tasks, then, suggests that whenever possible existing and fractionalized tasks should be put together to form new and larger modules of work. At the Medfield, Massachusetts plant of Corning Glass Works the assembly of a laboratory hot plate has been redesigned along the lines suggested here. Each hot plate now is assembled from start to finish by one operator, instead of going through several separate operations that are performed by different people.

Some tasks, if combined into a meaningfully large module of work, would be more than an individual could do by himself. In such cases, it is often useful to consider assigning the new, larger task to a small *team* of workers—who are given great autonomy for its completion. At the Racine, Wisconsin plant of Emerson Electric, the assembly process for trash disposal appliances was restructured this way. Instead of a sequence of moving the appliance from station to station, the assembly now is done from start to finish by one team. Such teams include both men and women to permit switching off the heavier and more delicate aspects of the work. The team responsible is identified on the appliance. In case of customer complaints, the team often drafts the reply.

As a job-design principle, task combination, like natural units of work, expands the task identity of the job. For example, the hot-plate assembler can see and identify with a finished product ready for shipment, rather than a nearly invisible junction of solder. Moreover, the more tasks that are combined into a single worker's job, the greater the variety of skills he must call on in performing the job. So task combination also leads directly to greater skill variety—the third core dimension that contributes to the overall experienced meaningfulness of the work.

♦ Establishing client relationships. One consequence of fractionalization is that the typical worker has little or no contact with (or even awareness of) the ultimate user of his product or service. By encouraging and enabling employees to establish direct relationships with the clients of their work, improvements often can be realized simultaneously on three of the core dimensions. Feedback increases, because of additional opportunities for the individual to receive praise or criticism of his work outputs directly. Skill variety often increases, because of the necessity to develop and exercise one's interpersonal skills in maintaining the client relationship. And autonomy can increase because the individual often is given personal responsibility for deciding how to manage his relationships with the clients of his work.

Creating client relationships is a three-step process. First, the client must be identified. Second, the most direct contact possible between the worker and the client must be established. Third, criteria must be set up by which the client can judge the quality of the product or service he receives. And whenever possible, the client should have a means of relaying his judgments directly back to the worker.

The contact between worker and client should be as great as possible and as frequent as necessary. Face-to-face contact is highly desirable, at least occasionally. Where that is impossible or impractical, telephone and mail can suffice. In any case, it is important that the performance criteria by which the worker will be rated by the client must be mutually understood and agreed upon.

♦ Vertical loading. Typically the split between the "doing" of a job and the "planning" and "controlling" of the work has evolved along with horizontal fractionalization. Its rationale, once again, has been "efficiency through specialization." And once again, the excess of specialization that has emerged has resulted in unexpected but significant costs in motivation, morale, and work quality. In vertical loading, the intent is to partially close the gap between the doing and the controlling parts of the job—and thereby reap some important motivational advantages.

Of all the job-design principles, vertical loading may be the single most crucial one. In some cases, where it has been impossible to implement any other changes, vertical loading alone has had significant motivational effects.

When a job is vertically loaded, responsibilities and controls that formerly were reserved for higher levels of management are added to the job. There are many ways to accomplish this:

• Return to the job holder greater discretion in setting schedules, deciding on work methods, checking on quality, and advising or helping to train less experienced workers.

• Grant additional authority. The objective

should be to advance workers from a position of no authority or highly restricted authority to positions of reviewed, and eventually, near-total authority for his own work.

- Time management. The job holder should have the greatest possible freedom to decide when to start and stop work, when to break, and how to assign priorities.

- Troubleshooting and crisis decisions. Workers should be encouraged to seek problem solutions on their own, rather than calling immediately for the supervisor.

- Financial controls. Some degree of knowledge and control over budgets and other financial aspects of a job can often be highly motivating. However, access to this information frequently tends to be restricted. Workers can benefit from knowing something about the costs of their jobs, the potential effect upon profit, and various financial and budgetary alternatives.

When a job is vertically loaded it will inevitably increase in *autonomy*. And as shown in Figure 4, this increase in objective personal control over the work will also lead to an increased feeling of personal responsibility for the work, and ultimately to higher internal work motivation.

- Opening feedback channels. In virtually all jobs there are ways to open channels of feedback to individuals or teams to help them learn whether their performance is improving, deteriorating, or remaining at a constant level. While there are numerous channels through which information about performance can be provided, it generally is better for a worker to learn about his performance *directly as he does his job*—rather than from management on an occasional basis.

Job-provided feedback usually is more immediate and private than supervisor-supplied feedback, and it increases the worker's feelings of personal control over his work in the bargain. Moreover, it avoids many of the potentially disruptive interpersonal problems that can develop when the only way a worker has to find out how he is doing is through direct messages or subtle cues from the boss.

Exactly what should be done to open channels for job-provided feedback will vary from job to job and organization to organization. Yet in many cases the changes involve simply removing existing blocks that isolate the worker from naturally occurring data about performance—rather than generating entirely new feedback mechanisms. For example:

- Establishing direct client relationships often removes blocks between the worker and natural external sources of data about his work.

- Quality-control efforts in many organizations often eliminate a natural source of feedback. The quality check on a product or service is done by persons other than those responsible for the work. Feedback to the workers—if there is any—is belated and diluted. It often fosters a tendency to think of quality as "someone else's concern." By placing quality control close to the worker (perhaps even in his own hands), the quantity and quality of data about performance available to him can dramatically increase.

- Tradition and established procedure in many organizations dictate that records about performance be kept by a supervisor and transmitted up (not down) in the organizational hierarchy. Sometimes supervisors even check the work and correct any errors themselves. The worker who made the error never knows it occurred—and is denied the very information that could enhance both his internal work motivation and the technical adequacy of his performance. In many cases it is possible to provide standard summaries of performance records directly to the worker (as well as to his superior), thereby giving him personally and regularly the data he needs to improve his performance.

- Computers and other automated operations sometimes can be used to provide the individual with data now blocked from him. Many clerical operations, for example, are now performed on computer consoles. These consoles often can be programmed to provide the clerk with immediate feedback in the form of a CRT display or a printout indicating that an error has been made. Some systems even have been programmed to provide the operator with a positive feedback message when a period of error-free performance has been sustained.

Many organizations simply have not recognized

the importance of feedback as a motivator. Data on quality and other aspects of performance are viewed as being of interest only to management. Worse still, the *standards* for acceptable performance often are kept from workers as well. As a result, workers who would be interested in following the daily or weekly ups and downs of their performance, and in trying accordingly to improve, are deprived of the very guidelines they need to do so. They are like the golfer we mentioned earlier, whose efforts to correct his hook are stopped dead by fog over the driving range.

The Strategy in Action:
How Well Does It Work?

So far we have examined a basic theory of how people get turned on to their work; a set of core dimensions of jobs that create the conditions for such internal work motivation to develop on the job; and a set of five implementing concepts that are the action steps recommended to boost a job on the core dimensions and thereby increase employee motivation, satisfaction, and productivity.

The remaining question is straightforward and important: *Does it work?* In reality, that question is twofold. First, does the theory itself hold water, or are we barking up the wrong conceptual tree? And second, does the change strategy really lead to measurable differences when it is applied in an actual organizational setting?

This section summarizes the findings we have generated to date on these questions.

Is the job-enrichment theory correct? In general, the answer seems to be yes. The JDS instrument has been taken by more than 1,000 employees working on about 100 diverse jobs in more than a dozen organizations over the last two years. These data have been analyzed to test the basic motivational theory—and especially the impact of the core job dimensions on worker motivation, satisfaction, and behavior on the job. An illustrative overview of some of the findings is given below.[8]

1. People who work on jobs high on the core dimensions are more motivated and satisfied than are people who work on jobs that score low on the dimensions. Employees with jobs high on the core dimensions (MPS scores greater than

240) were compared to those who held unmotivating jobs (MPS scores less than 40). As shown in Figure 5, employees with high MPS jobs were higher on (a) the three psychological states, (b) internal work motivation, (c) general satisfaction, and (d) "growth" satisfaction.

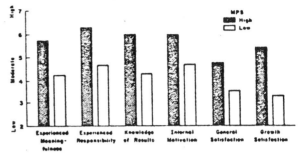

Figure 5. Employee reactions to jobs high and low in motivating potential for two banks and a steel firm.

2. Figure 6 shows that the same is true for measures of actual behavior at work—absenteeism and performance effectiveness—although less strongly so for the performance measure.

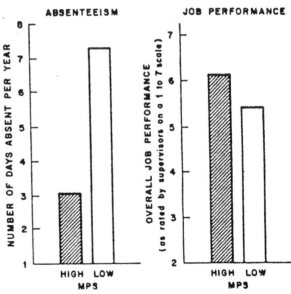

Figure 6. Absenteeism and job performance for employees with jobs high and low in motivating potential.

3. Responses to jobs high in motivating potential are more positive for people who have strong growth needs than for people with weak needs for growth. In Figure 7 the linear relationship between the motivating potential of a job and employees' level of internal work motivation is shown, separately for people with high versus

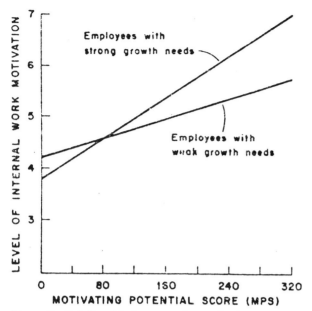

Figure 7. Relationship between the motivating potential of a job and the internal work motivation of employees. (Shown separately for employees with strong versus weak growth-need strength.)

low growth needs as measured by the JDS. While both groups of employees show increases in internal motivation as MPS increases, the *rate* of increase is significantly greater for the group of employees who have strong needs for growth.

How does the change strategy work in practice? The results summarized above suggest that both the theory and the diagnostic instrument work when used with real people in real organizations. In this section, we summarize a job-enrichment project conducted at The Travelers Insurance Companies, which illustrates how the change procedures themselves work in practice.

The Travelers project was designed with two purposes in mind. One was to achieve improvements in morale, productivity, and other indicators of employee well-being. The other was to test the general effectiveness of the strategy for job enrichment we have summarized in this article.

The work group chosen was a keypunching operation. The group's function was to transfer information from printed or written documents onto punched cards for computer input. The work group consisted of ninety-eight keypunch operators and verifiers (both in the same job classification), plus seven assignment clerks. All reported to a supervisor who, in turn, reported

to the assistant manager and manager of the data-input division.

The size of individual punching orders varied considerably, from a few cards to as many as 2,500. Some work came to the work group with a specified delivery date, while other orders were to be given routine service on a predetermined schedule.

Assignment clerks received the jobs from the user departments. After reviewing the work for obvious errors, omissions, and legibility problems, the assignment clerk parceled out the work in batches expected to take about one hour. If the clerk found the work not suitable for punching it went to the supervisor, who either returned the work to the user department or cleared up problems by phone. When work went to operators for punching, it was with the instruction, "Punch only what you see. Don't correct errors, no matter how obvious they look."

Because of the high cost of computer time, keypunched work was 100 percent verified—a task that consumed nearly as many man-hours as the punching itself. Then the cards went to the supervisor, who screened the jobs for due dates before sending them to the computer. Errors detected in verification were assigned to various operators at random to be corrected.

The computer output from the cards was sent to the originating department, accompanied by a printout of errors. Eventually the printout went back to the supervisor for final correction.

A great many phenomena indicated that the problems being experienced in the work group might be the result of poor motivation. As the only person performing supervisory functions of any kind, the supervisor spent most of his time responding to crisis situations, which recurred continually. He also had to deal almost daily with employees' salary grievances or other complaints. Employees frequently showed apathy or outright hostility toward their jobs.

Rates of work output, by accepted work-measurement standards, were inadequate. Error rates were high. Due dates and schedules frequently were missed. Absenteeism was higher than average, especially before and after weekends and holidays.

The single, rather unusual exception was turnover. It was lower than the companywide average for similar jobs. The company has attributed this fact to a poor job market in the base period just before the project began, and to an older, relatively more settled work force—made up, incidentally, entirely of women.

The diagnosis. Using some of the tools and techniques we have outlined, a consulting team from the Management Services Department and from Roy W. Walters & Associates concluded that the keypunch-operator's job exhibited the following serious weaknesses in terms of the core dimensions.

● Skill variety: there was none. Only a single skill was involved—the ability to punch adequately the data on the batch of documents.

● Task identity: virtually nonexistent. Batches were assembled to provide an even workload, but not whole identifiable jobs.

● Task significance: not apparent. The keypunching operation was a necessary step in providing service to the company's customers. The individual operator was isolated by an assignment clerk and a supervisor from any knowledge of what the operation meant to the using department, let alone its meaning to the ultimate customer.

● Autonomy: none. The operators had no freedom to arrange their daily tasks to meet schedules, to resolve problems with the using department, or even to correct, in punching, information that was obviously wrong.

● Feedback: none. Once a batch was out of the operator's hands, she had no assured chance of seeing evidence of its quality or inadequacy.

Design of the experimental trial. Since the diagnosis indicated that the motivating potential of the job was extremely low, it was decided to attempt to improve the motivation and productivity of the work group through job enrichment. Moreover, it was possible to design an experimental test of the effects of the changes to be introduced: the results of changes made in the target work group were to be compared with trends in a control work group of similar size and demographic make-up. Since the control group was located more than a mile away, there

appeared to be little risk of communication between members of the two groups.

A base period was defined before the start of the experimental trial period, and appropriate data were gathered on the productivity, absenteeism, and work attitudes of members of both groups. Data also were available on turnover; but since turnover was already below average in the target group, prospective changes in this measure were deemed insignificant.

An educational session was conducted with supervisors, at which they were given the theory and implementing concepts and actually helped to design the job changes themselves. Out of this session came an active plan consisting of about twenty-five change items that would significantly affect the design of the target jobs.

The implementing concepts and the changes. Because the job as it existed was rather uniformly low on the core job dimensions, all five of the implementing concepts were used in enriching it.

● Natural units of work. The random batch assignment of work was replaced by assigning to each operator continuing responsibility for certain accounts—either particular departments or particular recurring jobs. Any work for those accounts now always goes to the same operator.

● Task combination. Some planning and controlling functions were combined with the central task of keypunching. In this case, however, these additions can be more suitably discussed under the remaining three implementing concepts.

● Client relationships. Each operator was given several channels of direct contact with clients. The operators, not their assignment clerks, now inspect their documents for correctness and legibility. When problems arise, the operator, not the supervisor, takes them up with the client.

● Feedback. In addition to feedback from client contact, the operators were provided with a number of additional sources of data about their performance. The computer department now returns incorrect cards to the operators who punched them, and operators correct their own errors. Each operator also keeps her own file of copies of her errors. These can be reviewed to determine trends in error frequency and types of errors. Each operator receives weekly a computer printout of her errors and productivity, which is sent to her directly, rather than given to her by the supervisor.

• Vertical loading. Besides consulting directly with clients about work questions, operators now have the authority to correct obvious coding errors on their own. Operators may set their own schedules and plan their daily work, as long as they meet schedules. Some competent operators have been given the option of not verifying their work and making their own program changes.

Results of the trial. The results were dramatic. The number of operators declined from ninety-eight to sixty. This occurred partly through attrition and partly through transfer to other departments. Some of the operators were promoted to higher-paying jobs in departments whose cards they had been handling—something that had never occurred before. Some details of the results are given below.

• Quantity of work. The control group, with no job changes made, showed an increase in productivity of 8.1 percent during the trial period. The experimental group showed an increase of 39.6 percent.

• Error rates. To assess work quality, error rates were recorded for about forty operators in the experimental group. All were experienced, and all had been in their jobs before the job-enrichment program began. For two months before the study, these operators had a collective error rate of 1.53 percent. For two months toward the end of the study, the collective error rate was 0.99 percent. By the end of the study the number of operators with poor performance had dropped from 11.1 percent to 5.5 percent.

• Absenteeism. The experimental group registered a 24.1 percent decline in absences. The control group, by contrast, showed a 29 percent *increase.*

• Attitudes toward the job. An attitude survey given at the start of the project showed that the two groups scored about average, and nearly identically, in nine different areas of work satisfaction. At the end of the project the survey was repeated. The control group showed an insignificant 0.5 percent improvement, while the experi-

mental group's overall satisfaction score rose 16.5 percent.

• Selective elimination of controls. Demonstrated improvements in operator proficiency permitted them to work with fewer controls. Travelers estimates that the reduction of controls had the same effect as adding seven operators—a saving even beyond the effects of improved productivity and lowered absenteeism.

• Role of the supervisor. One of the most significant findings in the Travelers experiment was the effect of the changes on the supervisor's job, and thus on the rest of the organization. The operators took on many responsibilities that had been reserved at least to the unit leaders and sometimes to the supervisor. The unit leaders, in turn, assumed some of the day-to-day supervisory functions that had plagued the supervisor. Instead of spending his days supervising the behavior of subordinates and dealing with crises, he was able to devote time to developing feedback systems, setting up work modules and spearheading the enrichment effort in other words, managing. It should be noted, however, that helping supervisors change their own work activities when their subordinates' jobs have been enriched is itself a challenging task. And if appropriate attention and help are not given to supervisors in such cases, they rapidly can become disaffected—and a job-enrichment "backlash" can result.[11]

Summary. By applying work-measurement standards to the changes wrought by job enrichment—attitude and quality, absenteeism, and selective administration of controls—Travelers was able to estimate the total dollar impact of the project. Actual savings in salaries and machine rental charges during the first year totaled $64,305. Potential savings by further application of the changes were put at $91,937 annually. Thus, by almost any measure used from the work attitudes of individual employees to dollar savings for the company as a whole The Travelers test of the job-enrichment strategy proved a success.

Conclusions

In this article we have presented a new strategy for the redesign of work in general and for job enrichment in particular. The approach has four main characteristics:

1. It is grounded in a basic psychological theory of what motivates people in their work.

2. It emphasizes that planning for job changes should be done on the basis of *data* about the jobs and the people who do them—and a set of diagnostic instruments is provided to collect such data.

3. It provides a set of specific implementing concepts to guide actual job changes, as well as a set of theory-based rules for selecting *which* action steps are likely to be most beneficial in a given situation.

4. The strategy is buttressed by a set of findings showing that the theory holds water, that the diagnostic procedures are practical and informative, and that the implementing concepts can lead to changes that are beneficial both to organizations and to the people who work in them.

We believe that job enrichment is moving beyond the stage where it can be considered "yet another management fad." Instead, it represents a potentially powerful strategy for change that can help organizations achieve their goals for higher quality work—and at the same time further the equally legitimate needs of contemporary employees for a more meaningful work experience. Yet there are pressing questions about job enrichment and its use that remain to be answered.

Prominent among these is the question of employee participation in planning and implementing work redesign. The diagnostic tools and implementing concepts we have presented are neither designed nor intended for use only by management. Rather, our belief is that the effectiveness of job enrichment is likely to be enhanced when the tasks of diagnosing and changing jobs are undertaken *collaboratively* by management and by the employees whose work will be affected.

Moreover, the effects of work redesign on the broader organization remain generally uncharted. Evidence now is accumulating that when jobs are changed, turbulence can appear in the surrounding organization—for example, in supervisory-subordinate relationships, in pay and

benefit plans, and so on. Such turbulence can be viewed by management either as a problem with job enrichment, or as an opportunity for further and broader organizational development by teams of managers and employees. To the degree that management takes the latter view, we believe, the oft-espoused goal of achieving basic organizational change through the redesign of work may come increasingly within reach.

The diagnostic tools and implementing concepts we have presented are useful in deciding on and designing basic changes in the jobs themselves. They do not address the broader issues of who plans the changes, how they are carried out, and how they are followed up. The way these broader questions are dealt with, we believe, may determine whether job enrichment will grow up—or whether it will die an early and unfortunate death, like so many other fledgling behavioral-science approaches to organizational change.

Appendix:

For the algebraically inclined, the Motivating Potential Score is computed as follows

$$MPS = \left[\frac{\text{Skill Variety} + \text{Task Identity} + \text{Task Significance}}{3} \right]$$

X Autonomy   X Feedback

It should be noted that in some cases the MPS score can be *too* high for positive job satisfaction and effective performance—in effect overstimulating the person who holds the job. This paper focuses on jobs which are toward the low end of the scale—and which potentially can be improved through job enrichment.

Acknowledgments: The authors acknowledge with great appreciation the editorial assistance of John Hickey in the preparation of this paper, and the help of Kenneth Brousseau, Daniel Feldman, and Linda Frank in collecting the data that are summarized here. The research activities reported were supported in part by the Organizational Effectiveness Research Program of the Office of Naval Research, and the Manpower Administration of the U.S. Department of Labor, both through contracts to Yale University.

REFERENCES

1. F. Herzberg, B. Mausner and B. Snyderman, *The Motivation to Work* (New York: John Wiley & Sons, 1959).

2. F. Herzberg, *Work and the Nature of Man* (Cleveland: World, 1966).

3. F. Herzberg, "One More Time: How Do You Motivate Employees?" *Harvard Business Review* (1968), pp. 53-62.

4. W. J. Paul, Jr.; K. B. Robertson and F. Herzberg, "Job Enrichment Pays Off," *Harvard Business Review* (1969), pp. 61-78.

5. R. N. Ford, *Motivation Through the Work Itself* New York: American Management Association, 1969).

6. A. N. Turner and P. R. Lawrence, *Industrial Jobs and the Worker* (Cambridge, Mass.: Harvard Graduate School of Business Administration, 1965).

7. J. R. Hackman and E. E. Lawler, "Employee Reactions to Job Characteristics," *Journal of Applied Psychology Monograph* (1971), pp. 259-286.

8. J. R. Hackman and G. R. Oldham, *Motivation Through the Design of Work: Test of a Theory*, Technical Report No. 6, Department of Administrative Sciences, Yale University, 1974.

9. J. R. Hackman and G. R. Oldham, "Development of the Job Diagnostic Survey," *Journal of Applied Psychology* (1975), pp. 159-170.

10. R. W. Walters and Associates, *Job Enrichment for Results* (Cambridge, Mass.: Addison-Wesley, 1975).

11. E. E. Lawler III; J. R. Hackman, and S. Kaufman, "Effects of Job Redesign: A Field Experiment," *Journal of Applied Social Psychology* (1973), pp. 49-62.

Cases

CASE 1

KILKENNY LUMBER

KILKENNY LUMBER COMPANY

Discussion Questions

1. What factors may account for the formation of two distinct subgroups in the work team?

2. Why are the levels of productivity and satisfaction of the two subgroups different?

3. Why are the leader's efforts to increase the productivity of the "problem" group unsuccessful?

4. What alternative causes of action might the leader have taken which might have had a higher probability of success?

10. KILKENNY LUMBER COMPANY

Part 1[1]

THE KILKENNY LUMBER COMPANY owned and managed a large tract of forest in the northeastern United States. The company employed a number of men to maintain the tract according to modern forestry practice. In rotation, various areas of the tract were annually harvested by removing mature trees. Each winter, in preparation for harvesting and when other forestry tasks were at a standstill, a timber-marking crew composed of eight to ten regular company employees traveled through a selected area designating the trees to be cut and estimating the usable volume of lumber. In the spring, contractors moved over the area removing the marked trees.

Tree marking required considerable timbering knowledge and judgment. Once a tree was designated as mature and economical for harvest, height and diameter were calculated, defects estimated, and volume calculated. This volume was recorded along with a number code for the tree and was subsequently used as a basis for payment from the contractor. The code number was painted on the tree itself, as an indication of permission for cutting by the contract crew.

Tree-marking errors were costly. Missed trees or improper postponement of cutting meant lost sales and poor contractor relations, the latter depending on the maximum density of mature trees for his profit. Incorrect volume calculations meant lost money to Kilkenny or costly arbitration with the contractor. Designation of immature trees for cutting also cost Kilkenny money, particularly since the harvesting cycle was extremely long.

Several procedures had been adopted to reduce the chance of marking errors. The crew formed a moving line, each man fifty feet away from the men on either side. A man's place in the line was set by informal crew decision. The line was to keep within a predetermined strip of forest and the men kept in proper relation to each other by periodic shouts to determine relative positions and by supervisory observation. Supervisors also spent considerable time, particularly at the beginning of the winter, training the crew members to make judgments and measurements. Supervisors checked each man's work periodically to make sure it met standards. If not, additional training was given. If it still did not meet standards, the man was assigned to other work if it were available. Although there were no production quotas, the men were expected to keep up with the moving line and mark approximately the same number of trees. Despite occasional variations in terrain, disparity of work loads was not an issue.

Working conditions were arduous. Temperatures often fell below 0°F. Snow was heavy and often fell during working hours. The terrain

Exhibit 1

KILKENNY LUMBER COMPANY

TIMBER-MARKING CREW,

Title	Rank*	Pay Grade	Seniority	Age	Education
Leader...............Professional forester		9	3 years	25	College degree
Assistant leader........Subprofessional forester		7	30 years	55	College, 1 year
Crewman†..............Professional forester		7	6 years	28	College degree
Crewman†..............Professional forester		7	4 years	26	College degree
Crewman†..............Professional forester		5	3 years	25	College degree
Crewman...............Subprofessional forester		5	15 years	38	High school diploma
Crewman...............Subprofessional forester		5	1 year	22	College, 2 years
Crewman...............Subprofessional forester		3	4 years	45	High school diploma

* Rank was attained by formal education, examination and experience. Professional foresters normally were responsible for maintenance of forest districts, often supervising crews of subprofessional foresters and other lower-ranking woodsmen.

† These three men had been assigned to this crew from a distant and organizationally separate district of Kilkenny's land. They were assigned to the crew because of lack of other work and were expected to gain new practical experience from the marking assignment. They customarily worked together in their home district. Unlike the rest of the crew, which lived near the district being marked, these men lived away from home on a subsistence and transportation allowance during the week.

was uneven and the men had to carry food and supplies on their backs. Generally the men had no opportunity to dry out or warm up during the twelve hours of daylight in which they worked.

The crew which began work in December,　(see Exhibit 1), had received timber-marking training, though, as usual, all the men worked at other tasks during the rest of the year. A brief period of further training had been carried out by the leader and his assistant before the crew began regular work. Past timber-marking experience indicated that a crew like this could easily mark timber with the desired accuracy and speed.

The crew leader and his assistant were considered by Kilkenny management to be excellent foresters and teachers. In woodsman tradition, crew leaders were expected to carry out supervisory tasks and at the same time, turn out more individual marking than any one of their men. The leaders of this crew were able to live up to this tradition. Both leaders tended to allow the men privileges not strictly according to regulation, such as long lunch hours before a fire, early departures for home, and frequent work breaks, particularly when the weather was severe.

KILKENNY LUMBER COMPANY

Part 2

THE TIMBER-MARKING CREW split into two informal groups soon after work in the forest began. One group was composed of the three professional foresters who had been assigned to the crew from a distant district. They constantly complained about the weather, the inadequacy of equipment, and their leaders. They found the leader to be a task-master who worked them too hard, his assistant a busybody who was too fussy about quality. The quantity of work performed by these three ranged between one third and one half of that attained by the other crewmen who were considered to be performing at a normal pace. Efforts at retraining produced no change. Absences among the three were high and excuses, though plentiful, often proved to be fabricated. The three men kept to themselves, building their separate fire at lunch time.

The rest of the crew tended to stick together. Although some of these men lacked the skill and training possessed by professional foresters, the men helped each other and production and quality were high. The leaders, feeling rejected by the three professional foresters, ate with the subprofessionals.

The leaders were angered by the three recalcitrant crewmen. They interpreted the latter's behavior as an attempt to be reassigned to a more pleasant job. Since no other positions were open and because the leaders disliked the thought of giving in to what they considered a play for preferential treatment, they told the three men they would have to stay out in the cold, work or not. Conditions did not improve.

KILKENNY LUMBER COMPANY

Part 3

AFTER SEVERAL WEEKS, the leaders decided on two alternative strategies to increase the productivity of the professional foresters. First, the three men would be dispersed along the line and placed near the leader and his assistant instead of congregating at the far end of the line and trailing off as they had chosen to do (see Exhibit 2).

Exhibit 2
KILKENNY LUMBER COMPANY
POSITIONS IN LINE OF MARCH

A. BEFORE CONTEMPLATED CHANGE: *

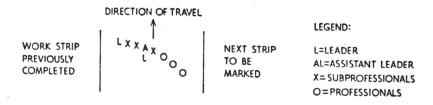

LEGEND:

L=LEADER
AL=ASSISTANT LEADER
X=SUBPROFESSIONALS
O=PROFESSIONALS

B: CONTEMPLATED CHANGE:

* The unevenness of the line was compensated for by stopping forward progress before the end of the day and bringing the tail end of the line up to par with the leading edge.

If this strategy failed, the leader would assume responsibility for the professionals as a separate group away from the rest of the crew and hope to increase their production by close supervision.

KILKENNY LUMBER COMPANY

Part 4

INSERTING the professionals between other crew members served to slow the entire work line. Although quality did not suffer, productivity for the whole crew dropped off to a total figure lower than that previously achieved. Consequently, the second strategy was attempted. However, while the subprofessional crew resumed their former pace, the professionals moved even slower than they had under the initial arrangement. The leaders were at a loss to find a way to attain the productivity which they felt certain the crew members were capable of achieving.

CASE 2

HOVEY AND BEARD COMPANY

From: W.F. Whyte, Money and Motivation. New York: Harper and Row, 1955, pp. 90-94. Used by Permission.

Hovey and Beard Company*

PART 1

THE HOVEY AND BEARD Company manufactured wooden toys of various kinds: wooden animals, pull toys, and the like. One part of the manufacturing process involved spraying paint on the partially assembled toys. This operation was staffed entirely by girls.

The toys were cut, sanded, and partially assembled in the wood room. Then they were dipped into shellac, following which they were painted. The toys were predominantly two-colored; a few were made in more than two colors. Each color required an additional trip through the paint room.

For a number of years, production of these toys had been entirely handwork. However, to meet tremendously increased demand, the painting operation had recently been re-engineered so that the eight girls who did the painting sat in a line by an endless chain of hooks. These hooks were in continuous motion, past the line of girls and into a long horizontal oven. Each girl sat at her own painting booth so designed as to carry away fumes and to backstop excess paint. The girl would take a toy from the tray beside her, position it in a jig inside the painting cubicle, spray on the color according to a pattern, then release the toy and hang it on the hook passing by. The rate at which the hooks moved had been calculated by the engineers so that each girl, when fully trained, would be able to hang a painted toy on each hook before it passed beyond her reach.

The girls working in the paint room were on a group bonus plan. Since the operation was new to them, they were receiving a learning bonus which decreased by regular amounts each month. The learning bonus was scheduled to vanish in six months, by which time it was expected that they would be on their own—that is, able to meet the standard and to earn a group bonus when they exceeded it.

* This case is taken from Alex Bavelas and George Strauss, *Money and Motivation* (New York: Harper Brothers, 1955), chap. 10, and was based on Dr. Bavelas' experience as a consultant. Reproduced by permission.

PART 2

By the second month of the training period trouble had developed. The girls learned more slowly than had been anticipated, and it began to look as though their production would stabilize far below what was planned for. Many of the hooks were going by empty. The girls complained that they were going by too fast, and that the time study man had set the rates wrong. A few girls quit and had to be replaced with new girls, which further aggravated the learning problem. The team spirit that the management had expected to develop automatically through the group bonus was not in evidence except as an expression of what the engineers called "resistance." One girl whom the group regarded as its leader (and the management regarded as the ringleader) was outspoken in making the various complaints of the group to the foreman: the job was a messy one, the hooks moved too fast, the incentive pay was not being correctly calculated, and it was too hot working so close to the drying oven.

PART 3

A consultant who was brought into this picture worked entirely with and through the foreman. After many conversations with him, the foreman felt that the first step should be to get the girls together for a general discussion of the working conditions. He took this step with some hesitation, but he took it on his own volition.

The first meeting, held immediately after the shift was over at four o'clock in the afternoon, was attended by all eight girls. They voiced the same complaints again: the hooks went by too fast, the job was too dirty, the room was hot and poorly ventilated. For some reason, it was this last item that they complained of most. The foreman promised to discuss the problem of ventilation and temperature with the engineers, and he scheduled a second meeting to report back to the girls. In the next few days the foreman had several talks with the engineers. They and the superintendent felt that this was really a trumped-up complaint, and that the expense of any effective corrective measure would be prohibitively high.

The foreman came to the second meeting with some apprehensions. The girls, however, did not seem to be much put out, perhaps because they had a proposal of their own to make. They felt that if several large fans were set up so as to circulate the air around their feet, they would be much more comfortable. After some discussion, the foreman agreed that the idea might be tried out. The foreman and the consultant discussed the question of the fans with the superintendent, and three large propeller-type fans were purchased.

PART 4

The fans were brought in. The girls were jubilant. For several days the fans were moved about in various positions until they were placed to the satisfaction of the group. The girls seemed completely satisfied with the results, and relations between them and the foreman improved visibly.

The foreman, after this encouraging episode, decided that further meetings might also be profitable. He asked the girls if they would like to meet and discuss other aspects of the work situation. The girls were eager to do this. The meeting was held, and the discussion quickly centered on the speed of the hooks. The girls maintained that the time study men had set them at an unreasonably fast speed and that they would never be able to reach the goal of filling enough of them to make a bonus.

The turning point of the discussion came when the group's leader frankly explained that the point wasn't that they couldn't work fast enough to keep up with the hooks, but that they couldn't work at that pace all day long. The foreman explored the point. The girls were unanimous in their opinion that they could keep up with the belt for short periods if they wanted to. But they didn't want to because if they showed they could do this for short periods they would be expected to do it all day long. The meeting ended with an unprecedented request: "Let us adjust the speed of the belt faster or slower depending on how we feel." The foreman agreed to discuss this with the superintendent and the engineers.

The reaction of the engineers to the suggestion was negative. However, after several meetings it was granted that there was some latitude within which variations in the speed of the hooks would not affect the finished product. After considerable argument with the engineers, it was agreed to try out the girls' idea.

With misgivings, the foreman had a control with a dial marked "low, medium, fast" installed at the booth of the group leader; she could now adjust the speed of the belt anywhere between the lower and upper limits that the engineers had set.

PART 5

The girls were delighted, and spent many lunch hours deciding how the speed of the belt should be varied from hour to hour throughout the day. Within a week the pattern had settled down to one in which the first half hour of the shift was run on what the girls called a medium speed (a dial setting slightly above the point marked "medium"). The next two and one-half hours were run at high speed; the half hour before lunch and the half hour after lunch were run at low speed. The rest of the afternoon was run at high speed with the exception of the last forty-five minutes of the shift, which was run at medium.

In view of the girls' reports of satisfaction and ease in their work, it is interesting to note that the constant speed at which the engineers had originally set the belt was slightly below medium on the dial of the control that had been given the girls. The average speed at which the girls were running the belt was on the high side of the dial. Few, if any, empty hooks entered the oven, and inspection showed no increase of rejects from the paint room.

Production increased, and within three weeks (some two months before the scheduled ending of the learning bonus) the girls were operating at 30 to 50 percent above the level that had been expected under the original arrangement. Naturally the girls' earnings were correspondingly higher than anticipated. They were collecting their base pay, a considerable piece rate bonus, and the learning bonus which, it will be remembered, had been set to decrease with time and not as a function of current productivity. The girls were earning more now than many skilled workers in other parts of the plant.

PART 6

Management was besieged by demands that this inequity be taken care of. With growing irritation between superintendent and foreman, engineers and foreman, superintendent and engineers, the situation came to a head when the superintendent revoked the learning bonus and returned the painting operation to its original status: the hooks moved again at their constant, time-studied designated speed, production dropped again, and within a month all but two of the eight girls had quit. The foreman himself stayed on for several months, but, feeling aggrieved, then left for another job.

CASE 3

BOB KNOWLTON

BOB KNOWLTON

Discussion Questions

1. What factors have contributed to Knowlton's dissatisfaction with his job?

2. Are the Factors contributing to his dissatisfaction based upon accurate perceptions of how he is being treated and what his prospects are with the company?

3. What should have been done differently by all of the people involved in order to have prevented Knowlton from making the decision to leave?

BOB KNOWLTON

Alex Bavelas

Bob Knowlton was sitting alone in the conference room of the laboratory. The rest of the group had gone. One of the secretaries had stopped and talked for a while about her husband's coming induction into the Army, and had finally left. Bob, alone in the laboratory, slid a little further down in his chair, looking with satisfaction at the results of the first test run of the new photon unit.

He liked to stay after the others had gone. His appointment as project head was still new enough to give him a deep sense of pleasure. His eyes were on the graphs before him, but in his mind he could hear Dr. Jerrold, the head of the laboratory, saying again, "There's one thing about this place that you can bank on. The sky is the limit for the person who can produce!" Knowlton felt again the tingle of happiness and embarrassment. Well, dammit, he said to himself, he had produced. He wasn't kidding anybody. He had come to the Simmons Laboratories 2 years ago. During a routine testing of some rejected Clanson components, he had stumbled onto the idea of the photon correlator, and the rest had just happened. Jerrold had been enthusiastic; a separate project had been set up for further research and development of the device, and he had gotten the job of running it. The whole sequence of events still seemed a little miraculous to Knowlton.

He shrugged out of the reverie and bent determinedly over the sheets when he heard someone come into the room behind him. He looked up expectantly; Jerrold often stayed late himself, and now and then dropped in for a chat. This always made the day's end especially pleasant for Bob. It wasn't Jerrold. The man who had come in was a stranger. He was tall, thin, and rather dark. He wore steel-rimmed glasses and had on a very wide leather belt with a large brass buckle. His wife remarked later that it was the kind of belt the pilgrims must have worn.

The stranger smiled and introduced himself. "I'm Simon Fester. Are you Bob Knowlton?" Bob said yes, and they shook hands. "Doctor Jerrold said I might find you in. We were talking about your work, and I'm very much interested in what you are doing." Bob waved to a chair.

Fester didn't seem to belong in any of the standard categories of visitors: customer, visiting fireman, stockholder. Bob pointed to the sheets on the table. "There are the preliminary results of a test we're running. We've got a new gadget by the tail and we're trying to understand it. It's not finished, but I can show you the section that we're testing."

He stood up, but Fester was deep in the graphs. After a moment, he looked up with an odd grin. "These look like plots of a Jennings surface. I've been playing around with some autocorrelation functions of surfaces—you know that stuff." Bob, who had no idea what he was referring to, grinned back and nodded, and immediately felt uncomfortable. "Let me show you the monster," he said, and led the way to the work room.

After Fester left, Knowlton slowly put the graphs away, feeling vaguely annoyed. Then, as if he had made a decision, he quickly locked up and took the long way out so that he would pass Jerrold's office. But the office was locked. Knowlton wondered whether Jerrold and Fester had left together.

The next morning, Knowlton dropped into Jerrold's office, mentioned that he had talked with Fester, and asked who he was. "Sit down for a minute," Jerrold said. "I want to talk to you about him. What do you think of him?" Knowlton replied truthfully that he thought Fester was very bright and probably very competent. Jerrold looked pleased.

"We're taking him on," he said. "He's had a very good background in a number of laboratories, and he seems to have ideas about the problems we're tackling here." Knowlton nodded in agreement, instantly wishing that Fester would not be placed with him.

"I don't know yet where he will finally land," Jerrold continued, "but he seems interested in what you are doing. I thought he might spend a little time with you by way of getting started." Knowlton nodded thoughtfully. "If his interest in your work continues, you can add him to your group."

"Well, he seemed to have some good ideas even without knowing exactly what we are doing," Knowlton answered. "I hope he stays; we'd be glad to have him."

Knowlton walked back to the laboratory with mixed feelings. He told himself that Fester would be good for the group. He was no dunce, he'd produce. Knowlton thought again of Jerrold's promise when he had promoted him—"the person who produces gets ahead in this outfit." The words seemed to carry the overtones of a threat now.

The next day, Fester didn't appear until mid-afternoon. He explained that he had had a long lunch with Jerrold, discussing his place in the laboratory. "Yes," said Knowlton, "I talked with Jerry this morning about it, and we both thought you might work with us for a while." Fester smiled in the same knowing way that he had smiled when he mentioned the Jennings surfaces. "I'd like to," he said.

Knowlton introduced Fester to the other members of the laboratory. Fester and Link, the mathematician of the group, hit it off well together, and spent the rest of the afternoon discussing a method of analysis of patterns that Link had been worrying over for the last month.

It was 6:30 when Knowlton left the laboratory that night. He had waited almost eagerly for the end of the day to come—when everyone would be gone and he could sit in the quiet rooms, relax, and think it over. "Think what over?" he asked himself. He didn't know. Shortly after 5 p.m. everyone had gone except Fester, and what followed was almost a duel. Knowlton was annoyed that he was being cheated out of his quiet period, and finally resentfully determined that Fester should leave first.

Fester was reading at the conference table, and Knowlton was sitting at his desk in the little glass-enclosed cubicle that he used during the day when he needed to be undisturbed. Fester was carefully studying the last year's progress reports. The time dragged. Knowlton doodled on a pad, the tension growing inside him. What the hell did Fester think he was going to find in the reports?

Knowlton finally gave up and they left the laboratory together. Fester took several reports with him to study in the evening. Knowlton asked him if he thought the reports gave a clear picture of the laboratory's activities.

"They're excellent," Fester answered with obvious sincerity. "They're not only good reports; what they report is damn good, too!" Knowlton was surprised at the relief he felt, and grew almost jovial as he said goodnight.

Driving home, Knowlton felt more optimistic about Fester's presence in the laboratory. He had never fully understood the analysis that Link was attempting. If there was anything wrong with Link's approach, Fester would probably spot it. "And if I'm any judge," he murmured, "he won't be especially diplomatic about it."

He described Fester to his wife, who was amused by the broad leather belt and the brass buckle. "It's the kind of belt that pilgrims must have worn," she laughed.

"I'm not worried about how he holds his pants up." Knowlton laughed with her. "I'm afraid that he's the kind that just has to make like a genius twice each day. And that can be pretty rough on the group."

Knowlton had been asleep for several hours when he was abruptly awoken by the telephone. He realized it had rung several times. He swung off the bed muttering about damn fools and telephones. It was Fester. Without any excuses, apparently oblivious of the time, he plunged into an excited recital of how Link's patterning problem could be solved.

Knowlton covered the mouthpiece to answer his wife's stage-whispered "Who is it?" "It's the genius," replied Knowlton.

Fester, completely ignoring that it was 2 a.m., proceeded excitedly to start in the middle of an explanation of a completely new approach to certain photon laboratory problems that he had stumbled onto while analyzing past experiments. Knowlton managed to put some enthusiasm in his own voice and stood there, half-dazed and very uncomfortable, listening to Fester talk endlessly about what he had discovered. It was probably not only a new approach but also an analysis that showed the inherent weakness of the previous experiment and how experimentation along that line would certainly have been inconclusive. The following day Knowlton spent the entire morning with Fester and Link, the mathematician, the morning meeting having been called off so that Fester's work of the previous night could be gone over intensively. Fester was very anxious that this be done and Knowlton was not too unhappy to suspend the meeting for reasons of his own.

For the next several days, Fester sat in the back office that had been turned over to him and did nothing but read the progress reports of the work that had been done in the last 6 months. Knowlton felt apprehensive about the reaction that Fester might have to some of his work. He was a little surprised at his own feelings. He had always been proud (although he had put on a convincingly modest face) of the way in which new ground in the study of photon-measuring devices had been broken in his group. Now he wasn't sure, and it seemed to him that Fester might easily show that the line of research they had been following was unsound or even unimaginative.

The next morning, as was the custom in Bob's group, the members of the laboratory, including the secretaries, sat around a conference table. Bob always prided himself on the fact that the work of the laboratory was guided and evaluated by the group as a whole, and he was fond of repeating that it was not a waste of time to include secretaries in such meetings. Often, what started out as a boring recital of fundamental assumptions to a naive listener, uncovered new ways of regarding these assumptions that would not have occurred to the researcher who had long ago accepted them as a necessary basis for his or her work.

These group meetings also served Bob in another sense. He admitted to himself that he would have felt far less secure if he had had to direct the work out of his own mind, so to speak. With the group meeting as the principle of leadership, it was always possible to justify the exploration of blind alleys because of the general educative effect on the team. Fester was there; Lucy Jones and Martha Smith, the laboratory secretaries, were there. Link was sitting next to Fester, their conversation concerning Link's mathematical study apparently continuing from yesterday. The other members, Bob Davenport, George Thurlow, and Arthur Oliver, were waiting quietly.

Knowlton, for reasons that he didn't quite understand, proposed for discussion this morning a problem that all of them had spent considerable time on previously, with the conclusion that a solution was impossible, that there was no feasible way to treat it in an experimental fashion. When Knowlton proposed the problem, Davenport remarked that there was hardly any use in reviewing it again, that he was satisfied that there was no way to approach the problem with the equipment and the physical capacities of the laboratory.

This statement had the effect of a shot of adrenalin on Fester. He said he would like to know about the problem in detail, and walking to the blackboard, began to write the "factors" as various members of the group began to discuss the problem and simultaneously list the reasons for its abandonment.

Very early in the description of the problem, it was evident that Fester would disagree about the impossibility of attacking it. The group realized this and finally the descriptive materials and their recounting of the reasoning that had led to its abandonment dwindled away. Fester began his statement which, as it proceeded, might well have been prepared the previous night although Knowlton knew this was impossible. He could not help being impressed with the organized, logical way that Fester was presenting ideas that must have occurred to him only a few minutes before.

Fester had some things to say, however, that left Knowlton with a mixture of annoyance, irritation and, at the same time, a rather smug feeling of superiority over Fester in at least one area. Fester thought that the way the problem had been analyzed was really typical of group thinking and, with an air of sophistication that made it difficult for a listener to dissent, he proceeded to comment on the American emphasis on team ideas, satirically describing the ways in which they led to a "high level of mediocrity."

During this time, Knowlton observed that Link stared studiously at the floor, and he was very conscious of Thurlow's and Davenport's glances toward him at several points during Fester's speech. Inwardly, Knowlton couldn't help feeling that this was one point at least in which Fester was off on the wrong foot. The whole laboratory, following Jerry's lead, talked if not practiced the theory of small research teams as the basic organization for effective research. Fester insisted that the problem could be approached and that he would like to study it for a while himself.

Knowlton ended the morning session by remarking that the meetings would continue and that the very fact that a supposedly insoluble experimental problem was now going to receive another chance was another indication of the value of such meetings. Fester immediately remarked that he was not at all averse to meetings for the purpose of informing the group of the progress of its members—that the point he wanted to make was that creative advances were seldom accomplished in such meetings, that they were made by the individual "living with" the problem closely and continuously, a sort of personal relationship to it.

Knowlton went on to say to Fester that he was very glad that Fester had raised these points and that he was sure the group would profit by reexamining the basis on which they had been operating. Knowlton agreed that individual effort was probably the basis for making the major advances, but that he considered the group meetings useful primarily because of the effect they had on keeping the group together and on helping the weaker members of the group keep up with the members who were able to advance more easily and quickly in the analysis of problems.

It was clear as days went by and meetings continued as they did, that Fester came to enjoy them because of the pattern that the meetings assumed. It became typical for Fester to hold forth and it was unquestionably clear that he was more brilliant, better prepared on the various subjects that were germane to the problems being studied, and more capable of progress than anyone there. Knowlton grew increasingly disturbed as he realized that his leadership of the group had been, in fact, taken over.

Whenever the subject of Fester was mentioned in occasional meetings with Jerrold, Knowlton would comment only on Fester's ability and obvious capacity for work. Somehow he never felt that he could mention his own discomforts, not only because they revealed a weakness on his part but also because it was quite clear that Jerrold himself was considerably impressed with Fester's work and with the contacts he had with him outside the photon laboratory.

Knowlton now began to feel that perhaps the intellectual advantages that Fester had brought to the group did not quite compensate for what he felt were evidences of a breakdown in the cooperative spirit that he had seen in the group before Fester's coming. More and more of the morning meetings were skipped. Fester's opinion of the abilities of other group members, with the exception of Link, was obviously low. At times, during the morning meetings or in smaller discussions, he had been on the point of rudeness, refusing to pursue an argument when he claimed it was based on the other person's ignorance of the facts involved. His impatience with others led him to make similar remarks to Jerrold. Knowlton inferred this from a conversation with Jerrold in which Jerrold asked whether Davenport and Oliver were going to be continued on; and his failure to mention Link led Knowlton to believe that this was the result of private conversations between Fester and Jerrold.

It was not difficult for Knowlton to make a quite convincing case on whether the brilliance of Fester was sufficient compensation for the beginning of the breakup of the group. He took the opportunity to speak privately with Davenport and Oliver, and it was quite clear that both were uncomfortable because of Fester. Knowlton didn't press the discussion beyond the point of hearing them in one way or another say that they did feel awkward and that it was sometimes difficult for them to understand the arguments Fester advanced, but often embarrassing to ask him to provide the background on which his arguments were based. Knowlton did not interview Link.

About 6 months after Fester came to the photon laboratory, a meeting was scheduled in which the sponsors of the research would visit the laboratory to get an idea of the work and its progress. It was customary at these meetings for project heads to present the research being conducted in their groups. The members of each group were invited to other meetings, which were held later in the day and open to all, but the special meetings were usually attended only by project heads, the head of the laboratory, and the sponsors.

As the time for the special meeting approached, it seemed to Knowlton that he must avoid the presentation at all cost. He felt that he could not trust himself to present the ideas and work that Fester had advanced, because of his apprehension as to whether he could present them in sufficient detail and answer questions correctly. On the other hand, he did not feel he coud ignore these newer lines of work and present only the material that he had done or had been started before Fester's arrival. He also felt that it would not be beyond Fester at all, in his blunt and undiplomatic way (if he were present at the meeting, that is), to comment on his own presentation and reveal the inadequacy that Knowlton felt he had. It also seemed quite clear that it would not be easy to keep Fester from attending the meeting, even though he was not on the administrative level that was invited.

Knowlton found an opportunity to speak to Jerrold and raised the question. He remarked to Jerrold that, with the meetings coming up and with the interest in the work and with the contributions that Fester had been making, Fester would probably like to attend these meetings, but that there was a question of the feelings of the others in the group if Fester alone were invited. Jerrold dismissed this very lightly by saying that he didn't think the group would fail to understand Fester's rather different position, and that he thought Fester by all means should be invited. Knowlton then immediately agreed, adding that Fester should present the work because much of it had been done by him and that, as Knowlton put it, this would be an opportune way to recognize Fester's contributions and to reward him since he was eager to be recognized as a productive member of the laboratory. Jerrold agreed and so the matter was decided.

Fester's presentation was very successful and in some ways dominated the meeting. He attracted the interest and attention of many in attendance, and a long discussion followed his presentation. Later in the evening, with the entire laboratory staff present, a small circle of people formed about Fester in the cocktail period before the dinner. One of them was Jerrold himself, and a lively discussion took place concerning the application of Fester's theory. All of this disturbed Knowlton and his reaction and behavior were characteristic. He joined the circle, praised Fester to Jerrold and to the others, and remarked on the brilliance of the work.

Without consulting anyone, Knowlton began to take an interest in the possibility of a job elsewhere. After a few weeks he found that a new laboratory of considerable size was being organized in a nearby city, and that his training would enable him to secure a project-head job equivalent to his present one, with slightly more money.

He immediately accepted it and notified Jerrold by a letter, which he mailed on a Friday night to Jerrold's home. The letter was quite brief and Jerrold was stunned. The letter merely said that he had found a better position; that there were personal reasons why he didn't want to appear at the laboratory anymore; and that he would be glad to return at a later time from where he would be, some 40 miles away, to assist if there was any mixup at all in the past work. It also mentioned that he felt sure that Fester could supply any leadership for the group, and that his decision to leave so suddenly was based on some personal problems; he hinted at problems of health in his family, his mother and father. All of this was fictitious, of course. Jerrold took it at face value but still felt that this was very strange behavior and quite unaccountable since he had always felt his relationship with Knowlton had been warm and that Knowlton was satisfied and, as a matter of fact, quite happy and productive.

Jerrold was considerably disturbed, because he had already decided to place Fester in charge of another project that was going to be set up very soon. He had been wondering how to explain this to Knowlton, in light of the obvious help and value Knowlton was getting from Fester and the high regard in which he held him. He had, as a matter of fact, considered the possibility that Knowlton could add to his staff another person with Fester's kind of background and training, which had proven so valuable.

Jerrold did not make any attempt to meet Knowlton. In a way, he felt aggrieved about the situation. Fester, too, was surprised at the suddenness of Knowlton's departure and when Jerrold asked him whether he had reasons to prefer to stay with the photon group instead of the impending Air Force project, he chose the Air Force project and went on to that job the following week. The photon laboratory was hard hit. The leadership of the laboratory was temporarily given to Link until someone could be hired to take charge.

CASE 4

RANDLEY STORES (PART A)

RANDLEY STORES, INC. (A)

For this case, concentrate on analysing the management styles of District Manager 1 (DM1) and District Manager 2 (DM2).

1. Look at the goals of the organization in terms of decentralization. What is the organization trying to achieve?

2. Look at the styles of DM1 and DM2 to see whether both fit in well with the goals identified in question 1. For example, how does each manager handle:

   a) Task assignment
   b) Communication with subordinates
   c) Performance reviews

3. What reactions or responses are provoked among subordinates by each style of management?

4. Under what conditions would either management style be appropriate or inappropriate?

Randley Stores, Inc. (A)

PART 1

Randley Stores, Inc. was, in 1957, an expanding chain of over 75 supermarket stores in and around a large eastern metropolitan area. Although a few older and smaller grocery stores remained in the chain, most stores were large and modern with complete grocery, meat, and produce departments. Since the early 1950's the company had been building 6 to 10 stores a year, many in new suburban shopping centers.

In 1954 and 1955 Randley top management had concluded that the chain should be "decentralized." Formerly, each store had three separate departmental managers, each of whom was closely supervised by a different headquarters representative. Final decisions as to new equipment, merchandise displays, promotions, demotions, hiring and firing of permanent employees, etc., were made almost entirely by these representatives. Management agreed that this kind of "centralization" had been adequate during the early stages of the organization. New stores, however, were being built (a) further and further away from headquarters, (b) to handle a much larger variety of merchandise, and (c) for minimum volumes of $2 million a year.

Because of these three factors, management, in the spring of 1956, announced an organizational change that would create a new position in the stores, that of "store manager."

These men were to be picked from among the ranks, given a two months' training program in which they were to spend time in each of the three departments in a variety of stores, and placed in new stores as they were built. It was the hope of top management, although they were fully aware that it would not be easy, to then begin to "shift a substantial amount of responsibility" from headquarters to the store level. Moreover, they thought it should introduce a "unity into the store personnel" who had hitherto kept to their own departments—thereby adding to the payroll expense of the stores by not moving temporarily to a department needing assistance for a

brief time. In general, in the words of one executive, "We want some day to have real administrators running our stores—not just errand boys."

Some six months after the change was announced, a researcher from the Harvard Business School asked to observe some of the store situations in which these organizational changes were occurring.

After only a short period it became clear to the researcher that he could easily observe the ways individuals were responding to the change by watching the interactions between district managers and store managers and the way in which district managers talked about these interactions. (See Exhibit 1 for a chart of the formal relationships.) The store manager

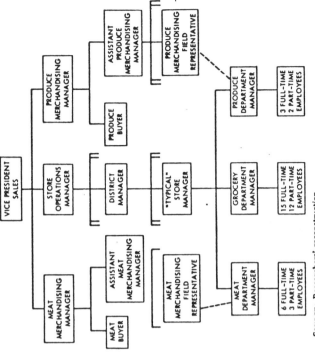

EXHIBIT 1

Partial Organization Chart, after Reorganization in 1956

Source: Researchers' reconstruction.

was being asked to "assume more overall administrative authority" in his stores and it was the district manager's job, according to the formal organizational change, to see to it that the store managers eventually behaved according to the new organizational expectations.

This case, then, focuses on two district managers—D.M.1 and D.M.2— as they talked with their subordinates and as they talked with the researcher. For purposes of comparison the two district managers picked were those closest together in certain "external" respects. Both were long-service employees of the company. They were in their fifties. They had for some time been the district managers of two of the largest and most important districts in the company. They had grown accustomed through the years to performing their duty in a way that was compatible with the "traditional" organizational patterns. Each had a reputation in the business as an expert in the field. Both were regarded by top management as high in quality of task performance.

Part 2 of this case includes selections from conversations the district managers had with the researcher in which they talked about their beliefs about themselves and their behavior in the organization, and about their attitudes towards subordinates, superiors, and the reorganization. Part 3 includes excerpts from conversations these men had with various store managers in their respective districts. In addition, it includes comments that two store managers made to the researcher about the district managers. Part 4 shows some quantitative data the researcher collected on the kinds of things these men discussed with their store managers and the ways in which they discussed them.

PART 2

The researcher talked with and observed the district managers over a period of several weeks and in a variety of contexts. The following statements were culled from these conversations and classified under "statements indicating a district manager's beliefs about himself as a district manager," "statements indicating a district manager's attitude towards subordinates," "statements indicating a district manager's attitude towards superiors," and, finally, "statements indicating a district manager's attitude towards the reorganization."

District Manager 1

Beliefs about Himself as a District Manager

One thing I've done lately is stop worrying about being fired. It happened mostly last summer when I was sick. I had a lot of time to think. I decided that it wasn't worth while worrying about things like that and that I might as well go ahead and do what I was going to do and stop worrying about it. I also decided I was going to speak up more when I disagreed about something. So, I go ahead and say what I want to say and I'm perfectly willing to take what follows. I don't think I'm going to get fired, because actually I think I'm doing a pretty good job as a district manager.

I'm the sort of person who is pretty critical of himself and so when I think I'm doing reasonably well, that must mean that my bosses think that I'm doing pretty well.

I don't think any of us should be too proud to use the good ideas that somebody else has.

The important thing is to teach yourself the new tricks first and then you might have a chance to teach someone else.

I've always been known as a maverick in this organization.

Attitudes toward Subordinates

My notion of a good supervisor is one who doesn't talk anymore than his subordinates do. Of course, you've got to do some of the talking to explain to him the kinds of things he ought to know about what the company wants him to do, but you have also got to give him plenty of chance to talk about his problems and the things he has on his mind or you are not going to get very far.

I'm interested in my store managers' opinions and, of course, I want them to know what mine are.

I won't do the same thing everytime I go into a store; if I did I would blow my brains out after a while because this job would be so dull. Of course, I don't do things the way I used to a few years ago. Even in the stores without store managers I've been letting the department managers handle more matters, like working out displays, than I used to, more than I imagine some of the other district managers do. Besides how the hell am I going to develop my men if I don't let them do things like that?

I believe that if a store manager can come up with his own answer to a problem, it is going to be the best answer in almost every case. It may not agree exactly with the way you would do it, but, unless he is really wrong, you ought to go ahead and let him do it in his own way and he'll be better off. That is the only way you can teach them to take the initiative on these matters.

I believe in giving my men suggestions instead of giving them hell!

He's a very good meat manager, but you have to be kind of careful how you talk to him because he is apt to take criticism in a rather childish way. He's apt to get sensitive and feel hurt if you criticize the way he runs his counter. That is why I step to one side to speak to him about his dirty floor. I've learned to handle him all right and he does a very good job.

You know you can't expect perfection out of people, and different people work differently. They can't all be as fast as some.

As far as I'm concerned, the number one part of a store manager's job is that he has got to have administrative ability. He's got to get people to do the job—that is the best definition of administration I know of.

I let the store manager know where he stands. At regular times I sit down with the fellow and we work out a written report evaluating and improving his performance. It is done with the man right there because it isn't going to do him any good if we just file a report in the head office. Sometimes these sessions are pretty frank and a little tough on the fellow, but as far as I am concerned he has to know his shortcomings and straighten them out.

Attitudes toward Superiors

The people who run this business make some mistakes, but they are really decent people. I don't hesitate to disagree with the vice president of sales on

costs up too much. To do that you have got to keep your shelves filled up with good merchandise properly presented. These are the fundamentals. If you are going to do those things right, it will show up in the figures.

I'm getting paid to have good merchandising ideas. Anybody who is a district manager has got to be interested in merchandise and selling merchandise, and in doing this you have to work with people to get them to understand this stuff so they can do it themselves.

I never give the store one figure on sales projections and the office another. The reason is that I simply can't lie. That is my biggest weakness. I'm not a diplomat. If I've got something on my mind, I just spill it. I can't fight it. When I get something on my mind I want to get it done today and not put it off. I suppose I carry that to such an extent that it is a fault of mine.

We've got too much heart in this company. We're just not businesslike.

Attitudes toward Subordinates

You really have to train store managers to look after those details and I have to follow up to make sure it is done. You see I've written out complete notes about everything I talked to this store manager about today so there is no excuse for his not doing something about them. Then I'll check these notes with him when I come back. You have to spend a lot of time with some of these fellows explaining these things to them.

I find in my own experience that I can work much better with the people under me who've learned to accept my criticisms, even welcome them, instead of those who seem to be fighting them.

[To store department heads:] I want each of you fellows to know that the store manager is constantly getting demands from above on how to do things. When he comes to you with something it is not just personal, he is getting orders from the district people to do things, and he has to follow through on them.

You saw that I had to go down and go all over with that store manager again what I want done on that drug counter down there. Now I've done all that before and I've gone into all those details before. He told me once before it couldn't work out there and I showed him how to make it work, and then today we have to go right back through the whole thing all over again. Now that is not the way you should have to treat the manager. I shouldn't have to spell things out that way for him. If I had store manager X here I would just say to him, "Put the drug counter up there." That would have been the end of it. It would have been done. Now that is my idea of a good store manager.

Attitudes toward Superiors

I may argue about something ahead of time, but once the decision is made, right or wrong, I will carry it out.

This is the first time I've found out what this new system is all about. Can you imagine that! They ought to tell us about these things if people are going to come in and put them into our store.

I used to be pretty outspoken and that was part of the thing that got me in trouble. I was known as the great dissenter, but I've stopped all of that now.

something or other and you can really discuss things with him. He's hardworking, too. Of course, after we have discussed things he has to decide what he is going to do and if he says we are going to do something, I'll do the best I can to make it work.

A couple of things came up recently that I think the district managers should have been consulted on by top managers. On one item I was so upset I got hold of my boss on the spot. It was a matter that affected the people in our stores and the district managers should have been consulted before the decision was made. We are closer to the situation and I think, actually, most of the top men would be glad to get our opinion. They just didn't bother to ask us.

This is a very friendly company, and I don't know anyone in the company who is afraid to speak up to anybody else. It has always been like that since I can remember and I think it stems largely from the top.

It is like in any organization you get into, there is always a certain amount of politics in it and you have to expect that.

I worked for Mr. Z. for many years, and I never did agree with his ideas about how to run things. I always did things somewhat differently than he would have. We grew to respect each other in spite of that.

Attitudes toward Reorganization

The store manager is my representative in the stores.

This store manager program is still pretty new . . . but I think it is already showing that it is paying for itself. We can add the store manager's salary to our store payroll and still have a better overall performance in that store. He can give us a lot of valuable supervision in there.

I have to keep watching myself in working consistently through the store manager. Every once in a while I slip back into the habit of speaking to whomever happens to be handy when I see something I don't like, but you really lose the effectiveness of what you are trying to do if you do that. Sometimes I have to remind other people, too, that come into the store to deal with the store manager.

District Manager 2

Beliefs about Himself as a District Manager

Mr. X is the best store manager in the whole chain. I never saw a guy who was so much like me in the way he acts in a store. He sometimes is tough on the people but he really gets the work out and done. For my money he is the best. I like a supervisor who is really the boss, really running things, a take-charge guy.

I was the one who started the first big self-service store in the chain. In that store we started a great many of the ideas that have since come into common use in the company.

I think the first thing you are in here for is to make some money for the company. In order to do that you have got to go out and get a volume of business. You've got to be selling things, and selling them in a way that doesn't run your

In this business you can't do anything right. It gets you one way or the other.

People at headquarters always accused me of not being patient enough to work out the problems that come along with new changes in the organization. I don't think they practice what they preach.

No one in the front office is much interested in my opinions.

Attitudes toward Reorganization

I'm one of the few people who doesn't like this new setup. I thought the old way was much better. I had a team with my two assistant district managers operating in my territory that you just couldn't beat.

I'm one of the few guys in the business who thinks this whole inventory control theory simply won't work.

I'm perfectly willing to live with the way things are. You sort of have to learn to do that, you know. I wasn't too happy when this country was being run by Democratic presidents but I lived through it, and there is something to be said for the things they did. It is the same way in this company. They have some reasons for doing what they are doing. I just don't happen to think it is right, but I'm perfectly willing to live with it.

PART 3

The researcher observed a number of interactions between the two district managers and some of their store managers. A few of these interactions are presented in Part 3 so that a comparison can be made between this aspect of the district managers' behavior and the other data in this case.

District Manager 1. D.M.1: Do you want to place an order for some new display steps with a formica top? Here is the story on them and this is what it would cost you to order them.

S.M.: Let's see what that would figure out to be. It sounds like it would run to $400 or $500.

D.M.1: Well, how many two- or three-tier displays do you have now?

S.M.: I've got three of the three-tier and two of the two-tier, so you see it would be a lot of money. I can't see spending that much.

D.M.1: That is what I feel too, that is an awful lot of money. You've got to sell a lot of merchandise to make $500. O.K., so much for that. Have you figured out how much the wage rate changes are going to affect your weekly payroll?

S.M.: I don't think it is going to be very much.

D.M.1: Well, I think you had better figure it out. I think you don't realize how much it is going to be. It turns out to be more in some of these stores than they think. It can easily be $100 a week.

S.M.: I don't think so. Last week we had a man out, but we also had some overtime and you see the figures didn't go up at all. I think it ought to go up at the most about $50.

D.M.1: Well, maybe that's right. You may be that lucky but I thought you might want to figure that out. Let's go on to something else.

On one occasion D.M.1 and a store manager were having a discussion when the grocery department manager took the researcher aside and pointed out that, as far as he was concerned, his store room was the nicest looking in the whole chain—the cleanest and the least inventory. He told the researcher that the inventory was down to less than two times weekly sales and that they were not on the new inventory control system that the company was slowly instituting "or anything else." He told the researcher, "It is all done by memory," and pointed to his forehead. When they rejoined the others, D.M.1 was talking about inventory handling.

D.M.1: Well, I think you fellows have a point but when our methods consultant sends in a report that we should mark merchandise when it goes on the selling floor and not in the basement I've got to listen to him, even though that does require a whole new system, because I'm not a technician and I don't know about these things. My only point is—I say that, let's not close our minds to this thing, because when a fellow like that comes up with a recommendation, I think we've got to consider it.

GROC. M.: What about the payroll in those stores? Is it the same?

D.M.1: Yes, it is. It doesn't cost any more the other way, and as a matter of fact, it costs a little bit less and they cut down the inventory.

S.M.: Well, our problem here is that our shipment from the headquarters warehouse comes in on Thursday. Everybody in the store is on the selling floor, waiting on customers, and you can't concentrate on the storage area. You simply couldn't handle a demand marking system here, because our part-timers come in Thursday at 3 o'clock and they are here for three hours. Well, if those fellows had to mark merchandise, they simply wouldn't be able to get it on the shelves by 6 o'clock, they just couldn't do it.

D.M.1: Well, I can certainly see that, and it is obvious that every store is not the same. But you fellows don't have the new shelf allocation system here, and when you do get that system you can go through a whole week on all but a very few items by just putting them up once. That is all part of the new inventory control system that is going in. Your shelves won't look as good—I know that, I won't argue that fact. The shelves and your display counters and tables may look very poor, and I don't like it. But it will cost you a lot less to put out merchandise on Monday, Tuesday, and Wednesday than on Thursday, Friday, and Saturday, when your whole selling area is packed with people. I think you are completely right, that when you don't have the shelf allocation system, you can't go to demand marking. You've certainly done a tremendous job here in this store, and I have no complaint at all about it.

GROC. M.: Well, yes, but it is all guesswork, though.

D.M.1: That is right. We've found, in the other stores, that you can cut your labor way down if you're on the shelf allocation system, no matter how good guesses you have made in the past about the kind of stuff you need and when you need it.

S.M.: Well, when they put us over on that shelf system, I'll consider it.

D.M.1: Well, you're right. I think that is the time to consider it. You have certainly done a hell of a job here and I think it is tremendous.

GROC. M.: Well, it's not just me, it's guys here like Bobbie. [Points to a young fellow who is opening a carton.]

District Manager 2. A researcher and D.M.2 entered a store one day, and D.M.2 walked immediately up to the store manager and said:

D.M.2: Boy, it's hot in here; what's going on?

S.M.: Yeah, it sure is hot. I just went down and turned off the heating system.

D.M.2: Well, it certainly is hot. Just what are you doing about it?

S.M.: Well, this happened once before and it got too hot. You see the thermostat is hooked up so it is tied in with the outside weather and it works that way. There was something that didn't work right about it so I got the repair people out here to look it over and they said they got it all fixed.

D.M.2: Well, what are you doing about it now?

S.M.: Well, I turned the heat off and I called the office.

D.M.2: Can you adjust the thermostat you've got?

S.M.: No, it is all locked up. You've got to get the maintenance people out here and they are coming out.

D.M.2: Boy, it's just too hot in here, it's too hot.

S.M.: For Christ's sake, of course it is too hot. What do you think I've got my coat off for; even in my shirt it's too hot.

D.M.2: Well, what can I do for you on this thing? Can I give you any help until you get it squared away?

S.M.: No, I don't think there is anything you can do. We are doing what we can. I've got the heat turned off now, so it should cool off.

On one occasion the researcher observed the opening day of a new store. During the morning the only interactions between D.M.2 and his new store manager were as follows:

D.M.2: You better keep an eye on the front entrance where they are passing out carriages, and keep the flow in and out going steadily.

The store manager nodded and for the next four hours remained at that task almost continuously.

At one point during the morning the opening surge fell off somewhat and the store manager went out to the back room for a cup of coffee, where he met D.M.2.

S.M.: Say, we have some awfully slow people on the cash registers out there.

D.M.2: I don't think so. Four out of your seven people are experienced, aren't they?

S.M.: Yes.

D.M.2: Well, that's about as good as you can expect on an opening day, with four good people in there.

S.M.: Well, yes, that is right.

D.M.2 told another store manager, once, to get some merchandise out of the employees' lunch room; and, when the store manager carried it out and set it in the hall, D.M.2 then told him to take it down to the store office and put it there.

S.M.: Well, the trouble is the office is too full to put it in.

D.M.2: What have you got down there?

S.M.: Some cases of cash register tapes.

D.M.2: Well, that shouldn't be. The thing for you to do is to move that tape out of there and then you can put this merchandise down there.

S.M.: O.K.

After discussing some further points with this store manager, the district manager continued:

D.M.2: What I suggest for you to do is to get yourself a notebook just like this one I carry, to keep these notes in, that I'm telling you to write down now. Then you will have them in one place and be able to keep track of them. It is sort of a little date book. Well, I guess that's all I've got. Any questions?

S.M.: No.

The researcher talked to the various store managers who worked for D.M.1 and D.M.2. The following comments from two such store managers seemed particularly interesting.

S.M. who worked for D.M.1: Yes, I've really got a good deal here in this store, because I've got good boys, and we work together pretty well. . . . There's a lot of little things that go together that make a good store. . . . The district manager has to be on your side. He can't be doing things that will keep you from moving in as boss, but there's a lot more to it besides that. You've got to have good personalities in the store on a department head level and on the store manager level, and, if your district manager is going to criticize somebody, or pay somebody a compliment, he should have you along and maybe he could mention it was the store manager's idea. So if you get all these things working together, and they are really all just little things, you're going to have a good store.

S.M. who worked for D.M.2: You know the district manager really goes by the book on things like special displays and does things the way the company wants, and that's the way they have to be done here. He really sticks by the book and that's the way it should be, because, of course, if you go by the book, you're going to keep out of trouble. Now I know there's a lot of D.M.'s who wink at stuff like that because they realize a fellow has got a few cases of junk that he wants to move, and island wings are usually a good way to do it. I know that Charlie has got a hell of a lot of stuff down there in the back room that he'd like to clean out but, gee, if I ever let him start putting up carriages of merchandise around the store, he'd have those carriages all over the place. You know they don't stay in one place either. You put a carriage down there by that drug table that has a few items on it, and you come back in a half hour and some damned little kid has pushed it way over there to the coke machine. And you just can't have stuff like that. Of course it's the same sort of thing in any job. You have to figure out what kind of a fellow your boss is and play the game his way. You figure out how your boss wants it done, and that's how you do it.

177

Organizational Change and Development

PART 4

The researcher wished to check the "feel" he had concerning the differences he saw in the behavior of D.M.1 and D.M.2 as well as some of the similarities. Consequently, he designed a simple method of recording interactions he observed between the two district managers and their various store managers. In this way he recorded: who talked; the length of each separate speech; the category of speech (i.e., asking a question, supplying information, giving an opinion, giving directions or suggestions); the type of topic involved (discussion of people, merchandise, record systems, physical plant, and small talk) and, finally, who initiated new topics.

As for the kinds of topics that were classified, such questions as, Is Joe doing a good job? What would you think of transferring Mary? Is Bill still asking for more money? Why did you assign that work to John? etc, were considered as "discussion of people." Under "merchandise" fell communications about the amount, kind, handling, and explaining of merchandise. Under "record systems" came all discussions of payroll records, procedures for scheduling people, sales figures, etc. Under "physical plants" were included discussions of store maintenance, housekeeping, new equipment, etc. "Small talk" was all joking, kidding, and talk not related to business.

The results follow in Exhibit 2. In Exhibit 2 the records of D.M.1 covered 227 minutes, of which 157 minutes occurred during early days of the week and 70 minutes late in the week. The number of separate comments were 1,115, recorded on nine separate store visits with three different store managers.

The record of D.M.2 covered 456 minutes, of which 293 were early and 173 late in the week. The number of separate comments was 2,092, recorded or four separate store visits with three different store managers.

EXHIBIT 2

D.M.–S.M. Interaction Analysis by Classification of Speech and Topics

Category	D.M.1	S.M.	D.M.2	S.M.
Average percent of talking time	58	42	75	25
Average percent of time spent:				
Asking questions	9	4	9	2
Giving information	17	23	26	17
Giving opinions	17	10	12	4
Giving suggestions/directions	15	5	28	2
Average percent of new topics initiated	77	23	86	14
Average percent of time both spent on:				
People	48		11.0	
Merchandise	10		32.0	
Record systems	22		47.0	
Physical plant	7		10.0	
Small talk	7		0.5	

CASE 5

DESERT SURVIVAL PROBLEM

The Desert Survival Problem

The Situation:

It is approximately 10:00 a.m. in mid-August and you have just crash landed in the Sonora Desert in southwestern United States. The light twin engine plane, containing bodies of the pilot and the co-pilot, has completely burned. Only the air frame remains. None of the rest of you has been injured.

The pilot was unable to notify anyone of your position before the crash. However, he had indicated before impact that you were 70 miles south-southwest from a mining camp which is the nearest known habitation and that you were approximately 65 miles off the course that was filed in your VFR Flight Plan.

The immediate area is quite flat and except for occasional barrel and saguaro cacti appears to be rather barren. The last weather report indicated the temperature would reach 110° that day which means that the temperature at ground level will be 130°. You are dressed in light weight clothing - short sleeved shirts, pants, socks and street shoes. Everyone has a handerkerchief. Collectively, your pockets contain $2.38 in change, $85.00 in bills, a pack of cigarettes, and a ballpoint pen.

The Problem:

Before the plane caught fire your group was able to salvage the 15 items listed below. Your task is to rank these items according to their importance to your survival starting with 1, the most important, to 15, the least important.

You should assume that all items are in good condition and that you are one of the actual people in the situation. Do not discuss the situation or problem with others in preparing your rankings.

	Expert's Ranks	Your Ranks	Your Error Points	Group Ranks	Group Error Points
Flashlight (4 battery size)					
Jack knife					
Sectional air map of area					
Plastic raincoat (large size)					
Magnetic compass					
Compress kit with gauze					
Forty-five caliber pistol (loaded)					
Parachute (red and white)					
Bottle of salt tablets (1,000 tablets)					
One quart of water per person					
A book entitled, Edible Animals of the Desert					
A pair of sunglasses per person					
Two quarts of 180 proof Vodka					
One top coat per person					
A cosmetic mirror					
TOTAL					

CASE 6

MAYFLOWER PAPER MILLS

MAYFLOWER PAPER MILLS

Discussion Questions

1. What is the evidence of the existence of intergroup conflict between people at the Quinault mill and members of the research department?

2. What factors are causing this conflict between the two groups?

3. How could this conflict be resolved?

MAYFLOWER PAPER MILLS

John Curtis was anxious about the pace of technical innovations
in the three paper mills for which he was general manager. The mills had
their own technical staff but for more long-term development and more
sophisticated work there was a small Research Department that the three
mills under Curtis shared with the Mayflower Company's other four mills
on the East Coast. "I am not really sure," he said, "that we have found
the best way of organizing research and development work for the mills.
The Research Department seems to work pretty well with most of the mills
but there is really no cooperation with the mill at Quinault. In fact,
the mill manager at Quinault thinks that Research is useless and I find
it difficult at the moment to persuade him to cooperate with them when
his mill is the most profitable in the group." (See Exhibits 1 and 2.)

Curtis added, however, that even though the Quinault mill was
working at full capacity, the newsprint sheet produced there was only of
medium quality. The quality of the paper produced depended on many
variables, such as fiber length, pulp consistency, machine speed, temperature, and water flow. The manipulation of these variables determined
weight, finish, thickness, softness, and moisture of the finished product. In the past the quality of the paper produced had depended entirely on the skill and experience of the machine operators as they adjusted the process variables. This dependence on human ability, while
still important, was decreasing, however, as scientific knowledge about
the factors influencing quality increased.

Curtis was mainly concerned about the lack of cooperation between the Quinault plant and the Research Department. "There is a real
running battle between the Quinault mill manager, Tom Moe, and the Director
of Research, Bob MacCaulay," he said, "and although I think it might be
having some harmful effects on our operations long term, I don't know how
to resolve the problem. I do think that the friction between Research and
Quinault has had some bad effects on technical innovations in the mill, but
I can't say that they are really significant. We should have something to
gain if Research had full access to Quinault. But all the things we want
Research to do up there have been solved by the mill technical people."

This case was prepared by Neil Millward, visiting scholar, at the Harvard
Business School under the direction of Associate Professor Jay W. Lorsch.
It was written as the basis for class discussion rather than to illustrate
effective or ineffective handling of an administrative situation.

The Mayflower Company

The three mills under John Curtis were part of a large and diversified "conglomerate" with sales of over one billion dollars in 1968. Mayflower corporate headquarters were located in Portland, Maine. The communications papers segment of the company's business, of which the paper mills were a part, contributed $130 million in sales and 13% of the company's profits in 1968.

. . . Mayflower paper mills produced 476,000 tons of communication papers during 1968 at 7 locations. . . . Both the Quinault and Vancouver newsprint mills operated at peak capacity despite the general leveling of US newsprint demand that characterized the 1967-1968 period. Newsprint accounts for just over half of Mayflower's communication paper production and is the largest single paper tonnage item produced by the company.

Of the seven mills in the communications papers group, the three western mills had originally been owned by the Washtenaw Pulp and Paper Company, either directly or through a wholly owned Canadian subsidiary. The Pulp and Paper Company was acquired by Mayflower in December 1964. Its assets consisted of three papers mills, one at Port Angeles, Washington, one just across the straits at Vancouver, British Columbia, and the third one, 150 miles north at Quinault, British Columbia, and research facilities in Port Angeles. The four original Mayflower mills were located on the East Coast.

Among the paper companies in the United States Mayflower ranked about average for introduction of new products; compared to companies with an equal sales volume, Mayflower was below average. Curtis believed that this was because management of the ten-year-old company was more concerned with current earnings than with future earnings which might accrue from investment in research.

Curtis had been manager of one of the Mayflower company's East Coast mills before becoming general manager of the three western mills. He had worked in the industry ever since he had obtained his degree in Pulp and Paper Technology, except for two years spent with the U. S. Army. He attended the Program for Management Development at Harvard six months after taking up his new appointment as general manager of the western mills in May 1967. Curtis maintained that a mill manager did not need to have a high degree of technical knowledge about paper making, but it was essential to have had some experience in the industry.

After the acquisition, the research laboratories at Port Angeles began to serve all seven of Mayflower's paper mills with the director of research reporting to the vice president of paper manufacturing. In January 1969 the director of research was Bob MacCaulay. After receiving his Ph.D. in Chemical Engineering, MacCaulay had started work in the research laboratories of Washtenaw Pulp and Paper and subsequently became laboratory manager. Within a year of the acquisition of Pulp and Paper by Mayflower he was made director of research for the paper group.

Tom Moe, the Quinault Mill Manager, had worked in the paper industry ever since he graduated as a chemical engineer in 1946. Early in his career he worked in Alberta in a newsprint mill and gradually worked his way up until he became technical director of the mill. When personal friction with some machine tenders in the mill caused him to resign, he joined another firm of paper manufacturers as a superintendent and was put in charge of starting up two new paper machines. Later on, when another company in British Columbia required an experienced man to start up a rebuilt paper machine he joined them as mill general superintendent and subsequently became mill manager. Some time later the problem of placing his children in a suitable school in a remote area caused him to look around for another job. He was appointed general superintendent of Mayflower's Vancouver Mill in December 1964. Within a year he was promoted to mill manager and then in June 1967 was appointed manager of the company's other Canadian paper mill at Quinault, British Columbia.

Tom Moe had become general superintendent of the Vancouver Mill on the day that the merger of Washtenaw Pulp and Paper with Mayflower was consummated.[1] Bob MacCaulay recollected that he was working on a problem with one of the pulp screens at Vancouver at the time that Moe was appointed. A small committee of technical and production people was discussing the screen problem and the question arose as to whether they should invite Tom Moe to the meeting. McCaulay said he thought the new superintendent would be too busy settling into his new job and so Moe wasn't invited. MacCaulay recalled that when Moe had found out about this he was very resentful and had held a grudge against him ever since.

Organization of the Paper Group

Exhibit 1 shows the formal positions of these two men in the management hierarchy of the paper group. The organization of the Mayflower Paper Group, comprising the seven mills and a number of service departments, was a complex one, involving differences in geography, product, nationality, technology, and date of acquisition. In financial terms, the paper mills were considered profit centers while the various service departments such as sales, research and engineering, were considered cost centers to the group. Both the Research Department and the Central Engineering Department received budget allocations from the vice president of paper manufacturing. Funds were also channeled from a particular mill to either of these departments if the project undertaken was specific to that mill only. For instance, when the Central Engineering Department did the design and commissioning for the rebuilding of a paper machine at the Quinault Mill the cost for this activity was charged against the mill. Similarly, when a mill manager requested that somebody in the Research Department carry out an investigation that was specific to his mill, the time spent by the Research Department was charged against the mill. A limit of 25% of the total time available to research personnel was to be used in this way, but this limit had never been reached.

---

[1] The general superintendent was responsible for the day-to-day operations of the mill's manufacturing departments and reports to the mill manager.

The Research Department at Port Angeles was small, with assets of approximately $600,000 at replacement cost. Besides Bob MacCaulay, the Director, there were nine professional engineers or chemists, including four Ph.D.'s and about twelve technicians and supporting staff members. In contrast, each of the seven paper mills represented an average investment of over $20,000,000 and each employed between 400 and 800 men. In 1969 the budgeted net sales for the seven paper mills were $160,000,000, while budgeted expenditure of the Research Department was $360,000.

In the early part of 1969 there were 16 projects on which research personnel were working. Of these, six were applicable to all seven paper mills, four others were applicable to either three or four of them, and the remaining six were each relevant to one mill only. Some of the more important projects were concerned with increasing the yield of pulp, general explorations into the chemical and physical characteristics of pulp from different species of wood, the development of new or improved finishes, and the improvement of testing procedures for new grades of paper. Bob MacCaulay described the nature of some of these projects:

> Most of the work we do now is on a pretty short-term basis and involves no real risk. We aren't really doing any new developments. The Washtenaw Pulp and Paper management had a longer term outlook and in their research department some completely new products were developed. The Mayflower management are much more short-term oriented and although things look good at the moment I think we might suffer long term from some of the decisions that have been made. For instance, last year we dropped our membership in the Canadian research center of the Institute of Paper Chemistry because of the high cost of subscription.

Managers of the paper mills which used the Research Department were asked about their attitude toward the Research Department. Tom Jacobs, Manager of the Vancouver Paper Mill, said:

> The people in the Eastern mills have a poor opinion of research, but the people here in my mill think highly of them. Charging for research time against the individual mill's profits doesn't affect or deter our use of them.

The Manager of the Port Angeles Mill, Ralph Jones, said:

> We are working on three or four new grades with Research. We do a lot of work with them, in fact I get a bill from them every month.

MacCaulay explained why it was that some of the paper mills used the Research Department more than others:

We do most of our work for the three mills here that used to be part of the old Pulp and Paper organization. At times our work with the mills over on the East Coast has been pretty small because of the distance, but relations with them are cordial and now our contacts with them seem to be increasing. Ralph Jones, the Manager of the Port Angeles Mill, drives us crazy with requests to carry out investigations and we also do a fair amount of work for the Vancouver Mill. But Quinault people prefer to go their own way - they think the research people are spies. We got on fine with the people at Quinault when Ralph Jones was manager there but when Tom Moe moved up there from Vancouver they cut us right out.

Tom Moe explained why:

My job as resident manager of the Quinault Mill is to run the mill, within the budget objectives and the goals set by top management, as a unit profit center. I see myself as a sort of team captain and I am trying to develop the people we have here so that the mill can be self-sufficient. If we haven't got enough people or we haven't got people with the specialized skills for a particular job then we go outside: for instance, we might get people from the Central Engineering Department or hire some outside consultants. The tendency now in the corporation is to say that you should give Central Engineering preference over outside consultants because we are paying the overhead anyway and it is good training for the engineers in the corporations. Personally, I try to get my own people here in the mill to do as many of the jobs as possible so that they can learn from the experience and build up technical expertise. Anyway, the same concept that applies to the use of Central Engineering is supposed to apply to Research. So if we have a job up here that we don't have the expertise to handle I could go to Research and ask them to help us out. But they don't like working under that arrangement. Before Washtenaw Pulp and Paper was taken over by Mayflower quite a few research projects were started without consultation with the mills and so they have got used to doing jobs which the mill managers haven't asked them to do. I feel that the Research people want to run the mill technically and not accept the responsibility for it.

I am trying to achieve a balance of technical and practical skills for the mill superintendents and the mill technical staff. The mill superintendents are the people who should define research problems. No man can serve two masters; how can the superintendents be carrying out tests for Research and running the machines in the most profitable way for the mill?

I have never asked the Research people to do anything for us since I have been here. But I have got research questions ironed out by our suppliers; for instance, we get a lot of chemicals from Dow and they haved helped us improve our utilization and reclamation of pulping chemicals. For other problems I will talk with my friends in other paper mills around the country. I know a lot of people in Canada through the paper industry associations and going to conventions and through working for different companies. We all try and help each other out as much as we can.

The Research Department here is on much too small a scale to be of any use. The Research people have an 8 to 4 job and that's a pretty soft touch compared with the technical people at the mill. I reckon the Research people make work so that they can stick to their soft jobs.

The ill feelings between Bob and Tom, and between their respective subordinates, were well known around the organization. The manager of Data Processing described what happened when he worked on a job with the two men themselves.

We were setting up a new quality control system for the newsprint that we shipped from Quinault down to one of the large daily newspapers in California: Bob was involved because the Research Department collects quality data on the paper from all the mills so that it can do standard statistical tests and maintain standardized test procedures. They didn't get along very well together. Whenever Bob made a suggestion Tom told him to stop telling him how to run his mill. One of the troubles is that Tom gets too involved with all the tiny details. When we were putting in that system we just couldn't have a meeting without Tom being there. He's a very hard-working guy but he just oversupervises. For instance, we had a small problem with data cards coming back which did not match the correct rolls of newsprint. Tom insisted on going down and seeing the customer himself to sort out the problem. I don't think the mill manager should need to go and sort out these problems - they aren't important enough for him.

It's a funny thing but Ralph Jones wants to get involved too much in the details as well and they are both Canadians. Perhaps this is one of the differences between Canadian and American managers?

Different people around the organization cited different factors as explaining the conflict between Research and Quinault. Besides the issue of nationality one of the popular explanations rested in the remoteness of the Quinault Mill from Port Angeles. The Research Department, the paper mill at Port Angeles, and the Vancouver Paper Mill were all within walking distance of each other, whereas the Quinault Mill was 150 miles north of Vancouver and occasionally, under bad weather conditions, it was impossible to get between the two places. Management personnel usually made the journey in a small company-owned plane and this was often grounded because of bad weather. To illustrate this point, it was not until the fourth day of his visit to Port Angeles in January 1969 that conditions were suitable for the casewriter to be flown to Quinault to visit the mill. Such constraints also affected the travel plans of top management personnel of Mayflower so that their appearance at the Quinault Mill was extremely uncommon. In contrast, the facilities at Port Angeles and Vancouver were accessible by regular scheduled airlines.

The Quinault Mill differed from the other two western mills in other respects. Its three high-speed paper-making machines were given over to the continuous production of newsprint. One of the three machines in the Vancouver Mill made newsprint about 40% of the time and all the rest of its machine capacity was used for making specialty papers.[1] A further difference was that, at least during the financial year 1968, Quinault was the most profitable mill in the group. In fact, some of the managers in the group said that Quinault "prints money."

Bob MacCaulay put it this way:

Because of the annual bonus system, which is related to the earnings per share of the total corporation, it is in my interest that the Quinault Mill makes more money, the same as it is for all the mills. The trouble is that they are making money so if you try to do any work there they think you are interfering.

The antagonism between the Research Department and the Quinault Mill was not confined to the two managers involved. The technical director of the Quinault Mill described how he dealt with technical problems.

My department is involved in all the technical aspects of the mill. This includes production, shipping, quality control, testing, and even statistics on the supply of pulpwood. We would like to think that technically we are self-sufficient here. If a problem arises that is outside our scope then I take it to the mill manager and he decides how it will be dealt with. The trouble with Research is that they feel the whole mill should be open for their investigation. We had some trouble with them recently over a screening improvement. We thought we had the expertise to deal with the problem and they thought they had more data avail-

---

[1]Specialty papers are those papers which are further processed by the customer to make a finished product.

able on which to base a decision. Well, anyway, we did the
work on it and were able to successfully improve the process.
Research shouldn't be involved with in-plant problems, they
should be developing new processes and new products. Research
should be technically ahead of the mills. The trouble is
that they do not have the resources to do new product development.

A young chemist, with about three years experience at the Quinault
Mill, had this to say:

When I first worked here as a summer student there were
people up here from Research working all the time. I worked
with some of the guys from Research sometimes but I never really
learned anything from them. Since I came here to work perma-
nently two years ago the mill has become much more self-sufficient, from a technical point of view. If we get into trouble
we usually talk to people we know in other paper mills and ask
them how they solved the problem. It's a really friendly
industry, the paper industry.

Typical of the views of the professional engineers and chemists from
the Research Department was the following:

We really have wonderful cooperation with the people in
the mill here at Port Angeles but if we go up to Quinault we
get the feeling that we are not wanted. Tom Moe has a technical background and he thinks he knows it all. When they
had a new technical director up there at first he was quite
okay but now he is as bad as the rest. We get better cooperation with the mills over on the East Coast than we do with
Quinault. If they ever ask you anything they are just satisfied with a short-term answer and then they shut you off.
Often they use our nationality as a justification for insult-
ing us. They are all Canadians and there are no Canadians
here in the Research Department.

One of the Ph.D.'s in the Research Department went on to describe
an incident which he said showed the "bad way" in which they were treated by
the people at Quinault. He had performed some tests at the Quinault Mill
which involved staying there for three weeks. Usually anyone visiting
Quinault stayed in the company staff house, provided there was room. When
he arrived he was told that he had to stay in a motel in the town. As far
as he could find out there were no people visiting the mill who would have
been occupying the staff house during that period. The group of researchers
suspected that this was just another case of "cussedness" on the part of the
mill manager. In fact, the casewriter was able to ascertain from the staff
house manager and the records in the guest register that at the particular
period in question the staff house had been completely occupied by a party
of important customers who were normally offered the facilities of the staff
house for fishing trips at that time of the year.

Problems also arose between the two groups because of different outlooks towards tests that were carried out on the machines in the mills. The machine operators thought that Research people should be sure of the results of what they were going to do, while the Research people complained that this showed that the men in the mill had no understanding of what it meant to have a research orientation. A mill hand said: "Those guys from Research always muck us up when they do their tests," while the researchers accused the men in the mill of being resistant to change and unreceptive to new ideas.

Besides the research projects carried out in the laboratories and the consulting-type investigations requested by mill managers or their technical directors, the Research Department carried out other activities. One important activity of the Research Department was to standardize the tests used for assessing paper quality and to calibrate the instruments used to perform these tests. There were many nationally recognized standards for paper color, brightness, strength, porosity, opacity, moisture content, ash content, etc., that made it important to have consistent and reliable instruments to insure that the quality of the finished product from the mill met customers' requirements. Some of these tests had to be carried out in specially controlled conditions and often required the use of an air-conditioned room. The Quinault Mill was the only mill in the Paper Group which did not have an air-conditioned room for test purposes. Such a facility was estimated by the Research Department as costing approximately $10,000. The brightness tester at the Quinault Mill was made by a different manufacturer than those used in all the other mills. These factors were regarded by the Research personnel as being partly responsible for some of the disputes they had about product quality with Quinault Mill personnel. As Bob MacCaulay put it:

The basis of research is standardized conditions and procedures and the people at Quinault don't use them. Our sales people are having a bad time getting tonnage for the newsprint mill that we are building in the South because of the poor quality of the Quinault newsprint. The reason why Quinault is full when other newsprint mills around the country are working on short time is that our sales people are building up the tonnage for when the new mill opens. Our two biggest newsprint customers say that our paper is the poorest for runability. Some time ago I sent Quinault a memo about runability and moisture content which they took offense at. They have been refusing to send me the summary of test results ever since as a punishment. They thought my memo was trying to tell them things that they knew. Well, everyone knows that runability and moisture content are related - the whole point is that they play it safe and don't use proper instruments. So they keep the moisture content too low and won't ease it up to the line.

The one function that the Research Department carried out which Quinault technical personnel agreed was useful was that of paying for a joint membership of the various industry and technical associations, thus reducing costs. Some of them also agreed that it would be useful to keep test equipment standardized through a central research department while a smaller number maintained that Research should be concerned with developing marketable by-products and totally new grades of paper. Twice per year there was a meeting of all mill managers, mill technical directors, the director of research and some of his professional staff. The mill managers received a monthly research report that described progress being made on current projects. Within the last year and a half technical directors at the mill had started sending monthly technical reports to the Research Department; Quinault was the last mill to adopt this practice. Bob MacCaulay said, "The technical report from Quinault was written by Tom Moe. You can't really call it a technical report because it contained no data - it was really just an essay from the manager's office."

In 1968 a major rebuild was completed on one of the paper machines at Quinault. This was the largest job that the western section of the Central Engineering Department had ever handled and the total contract involved 2.9 million dollars. The manager of the Central Engineering Department had this to say about the rebuild:

> Tom Moe was skeptical to start with but the job worked
> out well. He respects technical competence. Nowadays I think
> Quinault is the best mill for cooperative effort.

The technical director at Quinault said that a few of the start-up problems after the rebuild could have been eliminated if they had been better informed and consulted by the Central Engineering Department. Tom Moe added, "We don't have any real problems in dealing with Central Engineering."

In January of 1969 the vice president of paper manufacturing who was also concerned about the research organization asked the paper mill managers, the two general managers and the director of research and his assistant to submit their written comments on the following topics:

1) The guiding philosophy and basic objectives of research and development directed toward process improvement,

2) Increases, or other changes, in the personnel requirements of the Research Department and the technical departments at the mills,

3) Suggestions for suitable research projects to be carried out by the Research Department,

4) The best location of the facilities of the Research Department,

The suggestions made as a result of this request ranged from the establishment of a new research laboratory to serve the East Coast mills (made by a member of the Research Department to the abolition of the Research Department (made by Tom Moe).

Curtis wanted to see the conflict between the Research Department and the Quinault Mill resolved. He felt that such a resolution was his responsibility. He knew that Quinault was the most profitable mill in the company and that this was due to some extent to Tom Moe's skill. He also felt that the Quinault Mill would not lose volume or profit when the company's new mill opened. Yet the long-term health of the mill and improvement of quality necessitated better relations between Research and Quinault. He summarized his problem this way:

A lot of the problem is with Tom Moe, because of the way he is - his hang-ups. It's also Bob MacCaulay. He is quick, but somehow intense. So it's partly a personality clash. But it's mainly Tom, because he has problems with other people besides Bob.

I think Tom must feel really insecure although he has no reason to. If he would work with staff groups to get the benefit of their knowledge and experience he would be the best manager we have because he is without question the best paper man.

Curtis had discussed this problem on numerous occasions with John Dumont, Vice President of Paper Manufacturing. At Dumont's suggestion Curtis had also discussed the problem with Mayflower's new Corporate Director of Personnel, Phil Hanson, who had recently acquired his Ph.D. in Organizational Behavior from the Stanford Business School. Hanson had offered to help with the problem in any way he could. Curtis therefore wondered what he might do himself - or how he might involve Dumont and/or Hanson in solving the problem.

Exhibit 1

MAYFLOWER PAPER MILLS

Part of Organization Chart of Paper Group

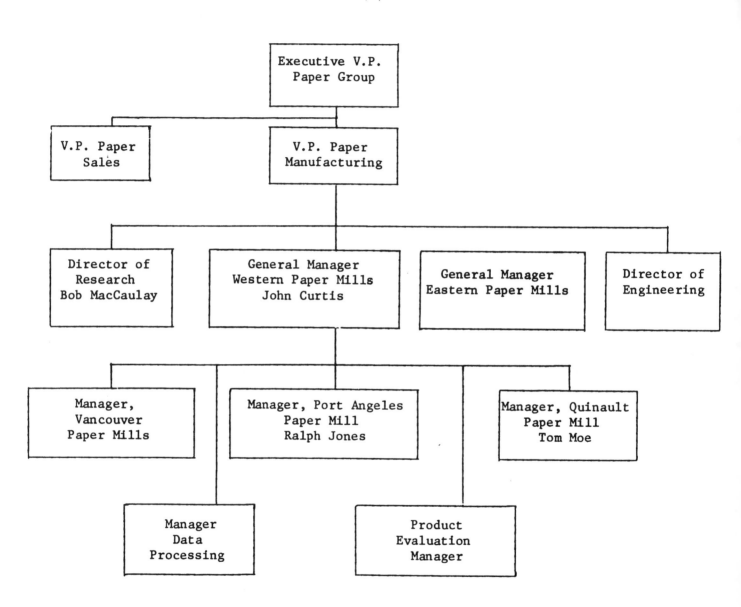

Exhibit 2

MAYFLOWER PAPER MILLS

Recent Operating Statistics for the Quinault Mill

	1966	1967	1968	1969 (6 Mos.)
Production (Tons)	218,548	239,915	239,949	130,410
Net Sales	$28,582,436	$31,896,698	$32,520,552	$17,928,430
Income*	$7,791,053	$7,880,985	$7,732,235	$4,844,880
R.O.I.**	27.7%	29.5%	29.5%	35.9%

*Before GS&A and before tax

**R.O.I $= \dfrac{\text{pretax income}}{\text{total investment}}$

Exhibit 3

MAYFLOWER PAPER MILLS

Excerpts from a Report Issued by Toronto Dominion Bank on

Paper and Allied Industries in Canada*

Pulp and Paper

Canadian Domestic Supply 1964 - 1968

	1964		1965		1966		1967		1968	
	1	2	1	2	1	2	1	2	1	2
A. Manufacturers' Shipments	1984	+10.6	2104	+ 6.0	2345	+11.4	2356	+ 0.5	2426	+ 2.8
B. Less: Exports	1359	+11.6	1432	+ 5.4	1576	+10.0	1595	+ 1.2	1718	+ 7.7
	625		672		769		761		708	
C. Add: Imports	65	+ 8.5	72	+10.9	71	- 2.1	70	- 0.6	78	+10.5
D. Domestic Supply	690	-17.4	744	+ 7.8	840	+12.9	831	- 1.1	786	- 6.4
Exports as a percentage of Manufacturers' Shipments (B/A)	68.5		68.1		67.2		67.7		70.8	
Imports as a percentage of Domestic Supply (C/D)	9.4		9.7		8.5		8.4		9.9	

1. Value in $ million.   Source: Based on DBS figures.
2. Per cent change over previous year.
*Includes pulp and paper, asphalt roofing, paper box and bag, and miscellaneous
   paper converters.

* * * * *

Conclusion

The faster rise of wages, compared to industry selling prices, particularly in 1966 and 1967, no doubt accounts for the reduction in net earnings in those years. In addition, the increasing capital investment in 1964
and after also led to a substantial surplus of productive capacity in newsprint and chemical pulp. Signs are, however, that the current year will see
better conditions, with improved exports. Mr. R. M. Fowler, President of
the Canadian Pulp and Paper Association, in the annual speech in January
1969, said "Nevertheless, by the end of 1968 there were signs that some of
the important problems that have plagued the industry for two years, problems
of growth, really, were beginning to ease. In particular, world markets were
considerably stronger, and for the immediate future, world demand for newsprint
and pulps seems likely to increase more rapidly than productive capacity."

Newspaper reports have appeared that some of the larger pulp and
paper companies expect improved profits this year, and newspaper reports
also mention a probable rise in the price of pulp and paper products some-
time this year.

CASE 7

WORDS IN SENTENCES COMPANY

From: D.T. Hall, D.W. Bowen, R. Lewicki & F. Hall. Experiences in
Management and Organizational Behavior (2nd ed.),
pp. 239-240. ©1982 by John Wiley and Sons, Inc.
Used by Permission.

ORGANIZATIONAL STRUCTURE AND DESIGN

WORDS-IN-SENTENCES COMPANY

INTRODUCTION

In this exercise you will form a "miniorganization" with several other people. You will be competing with other companies in your industry. The success of your company will depend on your (1) objectives, (2) planning, (3) organization structure, and (4) quality control. It may also depend on leadership style. It is important, therefore, that you spend some time thinking about the best design for your organization.

DIRECTIONS

You are a small company that manufactures words and then packages them in meaningful (English language) sentences. Market research has established that sentences of at least three words but not more than six words each are in demand. Therefore, packaging, distribution, and sales should be set up for three-to-six-word sentences.

The "words-in-sentences" (WIS) industry is highly competitive; several new firms have recently entered what appears to be an expanding market. Since raw materials, technology, and pricing are all standard for the industry, your ability to compete depends on two factors: (1) volume and (2) quality.

Group Task

Your group must design and participate in running a WIS company. You should design your organization to be as efficient as possible during each 10-minute production run. After the first production run, you will have an opportunity to reorganize your company if you want to.

Raw Materials

For each production run you will be given a "raw material word or phrase." The letters found in the word or phrase serve as the raw materials available to produce new words in sentences. For example, if the raw material word is "organization," you could produce the words and sentence: "Nat ran to a zoo."

Production Standards

There are several rules that have to be followed in producing "words-in-sentences." If these rules are not followed, your output will not meet production specifications and will not pass quality-control inspection.

1. The same letter may appear only as often in a manufactured word as it appears in the raw material word or phrase; for example, "organization" has two o's. Thus "zoo" is legitimate, but "zoonosis" is not. It has too many o's and s's.
2. Raw material letters can be used again in different manufactured words.
3. A manufactured word may be used only once in a sentence and in only one sentence during a production run; if a word—for example, a—is used once in a sentence, it is out of stock.
4. A new word may not be made by adding s to form the plural of an already used manufactured word.
5. A word is defined by its spelling, not its meaning.
6. Nonsense words or nonsense sentences are unacceptable.
7. All words must be in the English language.
8. Names and places are acceptable.
9. Slang is not acceptable.

Measuring Performance

The output of your WIS company is measured by the *total number of acceptable words* that are packaged in sentences. The sentences must be legible, listed on no more than two sheets of paper, and handed to the Quality Control Review Board at the completion of each production run.

Delivery

Delivery must be made to the Quality Control Review Board 30 seconds after the end of each production run.

Quality Control

If any word in a sentence does not meet the standards set forth above, *all* the words in the sentence will be rejected. The Quality Control Review Board (composed of one member from each company) is the final arbiter of acceptability. In the event of a tie vote on the Review Board, a coin toss will determine the outcome.

Step 3: 15 Minutes

Design your organization using as many group members as you see fit to produce your "words-in-sentences." There are many potential ways of organizing. Since some are more efficient than others, you may want to consider the following:

1. What is your company's objective?
2. How will you achieve your objective? How should you plan your work, given the time allowed?
3. What division of labor, authority, and responsibility is most appropriate, given your objective, your task, and the technology?
4. Which group members are most qualified to perform certain tasks?

Assign one member of your group to serve on the Quality Review Board. This person may also participate in production runs.

CASE 8

ECONOMY FASHIONS

DISCUSSION QUESTIONS

Economy Fashions

1. If you were Joe Smart, would you have restructured Economy Fashions? If so, how? If not, why?

2. What is the basic issue facing Joe Smart? Rank order secondary issues.

3. How would you characterize Joe Smart's management style and assumptions about people? Phil Samson's?

4. If you were the personnel manager at Economy Fashions what would you have done to alleviate the tension in the organization?

5. Regarding the firing of Jack Jones, what fallacy(ies) do you see in the statement that Mr. Knobel "had nothing to worry about as the personnel department had a number of first-class applicants for the position?"

6. What problems do you foresee in Economy Fashions's interactions with the consultants?

ECONOMY FASHIONS LIMITED

THOMAS KUBICEK AND HAROLD SHAFFER

When Joe Smart, president of Economy Fashions Limited, engaged the consulting firm of Fleischman and Katz Incorporated to review the organizational and management effectiveness of Economy Fashions Limited, he believed that they would assure him that he was perfectly capable of controlling Economy Fashion which he considered as easy as holding a paper tiger. However, after the first meeting between Fleischman and his chief executives, Smart had the uncomfortable feeling that he was holding a real tiger by the tail. Yet, looking back at his career in Economy Fashions, he had no idea how the tiger evolved and more perplexing what he should do about the beast or more precisely the predicament in which he now found himself.

Economy Fashions Limited were manufacturers of inexpensive men's ready-to-wear and made-to-measure suits, sports wear and young men's clothing with a 1976 sales volume of approximately eight million dollars. The company was founded by Joe's father, Harry, who had come to Canada from England in 1910 and opened an exclusive tailoring shop in Montreal. Harry soon developed a growing clientele as he had been trained by one of London's master tailors and his pleasing personality and English gentlemen's gentleman manner were easy to take by his customers. Soon he enlarged his premises and engaged one, then two, then three assistants.

Because Harry felt that he was working in a limited market he began to make made-to-measure suits for the more exclusive retailers in Montreal. These merchants were so pleased with Harry's tailoring expertise that they asked him to experiment with ready-made suits. Because of his training, he had to sell these suits at higher prices than most manufacturers, but as they contained excellent workmanship and styling, they were eagerly bought by his Montreal accounts. This encouraged him to give up his tailoring shop and go into the manufacturing of made-to-measure and ready-made suits for exclusive retail stores both inside and outside of Montreal.

However, in a few years he realized that the better suit market was limited and he looked for broader areas in which he could expand. He soon realized that mass merchandising was the answer and so he completely altered his production to turn out made-to-measure and ready-to-wear suits that could be sold in the bargain basements of Canada's largest department stores and in low-end men's wear chains. Again he was successful for no matter how inexpensive he made his suits, they still contained a touch of his early training and so they appeared to have more value and style than those of his competitors. In fact, he expanded so rapidly that he was forced to separate his production and rented space for his made-to-measure factory in another building.

In 1934 he saw the coming market for sports wear and decided to manufacture separate trousers, sports jackets and ski wear at a third factory. Again because he gave these garments the unique touch of the master tailor, he was successful even though they were sold to Canadians in the lower income brackets.

Harry's only son, Joe, has always liked the clothing business and even as a young lad he spent all his spare time doing odd jobs around the factories. In this way he learned how to lay out cloth, pack suits, work the pressing machines, etc., and, during his senior high school year, he began to wait on the trade. When he went to college he studied commerce and spent his vacations on the road with the salesmen. In each city that he visited, he talked to as many retailers as he could and from these interviews suggested to his dad a number of ways he thought his father could make Economy Fashion lines more attractive to retailers. Harry listened to his son with a smile but accepted very few of Joe's proposals. However, this never discouraged Joe as he decided that when he was president, he would inaugurate the ideas which he thought would improve Economy Fashions.

When Joe received his B. Comm. he decided that rather than continue college for his master's degree, he would enrol in a designing school in New York and then work for a few years in various men's clothing factories in the States. Then he planned to settle down and make his career in Economy Fashions. Harry was pleased with Joe's interest in Economy Fashions and proud of his academic and business accomplishments, and, after Joe's experiences in New York, Harry offered him a sales territory. Joe accepted and spent the next five years on the road and then moved into his dad's office as vice-president in charge of production and marketing. By this time Harry had begun to think of retiring and so made arrangements for Joe to buy him out. Shortly after the purchase arrangement had been concluded, Harry suffered a heart attack. When he recovered he turned the presidency of Economy Fashions over to Joe and retired to Florida.

It was soon apparent that Joe had inherited his father's tailoring genius and that his academic and practical experiences would make him a much more successful manufacturer than his dad, for the business prospered at a phenomenal rate. As Joe was an avid reader of trade and business papers, he became aware of the potential benefits of developing a specialized factory for young men's clothes and sports wear. After much thought he decided to organize a separate division for this segment of the Canadian population. This entailed renting a fourth factory site but it proved as successful a venture as his made-to-measure, and ready-to-wear and sports wear divisions.

However as Joe passed his middle forties he began to find it increasingly difficult to complete a day's work. He was fairly energetic in the morning but immediately after lunch his strength would ebb and he quickly reached a point

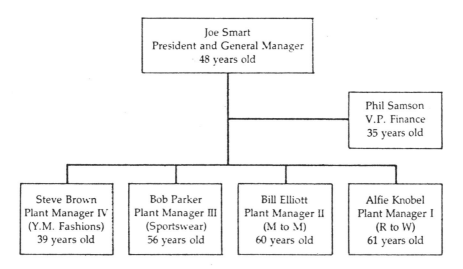

Exhibit 1   Economy Fashions Limited

where he ceased to function as he knew he must if he were to continue to run a successful business. He began to suffer from headaches, indigestion, and insomnia and finally became sufficiently worried about his health to consult his physician. The doctor assured him that his health was good but that he was suffering from too much business pressure. "Try taking things easy," the doctor said, "Go away on a leisurely holiday and when you are rested think about ways to organize your work so that you can take care of the business but still have time to relax and enjoy life."

Joe took the doctor's advice and for the first time in his life went to a small resort village where he knew no-one, and where life was conducted in a leisurely manner. At first Joe had trouble adjusting to the slow pace of the villagers, but eventually he began to accept their leisurely pace and this permitted him to think about Economy Fashions objectively.

To help him examine how the company was operating, he drew up an organizational chart (Exhibit 1). Although this chart gave the impression that Economy Fashions was highly decentralized, Joe knew that he and only he made decisions at all levels. Thus these could be as minor as purchasing another desk for the office or as important as finding the money to finance his operations, finalize style designs, or make changes in manufacturing techniques. He now realized that if he were to take the doctor's advice he would have to make the chart come true by really delegating authority to his executives and then letting them run the company. "I'll be the coach and my executives will be the team," Joe thought. "And in this way we will all work together for the betterment of Economy Fashions."

When he examined the chart more closely, he noticed that he had only one executive at the head office. This was Phil Samson, a smart young C. A. he had hired away from a competitor two years ago because he had heard that Samson was a good systems man and, at the time, Joe felt that systems organization was what he needed most. But although he gave Phil a good salary and the grandiose title of vice president-finance, Joe soon reduced Phil's real function to that of office manager. Before Joe left on his enforced vacation, he had heard rumors that Phil was very unhappy and was looking around for another position.

Joe decided that when he got back, he would elevate Phil to controller as well as vice president-finance and let him look after that end of the business. Moreover, he would hire another bright young man and make him assistant general manager and let him take care of such detailed work as minor analyses, interpretation of data, and so on. This would allow Joe to relax more frequently and still enable him to visit his factories and a certain number of his retail accounts. This was something he had wanted to do for a long time but had never managed because he was either too busy or too tired.

He recalled interviewing a Pierre Laurie who had an M.B.A. from Harvard and some experience in the needle trade. Laurie had claimed that he wanted a bigger challenge than his present position could give him. Joe decided he would hire Laurie when he got back and was pleased with this arrangement because he knew that Samson was about 35 and he thought Laurie was close to 30. Thus he would be a coach to a smart, educated young head-office team which was something he could boast about when he socialized with his competitors.

THE "COACH AND TEAM SYNDROME" CONCEPT

When he looked at the organization chart (the plant manager level), Joe Smart was not happy. All the managers except Steve Brown, who was in his late thirties and whom he hired when he went into young men's fashions were close to or in their sixties and had spent over twenty years with the company. Joe realized that the three older men had always been told what to do by his father and that he had continued with this practice when he took over. Could the four plant managers adjust to a real decentralized structure? Well he had no alternative. For his own good and that of the company he had to break down its functions into natural segments and permit the top executive of each one to run his own show. Joe and his head-office staff would act as advisors—like a head coach and his two assistants.

When Joe returned to his office, he hired young Laurie and within the week called Laurie and Samson into his office for a consultation. This consisted of an outline of his ideas for decentralization which he called his "coach-and-team syndrome" and said he wanted to put it into effect immediately. He was surprised when both young men cautioned a go-slow implementation policy and suggested that he should first test his ideas. Here he was the oldest in the group and he was pushing the youngsters instead of vice versa. Joe felt proud of

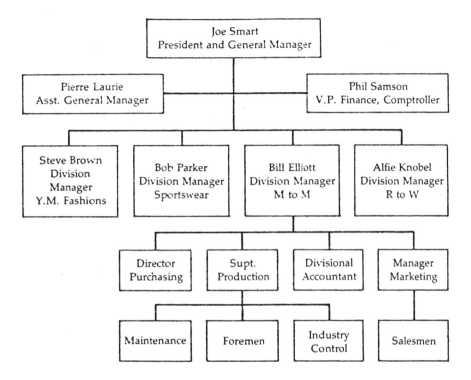

Exhibit 2   Economy Fashions Limited

Note: All divisions have the same internal organizations structures as M to M.

his new-found youth and vigor and dismissed his staff suggestions with "As far as I know, all progress in history is a result of trial and error."

Two weeks after this meeting and without further consultation with his head-office staff or the plant managers, Joe issued a memorandum that introduced his new organizational philosophy. Each plant was to be restructured as a separate division of Economy Fashions and the present managers of each plant would be elevated to the position of product divisional manager. The memo suggested that all executives below divisional manager refer to the revised organizational chart to check on their status (Exhibit 2).

This part of the memorandum concluded with

. . . we are satisfied that an organization on these lines will make the most effective use of the company resources. Furthermore, it will increase our potential to arrive at the best technical solutions aimed at the most valuable markets without incurring the duplication of expense by separate companies.

The memorandum then went on to explain that the divisional managers were to become responsible for all of their factory operations and that these would be judged on the "return-on-capital-employed concept" that had been suggested to Joe by Phil Samson shortly after Samson began to work for Economy Fashions. According to Mr. Samson's formula the following items were to be included in arriving at the amount of capital employed:

1. Fixed plant less depreciation

2. Total divisional volume of sales less the profit margin. (This included a portion of the head office overhead and current depreciation.)

3. Divisional inventories (raw materials, supplies and finished product.)

Each division would become responsible for formulating its own budget which would then become part of the over-all master plan. Divisional budgets were to be prepared by each divisional accountant, who was also responsible for the production of financial and cost statement which were to show two sets of figures: the current month, and the total-to-date. As these reports were considered an essential tool of planning and control, all projections of sales were to cover a period of 15 months. At the end of each quarter, the current budget was to be adjusted to the actual figure and then a new three-months' projection was to be added. The memorandum produced a sample of how the revolving type of budget would look.

	Actual	Budgeted	Tentative
At the beginning of the year	Oct.-Nov.-Dec.	Jan.-Feb.-Mar.	April thru Dec.
End of first quarter	Jan.-Feb.-Mar.	Apr.-May-June	July thru March
End of second quarter	Apr.-May-June	July-Aug.-Sept.	Oct. thru Jan.

As far as expenses were concerned, divisional managers were allowed to spend a thousand dollars without authorization. However, this did not include personal expenses which were to be approved by the corporate controller, nor did it encompass capital expenditures which were considered to be those items whose original costs were a hundred dollars or more and whose life extended over a one-year period. This included office furniture, equipment plant machinery etc.

Joe's memo produced considerable dismay among the newly designated divisional managers and their executives, and a foreboding awareness of the difficulties to come on the part of Laurie and Samson. It did not take long for inter-office memos to move from the divisions to the head office and back again. For example, Steve Brown writes Phil Samson:

Dear Mr. Samson:

It seems clear to me that for the purposes of which we are speaking the investment should be the assets employed by the Division minus the liabilities. To exclude the outstanding payables is in my opinion to deny that this form of financing is of importance to the operation. A rescheduling of our invoice paying only a short time ago served to free a very large sum of money for other purposes and we feel that this phase of the business should not be over-looked. Also it strikes me that monthly comparisons at the head office level would not be worthwhile. This of course is entirely your own affair. But I would suggest that a quarterly review of the divisional performance may be more meaningful.

Steve Brown

Dear Mr. Brown:

Your memo re: the use of the investment base minus the liabilities might have merit when considering the company as a whole. However, for divisional purposes I like to think that all assets used, rather then equity, constitutes the base upon which return is calculated. The rate of return should be determined from the stand point of the user rather than the supplier of capital.

Furthermore, I would like to comment on your discussion with Mr. Joe Smart re: the head office overhead. I would not be disturbed with some bookkeeping inequalities of this nature. I do not think that intention is to equate the different divisions. Since we cannot make the marketing conditions as fairly comparable as possible, I fail to see your concern about such differences of bookkeeping nature. For ultimately each division's performance will be compared against its own target, i.e.: the budget. The success or failure in meeting the target will then be equated and evaluated.

Phil Samson

The divisional managers continued to attack Samson's return-on-capital-employed concept. Mr. Alfie Knobel, manager Ready-To-Wear Division, pointed out that the return-on-capital-employed concept should be replaced by the "return-on-net-worth concept." Mr. Samson rejected this suggestion as impractical and continued to insist that divisional operating reports based on his concept be in his office not later than the seventh day of the following month. He would then review the results of each division with the president and if they indicated a serious departure from the budget, the divisional manager would be called in to explain the cause of the variances.

However, since the divisional managers continued to disagree with Mr. Samson on the return-on-capital-employed concept, divisional reports were often delayed. Jack Jones, the plant accountant in Mr. Knobel's division, strongly objected to Samson's concept and with the connivance of his divisional manager persisted in including certain adjustments in his monthly report which the controller was not ready to accept. This resulted in the correction and revision of several other reports and, thus, all the budgets were delayed. Phil Samson became very annoyed at Jack Jones and complained to the president that Jones was not qualified to do the job. Joe was inclined to believe Phil as for some time now he had had little use for divisional managers and other executives who in his opinion did not use modern management techniques and therefore did not know where they were going. Thus when Joe was on one of his usual plant visits to the ready-to-wear division, he asked Mr. Jones why he came to work at 10:00 a.m. instead of 9:00 a.m. The accountant replied that "My wife was visiting her relatives and unfortunately took the alarm clock with her. Being alone I slept in."

Later on when Mr. Smart asked for the amount of the net divisional contribution for the current month, Jones was somewhat indecisive. Angered by the accountant's apparent incompetency, Mr. Smart suggested that there was not much future for Jones in the company and that he might perhaps be better off if he looked for another position. When Mr. Knobel returned from out-of-town the following day and read Mr. Smart's memo regarding the dismissal of Mr. Jones he became very annoyed and immediately contacted the president. Smart assured Mr. Knobel that he had nothing to worry about as the Personnel

Department had a number of first-class applicants for the position of accountant for the Ready-To-Wear Division and that any of these would do a better job than Jones.

As noted by the above, Mr. Smart was extremely active and now he considered that he was not only head coach but the boss as well. He felt that he had to make every effort to visit each division and give the executives in charge all the help and consultation that his time permitted. Every morning, Joe toured one plant or another and talked to various supervisors and department heads, always stressing the point that he was just one of them; that in his company nobody should be afraid to talk to the boss because "here there was no boss, just one team with the same goal." Whether it was production, quality control, or choosing the right shades of fabrics, Joe was always ready to advise; for as he constantly reminded his team "he had had considerable experience in these lines." His afternoons were spent at the head office except when he would remember the doctor's advice and force himself to stay away from the office and pretend to relax.

Although the reports for the first quarter of 1976 indicated that it would be a good year for all lines of Economy Fashions Limited, both in terms of sales and profits, Mr. Smart felt a vague persistent uneasiness about the company's operations. In particular, he could not understand why Steve Brown had resigned as plant manager of the Young Men's Division and taken a less responsible position with a smaller salary with a competing company. Brown's resignation not only reinforced Joe's feeling that his managers seemed antagonistic to the various proposals that he made but it triggered a decision to engage a firm of management consultants to assess the effectiveness of Economy Fashions' organizational structure. The following is a transcript of the first of several meetings held by Mr. Arthur Fleischman of Fleischman and Katz, Inc. and the Economy Fashions management group that met to review the organizational and management effectiveness of Economy Fashions Limited.

Highlights of the Transcript of a Meeting of the Executive Committee of Economy Fashions Limited held in the Board Room of the company
On July 31st, 1976

PRESENT: Messrs. Smart, Parker, Elliott, Knobel, Samson and Fleischman

SMART: Gentlemen, thanks to your concerted effort we are in the happy position of being a company which, I feel, and the records indicate, is going places. But going places presents problems and I have asked you to attend this meeting so that we can have a frank and open discussion of these problems. I am sure that by now you have all met Mr. Fleischman whom I have retained to study our organization and to advise us on any possible improvements. At this point, I would like to ask Mr. Fleischman to take the Chair and come right to the point, Mr. Fleischman.

FLEISCHMAN: Gentlemen, this is the first of a series of meetings which I would like to utilize for a two-fold purpose: First, I would like to review our investigations of your operations in order to make sure we have a clear picture of how you are managing your company, and the problems you are facing. Second, I would like to start considering some of these issues in terms of their implications for your business. I would like to open this discussion with a question which I feel is indicative of the kind of problems you now face. Why did Steve Brown leave?

PARKER: If I may?

FLEISCHMAN: By all means.

PARKER: Steve and I had a good relationship, and we still meet occasionally. I posed some questions to him and he told me that he quit because of two things. Firstly, he saw no prospects for advancement shortly after Mr. Laurie joined the company, and secondly because he was fed up with heavy responsibilities but no freedom to manage.

SMART: How could he say that? With increasing sales, all our managerial jobs have been getting bigger and bigger, with salaries none of our competitors can match. Furthermore, ever since we decentralized, Steve commanded far more authority and responsibility than he had ever done before. For all practical purposes he was running his own business. If this isn't freedom to manage, I do not know what is. I cannot see what Laurie had to do with Steve.

PARKER: Assistant General Manager is a higher position than that of Division Manager. Steve is extremely ambitious, and with his experience and degree in Business he felt he was well qualified for the Assistant General Manager position. No doubt he saw it as a stepping stone to the position of General Manager.

SMART: General Manager? But Laurie was not hired with that end in mind— and I never even thought of him as part of my executive committee. His main job was to help me with paper work analysis, interpretation of data, and so on. I am sure Steve would not have liked that kind of work or not being on my executive team.

FLEISCHMAN: This seems to me to be a typical case of lack of communication. Normally, the title of Assistant General Manager conveys line relationship. If Mr. Laurie's position is that of a staff employee, don't you think it should be so designated?

KNOBEL: I would like to come back to Bob's remark (points to Parker) regarding the assumption of "heavy responsibilities but no freedom to manage." I believe that the financial set-up we have here is nothing but vaguely defined cost centers, in a centralized company. Yet, our performance, even our competence, is measured with data over which we have little or no control. On one hand, Joe insists on autonomous divisions; on the other he comes to my plant and fires my employees, in my absence, without my knowledge or approval. Would you call this freedom to manage?

SAMSON: If you are referring to Jack Jones, then I would answer. It was I who insisted to Joe, that Jones should be fired. You know very well, Alfie, that he was not qualified to do that particular job. I am sure Joe saved you the embarrassment of having to fire him yourself.

KNOBEL: Phil, was Jones working for you, or was he working for me? If he was working for me, then I was responsible for both his reports and their content. He reported what I told him to report, so any confusion in his reports could be a reflection on the deficiency of your system.

SMART: Don't tell me that you are still sulking over the Jones' case. We have discussed it too often, I don't want to hear about it again.

KNOBEL: Well you asked for a frank discussion. I have mentioned only one of the many causes why people are beginning to be dissatisfied around here. There are others. For instance, I do not believe that my performance can be measured by costs over which I have no control, such as apportioning the head office costs to divisions on the basis of divisional contribution to total sales. Neither do I believe in the formula of performance appraisal through return on capital employed.

ELLIOTT: I'd say Alfie is right. I find that some of my best men are becoming dissatisfied in spite of my trying hard to prevent it. You must realize that as the company gets bigger, its becoming more unwieldy and I believe that unless we stop and consolidate what we are now operating, Economy Fashions may get out of control before we realize it.

SMART: Well, this is exactly why we're here and what I am trying to do. To keep everything under control. With my experience I can assist with various operating problems. At the same time, my mixing with the people promotes an informal atmosphere. I do not want to stifle their initiative by governing them with an iron hand.

ELLIOTT: I don't agree!

SMART: What do you mean?

ELLIOTT: Well, your frequent visits to our plants, whatever the intention, are undermining our authority in the divisions. Instead of discussing operating problems with us, you go directly to our subordinates saying that, in fact, there is no boss in this company. For this reason, if my employees have a problem, they ignore me and wait for your next visit to approach you with it.

SMART: But the trend today is away from the structured organization. The team spirit facilitates a better environment and of course helps to build a better worker morale.

ELLIOTT: Do you feel that it is proper to go around the authority of your divisional managers rather than channeling everything through them? You know, with your attitude you may either encourage talebearing, or the divisional supervisors might acquire the habit of leaning on you as a crutch instead of trying to think for themselves.

SMART: I think that group participation rather than a strict superior versus subordinate relationship is highly stimulating and productive.

FLEISCHMAN: Your intention is a good one Mr. Smart. However, do your regular visits to the plants get the desired results? In my experience I have come across two different practices. One, that the top manager should be concerned solely with strategic functions; the other that both operating and strategic functions are his domain. Both of these seem to be correct. However, their applicability usually varies with the size of the company and the kind of its particular environment.

SAMSON: I have a feeling that we are wasting our time on trivial things, while neglecting bigger issues, such as: better communication, problem of reporting, control, etc.

FLEISCHMAN: I thought you were proud of your budgetary control system?

SAMSON: Well, it is true that we have a better system than a number of our competitors; however, there are still deficiencies in it which need correcting.

FLEISCHMAN: Why do you think your reports are late?

PARKER: I'll answer that! Because the division managers don't believe in them. There is not only a lack of planning but today we are told to do this, and tomorrow to do that. It looks like our only objective is opportunistic exploitation of changing situations regardless of the long-range consequences. Our accountants are overworked because of constant "crash programs" for the head office. I believe that, with a little more planning and organizing all this "extinguishing of business brushfires" could be avoided.

SMART: Our planning must be adaptable to fast movement. You mustn't forget that this is a constantly changing industry. If we miss an opportunity, it will never come back.

SAMSON: And under these circumstances, it takes time to establish smoothly running procedures.

KNOBEL: I agree, but it is not what we do not do here that is worrying us; rather it is what we do and how we are doing it. For instance, there is no doubt that control over expenditures must be maintained. But, I cannot see the practicality of the present limits. Don't you think that all such controls should be built into the divisional budget for which we are responsible, rather than deprive us of the opportunity to buy most of the things we need to operate?

SAMSON: Ours is a pretty common procedure which is followed by the best companies and while theoretically in decentralized operations the budgets should control both the capital and expense expenditures, in practice, some of the best-managed companies are keeping a grip on the purse strings, regardless of the amounts budgeted. Further, our formula of the return on capital employed is a valuable management appraisal tool. Do you know of any better?

FLEISCHMAN: Although this is a good way to check on the over-all company performance, there may be some doubt how equitable it would be for use in divisions like yours. Furthermore, I would call it a method of control rather than an appraisal system.

ELLIOTT: Do I understand you right, Phil, that you are seeking even more control, when I feel that the conflict here results from the fact that the head office controls all purchases, all salaries above common labour, and that most of our designs emanate from the head office? In fact, everything except production seems to be controlled by the head office.

SMART: I never made a secret about it. Our company is centralized for control purposes and decentralized for operating purposes. Under our system many items are budgeted, but must be re-approved by top management at the time actual expenditures are to be made. This procedure could be credited for our excellent cash position.

FLEISCHMAN: Well gentlemen we've made a good start. We have aired several issues. We are all aware of the fact that a lack of tight control over expenditures could run you out of house and home. However, there are other issues equally important we have not touched on yet. For example, how is your organizational structure to be built? Is it at present a typical staff and line organization or is it a functional one? Further, should the functions and the locus of accountability of the plant accountant, the purchasing agent, and the designer be more clearly defined than at present? Maybe we should even determine whether there is any need for job descriptions, or manpower planning, including the retirement age for executives and other personnel. All these areas are serious considerations in a company like yours. I would therefore like you to think about these and other problems which must be solved if we want to formulate a more viable organizational structure for Economy Fashions than it has at present.

Thank you, gentlemen, for coming, and this meeting is now adjourned.

CASE 9

HIGGINS DATA CORPORATION

DISCUSSION QUESTIONS

Higgins Data Corporation

1. Summarize your diagnosis of the major problem or problems in this organization.

2. What do you see as the major impediments to achieving integration and coordination among the various departments in the organization?

3. Why is Engineering Services not playing this integrating and coordinating role at the moment?

4. What do you believe should be done to alleviate the current organizational problems?

HIGGINS DATA CORPORATION

"God damn it, he's done it again!"

Steve Spencer threw the stack of prints and specifications down on his desk is disgust. The model 802 wide-band modulator, released to production the previous Thursday, had just come back to Steve's engineering services department, with a caustic note which began, "This one can't be produced, either..." It was the fourth time production had kicked the design back.

Stephen Spencer, director of engineering for Higgins Data Corp., was known as a peace-loving man. But the Model 802 was stretching his patience; it was beginning to look just like other new products which had hit delays and problems in the transition from design to production during the eight months Steve had worked for Higgins. These problems were nothing new at the Higgins factory; Steve's predecessor in the engineering job had run afoul of them too, and had finally been fired for protesting too vehemently about the other departments. But the Model 802 should have been different. Steve had met two months before (July 3, 1972) with the firm's president, John Howard, and with Factory Superintendent Gerry Browne, to smooth the way for the new mdoulator design. He thought back to the meeting...

"Now, we all know there's a tight deadline on the 802," John Howard said, "and Steve's done well to ask us to talk about its introduction. I'm counting on both of you to find any snags in the system, and to work together to get that first production run out by October 2. Can you do it?"

"We can do it in production if we get a clean design by July 17, as scheduled," answered Gerry Browne, grizzled factory superintendent. *"Steve and I have already talked about that, of course. I'm setting aside time in the card room and the machine shop, and we'll be ready. If the design goes over schedule, though, I'll have to fill in with other runs, and it will cost us a bundle to break in for the 802. How does it look in engineering, Steve?"*

"I've just frozen the design for the second time," Steve replied. "If Ralph Johnson can keep the salesmen out of our hair, and avoid any more last minute changes, we've got a shot. I've pulled the

---

draftsmen off of three other overdue jobs to get this one out. But Gerry, that means we can't spring engineers loose to confer with your production people on manufacturing problems."

"Well, Steve, most of those problems are caused by the engineers, and we need them to resolve the difficulties. We've all agreed that production bugs come from both of us bowing to sales pressure, and putting equipment into production before the designs are really ready. That's just what we're trying to avoid on the 802. But I can't have 500 people sitting on their hands waiting for an answer from your people. We'll have to have some engineering support."

John Howard broke in, *"So long as you two can talk calmly about the problem, I'm confident you can resolve it. What a relief it is, Steve, to hear the way you're approaching this. With Haverstick (the* previous director of engineering) *this conversation would have been a shouting match. Right, Gerry?"* Gerry nodded and smiled.

"Now there's one other thing you should both be aware of," Howard continued. *"Doc Sloane (Higgins' director of research) and I were talking last night about a new filtering technique, one that might improve the signal-to-noise ratio of the 802 by a factor of two. There's a chance Doc can come up with it before the 802 reaches production, and if it's possible, I'd like to use the new filters. This would give us a real jump on the competition."*

Four days after that meeting, Steve had found that two of his key people on the 802 design had been called to production for emergency consultation on a bug found in final assembly: two halves of a new data transmission interface wouldn't fit together, because recent changes in the front end required a different chassis design for the back end.

Another week later, Doc Sloane had walked into Steve's office, proud as a new parent, with the new filter design. "This won't affect the other modules of the 802 much," Doc had said. "Look, it takes three new cards, a few connectors, some changes in the wiring harness, and some new shielding, and that's all. I showed it to John last night; he's delighted with the improvement."

Steve had tried to resist the last-minute design changes, but John Howard had stood firm. With a lot of overtime by the engineers and draftsmen, engineering services would still be able to finish the prints in time.

Two engineers and three draftsmen went onto twelve-hour days to get the 802 ready, but the prints were still two weeks late reaching Gerry Browne. Two days later, the prints came back to Steve, heavily annotated in red. Browne had worked all day Saturday to review the job, and had found some two dozen discrepancies in the prints--most of them caused by the new filter design and insufficient checking time before the release. Browne's cover note to Steve Spencer indicated that the August production capacity previously reserved for the 802 had been allocated to other rush jobs.

Correction of the design faults flagged by Browne had brought on a new generation of discrepancies. On the third iteration of the prints and specs, Browne expressed concern about September's production schedule. Now, with his fourth refusal to accept the design, the factory superintendent reported he had re-allocated his machining capacity for the month, and would have to commit his photo and plating schedules within three days. By September 11, it was clear the Model 802 would be at least one month late, and more likely two. Ralph Johnson, Vice President for Sales, was furious. His customer needed 100 units NOW, he said as October began, and the damn things weren't even started in the factory yet. Higgins was the customer's only late supplier.

"Here we go again," thought Steve Spencer.

Company History

Higgins Data Corp. traced its lineage through several generations of electronics technology. Its original founder, Jack Higgins, had set the firm up in 1920 as "Higgins Equipment Co.," to manufacture several electrical testing devices he had invented as an engineering faculty member at a large university. The firm branched into radio broadcasting equipment in 1947, and into data transmission equipment in the early 1960s. A well-established corps of direct sales people, mostly engineers, called on industrial, scientific and government accounts, but concentrated heavily on original equipment manufacturers. In this market, Higgins had a long-standing reputation as a source of high-quality, innovative designs. The firm's salespeople fed a continual stream of challenging problems into the engineering department, where the creative genius of Roger "Doc" Sloane and several dozen other engineers "converted problems to solutions" (as the sales brochure bragged). Product design formed the spearhead of Higgins' growth.

By 1972, Higgins offered a wide range of products in its two major lines. Broadcast equipment sales had benefitted from the growth of FM radio and UHF television stations in the 1960s, but had faded in importance since; it now accounted for 35 percent of company sales. Data transmission had blossomed, and in this field an increasing number of orders called for unique specifications, ranging from specialized display panels to entirely untried designs.

The company had grown from 100 employees in 1947, to over 800 in 1972. (Exhibits 1 and 2 show the current organization chart and the backgrounds of key employees.) John Howard, who had been a student of the company's founder, had presided over most of that growth, and took great pride in preserving the "family spirit" of the old organization. Informal relationships between Higgins' veteran employees formed the backbone of the firm's day-to-day operations; all the managers relied on personal contact, and Howard often insisted that the absence of bureaucratic red tape was a key factor in recruiting outstanding engineering talent. The personal management approach extended throughout the factory. All exempt employees were paid on a straight salary plus a share of the profits. Higgins boasted an extremely loyal group of senior employees, and very low turnover in nearly all areas of the company.

The highest turnover job in the firm was Steve Spencer's. Steve had joined Higgins in January of 1972, replacing Max Haverstick, who had been director of engineering only ten months. Haverstick, in turn, had replaced Herb Jackson, an experienced Higgins engineer who had made a promising start after his promotion, but had taken to drink after a year in the job. Doc Sloan had refused the directorship in each of the recent changes, saying, "Hell, that's no job for a bench man like me. I'm no administrator."

Well before the promotion of Herb Jackson to head engineering, the firm had experienced a steadily increasing number of disputes between research, engineering, sales and production people--disputes generally centered on the problem of new product introduction. Quarrels between departments became more numerous under Jackson, Haverstick, and Steve Spencer. Some managers associated these disputes with the company's recent decline in profitability-- a decline which, in spite of higher sales and other backlogs, was beginning to bother people in 1971. President John Howard commented:

> Better cooperation, I'm sure, could increase our output by five to ten percent. I'd hoped Haverstick could solve the problems, but pretty obviously he was too young--too arrogant. People like Haver- stick--that conflict type of personality--bother me. I don't like strife, and with him it seemed I spent all my time smoothing out arguments. Haverstick tried to tell everyone else how to run their departments, without having his own house in order. That approach just wouldn't sell, here at Higgins. Steve Spencer, now, seems much more in tune with our style of organization. I'm really hopeful now.

> Still, we have just as many problems now as we did last year. Maybe even more. I hope Steve can get a handle on engineering services soon...

The Engineering Department: Research

According to the organization chart (see Exhibit 1), Steve Spencer was in charge of both research (really the product development function) and engineering services (which provided engineering support). To Spencer, however, the relationship with research was not so clear-cut. He commented:

> In some senses, I'm in charge of R&D and in others I'm not. In a nebulous way, Doc Sloane works through me and I through him. He's a creative genius, but he's not the least bit interested in manage- ment routines, and I can't count on him to take any responsibility in scheduling projects, or checking budgets, or what-have-you. Doc has more ideas per hour than most people have per year, and he keeps the whole engineering staff fired up. Everybody loves him-- and I have a great deal of affection and respect for him myself. In a way, he works for me, sure. But that's not what's important.

"Doc" Sloane--unhurried, contemplative, casual, and candid--tipped his stool back against the wall of his research cubicle and talked about what _was_ important:

Development engineering. That's where the company's future rests. Either we have it there, or we don't have it.

There's no kidding ourselves that we're anything but a bunch of Rube Goldbergs here. But that's where the biggest kicks come from-- from solving development problems, and dreaming up new ways of doing things. That's why I so look forward to the special contracts we get involved in. We accept them not for the revenue they represent, but because they subsidize the basic development work which goes into all our standard products.

I have a great crew here, and they can really deliver when the chips are down. Why, John Howard and I (he gestured toward the neighboring cubicle, where the president's name hung over the door) are likely to find as many people here at work at ten p.m. as at three in the afternoon. The important thing here is the relationships between people; they're based on mutual respect, not on policies and procedures. Administrative red tape is a pain. It takes away from development time.

Problems? Sure, there are problems now and then. There are power interests in production, where they sometimes resist change. But I'm not a fighting man, you know. I suppose if I were, I might go in there and push my weight around a little. But I'm an engineer, and can do more for Higgins sitting right here, or working with my own people. That's what brings results.

Other members of the research department echoed Doc's views, and added some additional sources of satisfactions with their work. They were proud of the personal contacts they built up with customers' technical staffs--contacts which increasingly involved travel to the customers' factories to serve as expert advisors in preparation of overall system design specifications. The engineers were also delighted with the department's encouragement of their personal development, continuing education, and independence on the job.

But there were problems, too. Dan Duffy, of the mechanical design section, noted:

In the old days I really enjoyed the work--and the people I worked with. But now there's a lot of irritation. I don't like someone breathing down my neck. You can be hurried into jeopardizing the design.

Russ Steinbeck, head of the radio electronic design section, was another designer with definite views, especially about ESD:

Production engineering is almost nonexistent in this company. Very little is done by the preproduction section in engineering services. Steve Spencer has been trying to get preproduction into the picture, but he won't succeed because you can't start from such an ambiguous position. There have been three directors of engineering in four years. Steve can't hold his own against the others in the company. Haverstick was too aggressive. Perhaps no amount of tact would have succeeded.

Jerry Stewart was head of special components in the R&D department. Like the rest of the department he valued bench work. But he complained of engineering services.

The services don't do things we want them to do. Instead, they tell us what they're going to do. I should probably go to Steve, but I don't get any decisions there. I know I should go through Steve, but this holds things up, so I often go direct.

The Engineering Department: Services

The engineering services department provided ancillary services to R&D, and served as liaison between engineering and the other Higgins departments. Among its main functions were drafting; management of the central technicians pool; scheduling and expediting engineering products; documentation and publication of parts lists and engineering orders; preproduction engineering (consisting of the final integration of individual design components into mechanically compatible packages); and quality control (which included inspection of incoming parts and materials, and final inspection of subassemblies and finished equipment). Top management's description of the department included the line, "ESD is responsible for maintaining cooperation with other departments, providing services to the development engineers, and freeing more valuable men in R&D from essential activities which are diversions from and beneath their main competence."

Many of Steve Spencer's 75 employees were located in other departments. Quality control people were scattered through the manufacturing and receiving areas, and technicians worked primarily in the research area or the prototype fabrication room. The remaining ESD personnel were assigned to leftover nooks and crannies near production or engineering sections.

Steve Spencer described his position:

My role in the company has never been well defined, really. It's complicated by Doc's unique position, of course, and also by the fact that ESD sort of grew by itself over the years, as the design engineers concentrated more and more on the creative parts of product development. I wish I could be more involved in the technical side. That's been my training, and it's a lot of fun. But in our setup, the technical side is the least necessary for me to be involved in.

My biggest problem is getting acceptance from the people I work with. I've moved slowly rather than risk antagonism. I saw what happened to Haverstick, and I want to avoid that. But although his precipitate action had won over a few of the younger R&D men, he certainly didn't have the department's backing. Of course, it was the resentment of other departments which eventually caused his discharge. People have been slow accepting me here. There's nothing really overt, but I get a negative reaction to my ideas.

Browne (production head) is hard to get along with. Before I came and after Haverstick left, there were six months intervening when no one was really doing any scheduling. No work loads were figured, and unrealistic promises were made about releases. This puts us in an awkward position. We've been scheduling way beyond our capacity to manufacture or engineer.

Certain people within R&D, for instance Russ Steinbeck, head of the radio electronic design section, understand scheduling well and meet project deadlines, but this is not generally true of the rest of the R&D department, especially the mechanical engineers who won't commit themselves. Most of the complaints come from sales and production department heads because items are going to production before they are fully developed, under pressure from sales to get out the unit, and this snags the whole process. Somehow, engineering services should be able to intervene and resolve these complaints, but I haven't made much headway so far.

I should be able to go to Howard for help, but he's too busy most of the time, and his major interest is the design side of engineering, where he got his own start. Sometimes he talks as though he's the engineering director as well as president. I have to put my foot down; there are problems here that the front office just doesn't understand.

Sales people were often observed taking their problems directly to designers, while production frequently threw designs back at R&D, claiming they could not be produced and demanding the prompt attention of particular design engineers. The latter were frequently observed in conference with production supervisors on the assembly floor. Steve went on:

The designers seem to feel they're losing something when one of us tries to help. They feel it's a reflection on them to have someone take over what they've been doing. They seem to want to carry a project right through to the final stages, particularly the mechanical boys. Consequently, engineering services people are used below their capacity to contribute and our department is denied functions it should be performing. There's not as much use made of engineering services as there should be.

Steve Spencer's technician foreman added his comments:

Production picks out the engineer who'll be the "bum of the month." They pick on every little detail instead of using their heads and making the minor changes that have to be made. The fifteen-to-twenty-year men shouldn't have to prove their ability any more, but they spend four hours defending themselves and four hours getting the job done. I have no one to go to when I need help. Steve Spencer is afraid. I'm trying to help him but he can't help me at this time. I'm responsible for fifty people and I've got to support them.

Jeff Hare, whom Steve had brought with him to the company as an assistant, gave another view of the situation:

I try to get our people in preproduction to take responsibility but they're not used to it and people in other departments don't usually see them as best qualified to solve the problem. There's a real barrier for a newcomer here. Gaining people's confidence is hard. More and more, I'm wondering whether there really is a job for me here. (Shortly after this interview, Jeff Hare left Higgins.)

Another of Spencer's subordinates gave his view:

If Doc gets a new product idea you can't argue. But he's too optimistic. He judges that others can do what he does--but there's only one Doc Sloane. We've had 900 production change orders this year--they changed 2,500 drawings. If I were in Steve's shoes I'd put my foot down on all this new development. I'd look at the re-working we're doing and get production set up the way I wanted it. Haverstick was fired when he was doing a good job. He was getting some system in the company's operations. Of course, it hurt some people. But, there is no denying that Doc is the most important person in the company. What gets overlooked is that Howard is a close second, not just politically but in terms of what he contributes technically and in customer relations.

This subordinate explained that he sometimes went out into the production department but that Browne, the production head, resented this. Men in production said that Haverstick had failed to show respect for old-timers and was always meddling in other departments' business. This was why he had been fired, they contended.

Olly Strauss, manager of quality control, commented:

I am now much more concerned with administration and less with work. It is one of the evils you get into. There is tremendous detail in this job. I listen to everyone's opinion. Everybody is important. There shouldn't be distinctions--distinctions between people. I'm not sure whether Steve has to be a fireball like Haverstick. I think the real question is whether Spencer is getting the job done. I know my job is essential. I want to supply service to the more talented men and give them information so they can do their jobs better.

The Sales Department

Ralph Johnson was angry. His job was supposed to be selling, he said, but instead it had turned into settling disputes inside the plant and making excuses to waiting customers.

"You see that telephone?" He jabbed a finger toward his desk. *"I'm actually afraid nowadays to hear it ring. Three times out of five, it will be a customer who's hurting because we've failed to deliver on schedule. The other two calls will be from production or ESD, telling me some schedule has slipped again.*

"The Model 802 is typical. Absolutely typical. We padded the delivery date by six weeks, to allow for contingencies. Within two months the slack had evaporated. Now it looks like we'll be lucky to ship it before Christmas. [It was now October 15.] *We're ruining our reputation in the market. Why, just last week one of our best customers--people we've worked with for 15 years--tried to hang a penalty clause on their latest order.*

"We shouldn't have to be after the engineers all the time. They should be able to see what problems they create without our telling them."

Max Kleindienst, head of broadcast sales under Johnson, noted that many sales decisions were made by top management. Sales was under-staffed, he thought, and had never really been able to get on top of the job:

We have grown further and further away from engineering. The director of engineering does not pass on the information that we give him. We need better relationships there. It is very difficult for us to talk to customers about development problems without technical help. We need each other. The whole of engineering is now too isolated from the outside world. The morale of ESD is very low. They're in a bad spot--they're not well organized.

People don't take much to outsiders here. Much of this is because the expectation is built up by top management that jobs will be filled from the bottom. So it's really tough when an outsider like Steve comes in.

Dan Fellman, order and pricing coordinator for data equipment, talked about his own relationships with the production department:

Actually, I get along with them fairly well. Oh, things could be better, of course, if they were more cooperative generally. They always seem to say, 'It's my bat and my ball, and we're playing by my rules.' People are afraid to make production mad; there's a lot of power in there.

But you've got to understand that production has its own set of problems. And nobody in Higgins is working any harder than Gerry Browne to try to straighten things out.

The Production Department

Gerald Browne had joined Higgins just after the Korean War, in which he had seen combat duty (at the Yalu River) and intelligence duty in

Pyong Yang. Both experiences had been useful in his first year of civilian employment: the wartime factory superintendent and several middle managers had been, apparently, indulging in highly questionable side deals with Higgins' suppliers. Gerry Browne had gathered evidence, revealed the situation to John Howard, and had stood by the president in the ensuing unsavory situation. Seven months after joining the company, Gerry was named factory superintendent.

His first move had been to replace the fallen managers with a new team from outside. This group did not share the traditional Higgins emphasis on informality and friendly personal relationships, and had worked long and hard to install systematic manufacturing methods and procedures. Before the reorganization, production had controlled purchasing, stock control, and final quality control (where final assembly of products in cabinets was accomplished). Because of the wartime events, management decided on a check-and-balance system of organization and removed these three departments from production jurisdiction. The new production managers felt they had been unjustly penalized by this reorganization, particularly since they had uncovered the behavior which was detrimental to the company in the first place.

By 1972, the production department had grown to 500 employees, of whom 60 percent worked in the assembly area—an unusually pleasant environment which had been commended by Factory magazine for its colorful decoration, cleanliness, and low noise level. An additional 30 percent of the work force, mostly skilled machinists, staffed the finishing and fabrication department. About 60 others performed scheduling, supervisory, and maintenance duties. Production workers were non-union, hourly-paid, and participated in both the liberal profit-sharing program and the stock purchase plan. Morale in production was traditionally high, and turnover was extremely low.

"To be efficient," Gerry Browne said, "production has to be a self-contained department. We have to control what comes into the department and what goes out. That's why purchasing, inventory control, and quality ought to run out of this office. We'd eliminate a lot of problems with better control here. Why, even Olly Strauss, in QC, would rather work for me than for ESD; he's said so himself. We understand his problems better.

"The other departments should be self-contained, too. That's why I always avoid the underlings, and go straight to the department heads with any questions. I always go down the line.

"I have to protect my people from outside disturbances. Look what would happen if I let unfinished, half-baked designs in here—there'd be chaos. The bugs have to be found before the drawings go into the shop, and it seems I'm the one who has to find them. Look at the 802, for example." (It was now October 23, and Gerry had spent most of the previous weekend red-pencilling the latest set of prints.) "ESD should have found every one of those discrepancies. They just don't check drawings properly. They change most of the things I flag, but then they fail to trace through the impact of those changes on the rest of the design. I shouldn't have to do that.

"And those engineers are tolerance crazy. They want everything to a millionth of an inch. I'm the only one in the company who's had any experience with actually machining things to a millionth of an inch. We make sure that the things that engineers say on their drawings actually have to be that way, and whether they're obtainable from the kind of raw material we buy.

"That shouldn't be production's responsibility, but I have to do it. Accepting bad prints wouldn't let us ship the order any quicker. We'd only make a lot of junk that had to be reworked. And that would take even longer.

"This way, I get to be known as the bad guy, but I guess that's just part of the job. The real fun here is in figuring how to make the basic products more efficiently--doing things the engineers thought couldn't be done. I never tell them how we do it; they ought to be as smart as we are." He paused with a wry smile. "Of course, what really gets them is that I don't even have a degree."

Gerry had fewer bones to pick with the sales department, because, he said, they trusted him.

"When we give Ralph Johnson a shipping date, he knows the equipment will be shipped then.

"You've got to recognize, though, that all of our new product problems stem from sales' making absurd commitments on equipment that hasn't been fully developed. That always means trouble. Unfortunately, Howard always backs sales up, even when they're wrong. He always favors them over us."

Tom Rawson, age 65, executive vice president of the company, had direct responsibility for Higgins' production department. He said:

There shouldn't really be a dividing of departments among top management in the company. The president should be czar over all. The production boys ask me to do something for them, and I really can't do it. It creates bad feelings between engineering and production, this special attention that they [R&D] get from Howard. But then Howard likes to dabble in design. Browne feels that production is treated like a poor relation.

The Executive Committee

At the executive committee meeting of November 6, it was duly recorded that Gerry Browne had accepted the prints and specifications for the model 802 modulator, and had set Friday, December 29 as the shipping date for the first 10 pieces. John Howard, in the chair, had shaken his head and changed the subject quickly when Steve tried to open the agenda to a discussion of interdepartmental coordination.

The executive committee itself was a brainchild of Higgins' controller, Dan Waldron, who was well aware of the disputes which swept the company. Waldron had convinced John Howard and Tom Rawson to meet every two weeks with their department heads, and the meetings were formalized with Howard, Rawson, Ralph Johnson, Gerry Browne, Steve Spencer, Doc Sloane, Waldron, and the personnel director attending. Waldron explained his intent and the results:

Doing things collectively and informally just doesn't work as well as it used to. Things have been gradually getting worse for at least two years now. We had to start thinking in terms of formal organizational relationships. I did the first organization chart, and the executive committee was my idea too--but neither idea is contributing much help, I'm afraid. It takes top management to make an organization click. The rest of us can't act much differently until the top people see the need for us to change.

I had hoped the committee, especially, would help get the department managers into a constructive planning process. It hasn't worked out that way, because Mr. Howard really doesn't see the need for it. He uses the meetings as a place to pass on routine information.

Merry Christmas

"Steve, I didn't know whether to tell you now, or after the holiday." It was Friday, December 22, and Steve Spencer was standing awkwardly in front of John Howard's desk.

"But I figured you'd work right through Christmas day if we didn't have this talk, and that just wouldn't have been fair to you. I can't understand why we have such poor luck in the engineering director's job lately. And I don't think it's entirely your fault. But...

Steve only heard half of Howard's words, and said nothing in response...He'd be paid through January 31...He should use the time for searching...Howard would help all he could...Max Haverstick was thought to be doing well at his own new job, and might need more help...

Steve cleaned out his desk, and numbly started home. The electronic carillion near his house was playing a Christmas carol. Steve thought again of Howard's rationale: conflict still plagued Higgins-- and Steve had not made it go away. Maybe somebody else could do it.

"And what did Santa Claus bring you, Stevie," he asked himself.

"The sack. Only the empty sack."

Exhibit 1

HIGGINS DATA CORPORATION

Organization Chart
1972

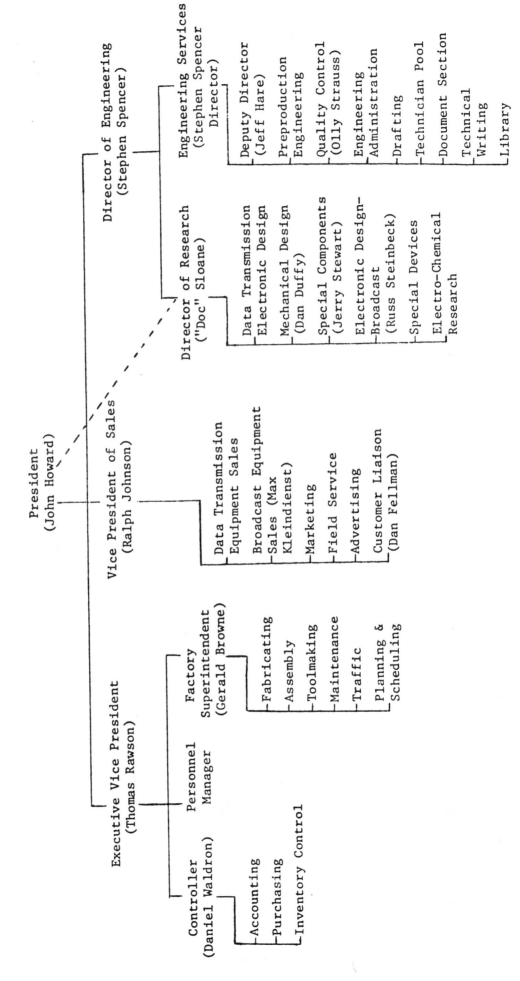

228

Exhibit 2

HIGGINS DATA CORPORATION

Background of Selected Higgins' Executives

John Howard - President, 63 years old: Engineering graduate of an Ivy League university; joined company in 1940 as an engineer. Worked on development exclusively for over a year and then split his time between development and field sales work, introducing the broadest equipment line, until he became Assistant to President in 1950. Became President in 1954. Howard and Tom Rawson, together, held sufficient Higgins stock to command effective control of the company.

Thomas Rawson - Executive Vice President, 65 years old: Joined company in 1939 as a traveling representative to collect debts from customers. In 1945 became company's first salesman and built up testing and instrument sales force. In 1950 was made Treasurer, but continued to spend time selling. In 1954 was appointed Executive Vice President with direct responsibility for financial matters and production.

Ralph Johnson - Vice President-Sales, 50 years old: B.S. in engineering; joined company in 1959 as a salesman, was influential in the establishment of the data transmission line and did early selling himself. In 1961 he was made Sales Manager, and completed recruitment and training of the sales force. Extensive contacts in trade associations and industrial shows. He was appointed Vice President-Sales in 1966.

Gerald Browne - Factory Superintendent, 62 years old: Trade school graduate; joined Higgins in 1957. Promoted to Production Manager seven months later. He was responsible for revision of production methods, and production control techniques, and brought a new cadre of production specialists to the company.

Stephen Spencer - Director of Engineering, 45 years old: Master's degree in engineering, previously division director of engineering for a large industrial firm. Joined company in 1972 as Director of Engineering, replacing man who had been dismissed because of his inability to work with sales and production personnel. As Director of Engineering was responsible for administration of research personnel and had complete responsibility for engineering services.

Roger Sloane - Director of Research, 47 years old: Master's degree in engineering; joined Higgins in 1948, working directly with John Howard to develop major innovations in broadcast equipment. Continuing their creative teamwork after Howard's promotion to head the firm, these two engineers invented the basic equipment for transmitting digital data by telephone. Sloane was appointed Director of Research in 1954.

Daniel Waldron - Controller, 48 years old: BA in business administration; joined Higgins in 1952 while attending night classes. Held several jobs, including production scheduling, accounting, and cost control. Named Controller in 1963.

CASE 10

COMPLAN INTERACTIVE SERVICES

Complan Interactive Services

Assume that you have been given the job of developing a proposed organization structure for Complan. Assume that the material listed under "Major Tasks" on the front two pages of the case constitutes a statement of the strategy Complan plans to pursue.

1. What are the key tasks and functions that will need to be performed in the company?

2. How should these tasks be grouped together into departments?

3. How should integration and coordination among the departments be achieved?

COMPLAN INTERACTIVE SYSTEMS, INC.

In 1969 and early 1970 the computer time-sharing industry, then only four years old, was experiencing a shakeout. At a time when the stock market had shown a year of nearly steady decline and the computer software and services industries had fallen into disfavor with investors, many time-sharing companies were merging and others were falling by the wayside or being acquired at fire-sale prices.

The Time-Sharing Industry

The development and growth of the time-sharing industry was described in volume twelve of Innovation Magazine: "Time-sharing is a special kind of service industry based on the remote manipulation of data via certain combinations of technology - computers, communications, software. This is a viable business largely because the technology becomes attractively inexpensive to use when its essential costs are shared..."

The customers use keyboard (i.e., teletypes) or graphic terminals linked to a central computer by telephone lines. In effect, each customer finds that the computer seems to operate exclusively in his or her behalf, for certain supervisory programs within the machine analyze the demands made by various customers "so that the response to demands by individual users optimally is given with no noticeable delay resulting from other customers' uses of the machine."

The article described the entry of some companies into the young time-sharing industry: "...after suitable juggling had been accomplished among potential customers, a computer supplier, and the phone company, you hired some smart programmers and whipped them like galley slaves in order to have the software ready on time to meld the whole affair together into an operating system..."

Technically creative people headed most time-sharing companies. Many companies were started by programmers who were attracted by the idea of capitalizing on what they knew - of squeezing the most out of computer hardware.

This case was prepared by Martin P. Charns, Research Associate, under the supervision of Professor Paul R. Lawrence, as a basis for class discussion rather than to illustrate either effective or ineffective handling of an administrative situation.

The time-sharing companies soon found that operations were more complex than they had anticipated. Customers could call at any time of the day or night, which was fine until too many customers called at the same time. Then the operating system - a sophisticated design of hardware and software - could answer each individual request only after much longer response times than were desirable. If this situation occurred too frequently, customers complained and eventually discontinued the service. On the other hand, the time-sharing company saw its machine being underutilized. The incremental cost of putting on new customers appeared very low, as the hardware was already there and each additional customer had only a small effect on the system's performance. The Innovation article described the outcome of this type of analysis:

> If enough companies put enough computer time on the market based on such an incremental pricing strategy, it doesn't take long before the cost competition has all of them selling at below real operating costs unless their computers do run at capacity which...degrades service and drives customers away. Then, when people find their services aren't selling, they cut price. This iteration becomes disastrous when there is no distinction between time-sharing services except price.

As time-sharing technology was commercially developed, many technical problems appeared. Since the technology for time-sharing was much more advanced than for traditional batch-mode service, and had not been completely debugged, many hardware and software problems were found only after customers began using the systems. Some problems occurred only when special circumstances, such as a unique sequence and timing of customer demands revealed a systems design flaw. These errors were especially difficult to correct. The error situation had to be first discovered and recreated but too often little information remained after the event to determine what had actually happened. Since customers had direct access to the system, it was more vulnerable than batch operations where the computer was in a protected environment and was accessible only to the operator. Furthermore, the fact that several customers were using the system at any one time increased the potential damage that a system error could cause; users could find that midway through a session with the system it would "crash" and possibly cause the loss of all of the work they had done to that point.

Many of the time-sharing companies' customers were not technically oriented, and the companies offered their customers little help in using the service. Innovation described this situation:

Few of the companies had made any real investment in a marketing force. Many of them acquired a good peddler, knighted him with a title of vice-president for marketing, paid him $25,000 per year plus stock options, and expected him to scare up customers for the computer waiting in the back room....Early in 1968 a salesman who knew little about programming could still go into a scientific research or engineering establishment and offer raw computer time on a central machine via teletype link: the client could then do as he pleased with the system. But it became more difficult to sell this way because there were lots of other customers who examined an offer of a computer and asked: But what do we do with it?

There followed a great rush through 1968 and 1969 to produce libraries of computer application programs....After two years the great flurry of programming activity hadn't produced much of a distinction between time-sharing services after all. Almost every service, large or small, offered the same computer languages and somewhat the same kinds of programs. This similarity of services continued to depress the time-sharing market.

The programming activity had absorbed many of the resources of the companies that had relied on this marketing strategy. Often, however, it became clear only after a program had been developed that it did not have as wide an application as was expected. Often the market for a program was severely limited by the fact that the program itself was technically a fine development but too difficult to understand and too sophisticated for use, for more than a small number of customers.

The Time-Sharing Industry in 1970

In 1970 time-sharing companies were retrenching. Few were profitable. As a result of the several mergers in the industry, some time-sharing companies had operations in more than one city (some all across the nation). The computer facilities in these situations could either be one large computer with leased telephone lines feeding to this computer, or separate computers with similar programs in different cities. The choice between these two alternatives was based upon an analysis of the capital investments and operating costs.

Complan Interactive Systems

In mid-1970 Complan Interactive Systems, Inc. was formed as a new time-sharing service. The company's founders believed that if they followed the right strategy and organized properly they could profitably offer time-sharing services. Basing their strategy upon experience they had gained from observing other time-sharing companies, CIS's founders decided to differentiate themselves from the rest of the industry by offering a specialized package of programs and services to, initially, one specialized market. CIS's potential clients had little knowledge of computer technology, but had several applications in which the use of time-sharing could make a major contribution. The company offered its clients a package which included the use of a terminal, access to the company's programs (which were designed to be both flexible in their application and easy to use), initial instruction in the use of the system and applications programs, detailed instruction manuals, and on-going support services. CIS priced its services significantly higher than the time-sharing industry's average. The company considered its marketing area to be the United States and Canada, and it based its operations on one central computer facility.

Major Tasks

The company believed that to be successful, it had to offer:

1. A dependable time-sharing system, which meant:

   a. Modifying and enhancing the system provided by the computer hardware manufacturer.

   b. Providing dependable operations and maintenance of the hardware and software.

2. Specialized applications programs that:

   a. Met specific customer needs.

   b. Were easy to use while still being effective.

   c. Were modified and augmented as required.

3. Extensive customer service and training that would:

   a. Assist the customer in effectively using the service, often answering questions that were relatively simple technically.

b. Answer occasional highly technical customer questions.

c. Provide feedback on the customers' views of the system's performance.

d. Provide information on additional applications and market potentials.

4. Reasonable (but higher than average) prices.

CIS's president esimtated that it would be necessary to assemble an organization of about 100 people, including support staff. He was trying to determine what organizational arrangements would best meet his company's objectives.

CASE 11

TYPE A/B QUESTIONNAIRE

■ *Skill Preassessment*

Social Readjustment Rating Scale

Which of the following have you experienced in the past year? Using the weightings at the right, total up your score.

Life Event	Mean Value
1. Death of spouse	100
2. Divorce	73
3. Marital separation from mate	65
4. Detention in jail or other institution	63
5. Death of a close family member	63
6. Major personal injury or illness	53
7. Marriage	50
8. Being fired at work	47
9. Marital reconciliation with mate	45
10. Retirement from work	45
11. Major change in the health or behavior of a family member	44
12. Pregnancy	40
13. Sexual difficulties	39
14. Gaining a new family member (e.g., through birth, adoption, oldster moving in, etc.)	39
15. Major business readjustment (e.g., merger, reorganization, bankruptcy, etc.)	39
16. Major change in financial state (e.g., a lot worse off or a lot better off than usual)	38
17. Death of a close friend	37
18. Changing to a different line of work	36
19. Major change in the number of arguments with spouse (e.g., either a lot more or a lot less than usual regarding childrearing, personal habits, etc.)	35
20. Taking out a mortgage or loan for a major purchase (e.g., for a home, business, etc.)	31
21. Foreclosure on a mortgage or loan	30
22. Major change in responsibilities at work (e.g., promotion, demotion, lateral transfer)	29
23. Son or daughter leaving home (e.g., marriage, attending college, etc.)	29
24. Trouble with in-laws	29
25. Outstanding personal achievement	28
26. Wife beginning or ceasing work outside the home	26
27. Beginning or ceasing formal schooling	26
28. Major change in living conditions (e.g., building a new home, remodeling, deterioration of home or neighborhood)	25
29. Revision of personal habits (dress, manners, association, etc.)	24
30. Troubles with the boss	23
31. Major change in working hours or conditions	20
32. Change in residence	20

SOURCE: T. H. Holmes and R. H. Rahe, Social readjustment rating scale, *Journal of Psychosomatic Research*, 1967, 11, 213–218.

33. Changing to a new school　　　　　　　　　　　　　　　　　　　　20
34. Major change in usual type and/or amount of recreation　　　　　　　19
35. Major change in church activities (e.g., a lot more or a lot less than usual)　　19
36. Major change in social activities (e.g., clubs, dancing, movies, visiting, etc.)　　18
37. Taking out a mortgage or loan for a lesser purchase (e.g., for a car, TV, freezer, etc.)　　17
38. Major change in sleeping habits (a lot more or a lot less sleep, or change in part of day when asleep)　　　　　　　　　　　　　　　　　　16
39. Major change in number of family get-togethers (e.g., a lot more or a lot less than usual)　　　　　　　　　　　　　　　　　15
40. Major change in eating habits (a lot more or a lot less food intake, or very different meal hours or surroundings)　　　　　　　　　　　　15
41. Vacation　　　　　　　　　　　　　　　　　　　　　　　　　13
42. Christmas　　　　　　　　　　　　　　　　　　　　　　　　12
43. Minor violations of the law (e.g., traffic tickets, jaywalking, disturbing the peace, etc.)　　　　　　　　　　　　　　　　　　　　　　11

Type A Behavior Pattern Inventory

Rate the extent to which each of the following statements is typical of you *most of the time.* Try to describe your general way of behaving or feeling, not isolated incidents. There are no correct answers. Scoring instructions for the instrument will be provided by the instructor. In responding to each statement, use the following scale:

5—The statement is *true.* It is *typical* of me.
4—The statement is *somewhat true.* It is *somewhat typical* of me.
3—The statement is *neither true nor untrue,* or I *can't decide.*
2—The statement is *somewhat untrue.* It is *somewhat atypical* of me.
1—The statement is *untrue.* It is *not typical* of me at all.

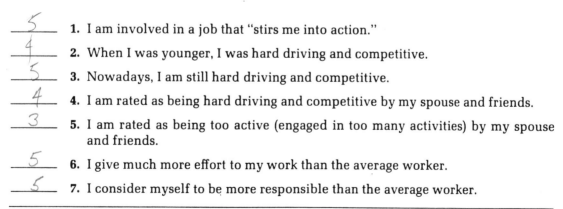

_5_ **1.** I am involved in a job that "stirs me into action."

_4_ **2.** When I was younger, I was hard driving and competitive.

_5_ **3.** Nowadays, I am still hard driving and competitive.

_4_ **4.** I am rated as being hard driving and competitive by my spouse and friends.

_3_ **5.** I am rated as being too active (engaged in too many activities) by my spouse and friends.

_5_ **6.** I give much more effort to my work than the average worker.

_5_ **7.** I consider myself to be more responsible than the average worker.

Adapted from Stephen J. Zyzanski and C. David Jenkins, Basic dimensions within the coronary-prone behavior pattern. *Journal of Chronic Diseases,* 1970, 22, 781–795.

_____4_____ **8.** I hurry in my work more than the average worker.

_____5_____ **9.** I consider myself to be more precise than the average worker.

_____5_____ **10.** I approach life more seriously than the average worker.

_____3_____ **11.** I often have trouble finding time for a haircut.

_____5_____ **12.** I eat more rapidly than most people.

_____5_____ **13.** I am often told that I eat too fast.

_____4_____ **14.** I frequently hurry a speaker to make the point.

_____4_____ **15.** I frequently put words into the speaker's mouth.

_____5_____ **16.** I find myself often inattentive to lengthy comments.

_____5_____ **17.** I often think of other things when listening to someone talk.

_____5_____ **18.** I find everyday life filled with challenges to be met.

_____3_____ **19.** I frequently set deadlines for myself at home.

_____4_____ **20.** I generally keep two jobs moving forward simultaneously.

_____4_____ **21.** I prefer a promotion to an increase in pay.

_____5_____ **22.** My income has considerably increased in the last three years.

_____5_____ **23.** I have more responsibility in my work than I did 10 years ago.

_____5_____ **24.** My present work has more prestige than it did 10 years ago.

_____4_____ **25.** I frequently do not leave work until well after closing time.

_____3_____ **26.** I frequently bring work home to do during the evenings.

_____2_____ **27.** I have held an office in an activity group while in school.

Total score for the total instrument:
Total score for items 1 through 10:
Total score for items 11 through 17:
Total score for items 18 through 27:

CASE 12

PERFORMANCE APPRAISAL AT DIGITAL ELECTRONICS

Performance Appraisal at Digital Electronics

Digital Electronics was a newly established company which specialized in the manufacture of electronic components for the auto parts industry. Many of the components were purchased from off-shore suppliers, but some were manufactured in Digital's own plant. A large part of the plant was occupied with the assembly of the electronic components into auto parts, such as "cruise-controls", automatic brake adjustment controls, fuel injection systems, etc.

There were three basic types of hourly-paid jobs in the plant: Shipping and Inventory; Electronic Manufacturing; and Final Assembly of products. The basic content of each of the three jobs was as follows:

Shipping and Inventory: these people did visual inspection of incoming shipments of components from offshore suppliers and then stocked acceptable parts in storage bins for inventory. Next, they prepared kits of parts from inventory for delivery to both the Electronics Manufacturing sites, and the Final Assembly sites. Lastly, they collected finished products from Final Assembly to prepare for shipping to customers. Key skills in the Shipping jobs were the clerical skills of reading and preparing shipping and order documents, and preparing kits of parts from inventory by reading specifications for parts from manufacturing orders. Shipping employees worked mostly on their own without close supervision.

Electronic Manufacturing: these people did precision soldering and wiring of tiny electronics parts onto circuit boards, using parts from kits supplied from Inventory. In addition to the high level of manual skill required, these people also had to be able to read wiring diagrams in order to know where and how the parts were to be installed and connected on the circuit boards. Electronics employees worked in an assembly line under close supervision to ensure high standards of product quality.

Final Assembly: these people put together completed auto parts using both the circuit boards from Electronics and components from kits supplied from Inventory. While it was necessary to be able to read product specification forms to know where and how the components were to be installed and connected, the skill level required for connecting components was not high. For this reason, most new employees in the plant started work in Final Assembly. Once a person had been trained in Final Assembly, supervision was relatively light, unless Quality Control started to detect problems with the final products before shipping.

When the company first started up, all performance ratings on employees were done by supervisors informally. Those employees whom the supervisors considered to be good employees were retained and some were promoted, while others were let go.

However, the company has now grown to a size where the informality of supervisor ratings, as done in the past, is no longer practical. There are too many employees now for the supervisors to get to know well and the President would like some more systematic appraisal procedure installed. In addition to a more systematic procedure, the President wants a procedure which is simple and quick to use, and which will provide useful information about an employee's level of performance.

All personnel administration in the plant was formally done by an Office Manager, but the President also felt that the scope of personnel administration has also grown too large for the Office Manager to handle. Consequently the President hired an experienced personnel administrator to take over these duties.

One of the first assignments given to the new Personnel Administrator was to prepare a new appraisal system for the hourly paid employees in the plant. (The President still intended to do appraisals on all the salaried employees). The new Personnel Administrator prepared the form shown in Appendix 1.

1. Analyze the proposed appraisal form for Digital Electronics in terms of its suitability for use for the hourly paid jobs.

2. What sort of appraisal system would you develop for the hourly paid jobs in this company?

Appendix A   Digital Electronics annual performance appraisal form

| Employee's Name _____ | Rating Period: Year Ended Dec. 31, 19____ |

Present Position	Code	Position Grade Level	Department	Section #	Division

	Below Standard	Satisfactory	Outstanding
1. ADAPTABILITY—Adjusts easily to changing conditions and assignments.	☐	☐	☐
2. APPEARANCE—Suitability in relation to the position.	☐	☐	☐
3. TEAMWORK—Cooperation with the fellow employees, works well with others.	☐	☐	☐
4. DEPENDABILITY—Degree to which employee can be relied upon to meet deadline without close supervision.	☐	☐	☐
5. DISPOSITION AND ATTITUDE—Obedient in carrying out orders; willingness to accept suggestions for work improvement; gives constant support to the organization.	☐	☐	☐
6. INITIATIVE—Has seen what needed to be done, and has shown initiative when the occasion called for it.	☐	☐	☐
7. JUDGMENT AND COMMON SENSE—Thinks clearly, weighs each problem, handles each situation with a minimum of supervision and readily adapts himself to meet the problem.	☐	☐	☐
8. SKILL LEVEL—Has skills required for present position.	☐	☐	☐
9. QUALITY OF WORK—Accuracy, completeness and neatness in performing special tasks.	☐	☐	☐
10. QUANTITY OF WORK—Amount completed in relation to job requirements.	☐	☐	☐
11. WORK HABITS—Punctuality, organization of work, care of equipment, and attention to safety.	☐	☐	☐
12. MORALS—Strength of morals and character.	☐	☐	☐
13. DEVELOPMENT—Potential shown for advancement and development.	☐	☐	☐
14. EMPLOYEE NEEDS & GOALS—Are employee needs and goals being met?	☐	☐	☐

Appraised by: _____   Date: _____

Appraisal review by: _____   Date: _____

CASE 13

MAKING SALARY DECISIONS

EMPLOYEE PROFILE SHEET

You have to make salary increase recommendations for eight managers that you supervise. They have just completed their first year with the company and are now to be considered for their first annual raise. Keep in mind that you may be setting precedents and that you need to keep salary costs down. However, there are no formal company restrictions on the kind of raises you can give. Indicate the size of the raise that you would like to give each manager by writing a dollar amount next to their names. You have a total of $17,000 available in your salary budget to use for pay raises.

$_____A. J. Adams. Adams is not, as far as you can tell, a good performer. You have checked your view with others, and they do not feel that Adams is effective either. However, you happen to know Adams has one of the toughest work groups to manage. Adams's subordinates have low skill levels, and the work is dirty and hard. If you lose Adams, you are not sure whom you could find as a replacement. *Salary: $20,000.*

$_____B. K. Berger. Berger is single and seems to live the life of a carefree swinger. In general, you feel that Berger's job performance is not up to par, and some of Berger's "goofs" are well known to the other employees. *Salary: $22,500.*

$_____C. C. Carter. You consider Carter to be one of your best subordinates. However, it is quite apparent that other people don't agree. Carter has married into wealth, and, as far as you know, doesn't need additional money. *Salary: $24,600.*

$_____D. Davis. You happen to know from your personal relationship that Davis badly needs more money because of certain personal problems. As far as you are concerned, Davis also happens to be one of the best of your subordinates. For some reason, your enthusiasm is not shared by your other subordinates, and you have heard them make joking remarks about Davis's performance. *Salary: $22,700.*

$_____E. J. Ellis. Ellis has been very successful so far. You are particularly impressed by this, since it is a hard job. Ellis needs money more than many of the other people and is respected for good performance. *Salary: $23,500.*

$_____F. M. Foster. Foster has turned out to be a very pleasant surprise to you, has done an excellent job, and is seen by peers as one of the best people in your group. This surprises you because Foster is generally frivolous and doesn't seem to care very much about money and promotion. *Salary: $21,800.*

$_____G. K. Gomez. Your opinion is that Gomez just isn't cutting the mustard. Surprisingly enough, however, when you check with others to see how they feel about Gomez, you discover that Gomez is very highly regarded. You also know that Gomez badly needs a raise. Gomez was just recently divorced and is finding it extremely difficult to support a house and a young family of four as a single parent. *Salary: $20,500.*

$_____H. A. Hunt. You know Hunt personally. This employee seems to squander money continually. Hunt has a fairly easy job assignment, and your own view is that Hunt doesn't do it particularly well. You are, therefore, quite surprised to find that several of the other new managers think that Hunt is the best of the new group. *Salary: $21,000.*

CASE 14

JOB REDESIGN

Developed by Hugh J. Arnold based upon materials
supplied by J. Richard Hackman.

Exhibit I

THE HACKMAN OLDHAM WORK DESIGN MODEL

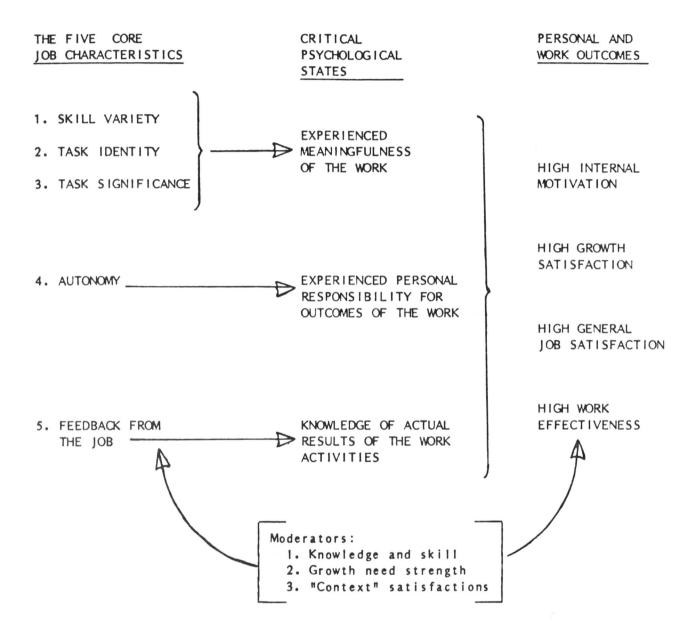

Exhibit 2

DEFINITION OF TERMS FROM THE HACKMAN-OLDHAM JOB DIAGNOSTIC SURVEY

Job Dimensions:

Skill Variety: The degree to which a job requires a variety of different activities in carrying out the work, which involve the use of a number of different skills and talents of the employee.

Task Identity: The degree to which the job requires completion of a "whole" and identifiable piece of work — that is doing a job from beginning to end with a visible outcome.

Task Significance: The degree to which the job has a substantial impact on the lives of work of other people — whether in the immediate organization or the external environment.

Autonomy: The degree to which the job provides substantial freedom, independence, and discretion to the employee in scheduling the work and in determining the procedures to be used in carrying it out.

Feedback from the job itself: The degree to which carrying out the work activities required by the job results in the employee obtaining direct and clear information about the effectiveness of his or her performance.

Critical Psychological States

Experienced meaningfulness of the work: The degree to which the employee experiences the job as one which is generally meaningful, valuable and worthwhile.

Experienced responsibility for work outcomes: The degree to which the employee feels personally accountable and responsible for the results of the work he or she does.

Knowledge of results: The degree to which the employee knows and understands, on a continuous basis, how effectively he or she is performing the job.

Affective Reactions to the Job

General satisfaction: An overall measure of the degree to which the employee is satisfied and happy with the job.

Internal work motivation: The degree to which the employee is self-motivated to perform effectively on the job — that is, the employee experiences positive internal feelings when working effectively on the job and negative feelings when doing poorly.

Specific satisfactions: Separate measures of satisfaction with specific factors.

The model states that five core dimensions of work or jobs lead to the experiencing of three different critical psychological states. These in turn lead to a variety of personal and work outcomes including high internal (intrinsic) motivation, high growth and general job satisfaction, and high work effectiveness. These relationships are moderated by the knowledge and skill, growth need strengh, and context satisfaction of the individuals involved.

Hackman & Oldham have developed a standardized questionnaire to administer to employees to measure each of the terms in the model. The terms as defined in the model and used in the questionnaire can be seen in Exhibit 2. The questionnaire is used to develop a total score for a job, called the "motivating potential score" or MPS. The MPS scores is calculated from the combined questionnaire item scores (individual questions are averaged into scale scores for each variable) which range from "1" (low) to "7" (high). The total score is calculated as follows:

$$MPS = \frac{SKILL\ VARIETY + TASK\ IDENTITY + TASK\ SIGN.}{3} \times AUTONOMY \times FEEDBACK$$

After diagnosis with this instrument, several approaches to improving the design of work are outlined. These approaches include:

1. Forming natural work units

2. Combining tasks

3. Establishing client relationships

4. Vertical loading

5. Opening feedback channels

Attachments

Attached are some sample printouts and information from a job diagnosis performed using the Hackman-Oldham model and instruments. The first three pages include printouts from the Job Diagnostic Survey for three different jobs: a college professor, an aircraft brake assembler, and a peripheral machine operator (operating peripheral computer equipment such as card sorters, key punches, etc. in a brokerage office). Following these listings is additional information on the third job (aircraft brake assembler) including a job description and diagram of the work flow.

JOB DIAGNOSTIC SURVEY - JOB 01 - COLLEGE PROFESSOR

JOB DIMENSIONS	JOB	PROFESSIONAL NORMS
SKILL VARIETY	6.85	5.40
TASK IDENTITY	5.25	5.10
TASK SIGNIFICANCE	6.30	5.60
AUTONOMY	5.74	5.40
FEEDBACK FROM THE JOB	4.95	5.10
EXPER. PSYCHOLOGICAL STATES		
MEANINGFULNESS OF WORK	6.75	5.40
RESPONSIBILITY FOR WORK	6.05	5.80
KNOWLEDGE OF RESULTS	4.80	5.00
AFFECTIVE RESPONSES TO JOB		
GENERAL SATISFACTION	4.80	4.90
INTERNAL WORK MOTIVATION	6.50	5.80
SPECIFIC SATISFACTIONS		
PAY SATISFACTION	2.20	4.40
SECURITY SATISFACTION	6.50	5.00
SOCIAL SATISFACTION	6.33	5.50
SUPERVISORY SATISFACTION	2.57	4.90
GROWTH SATISFACTION	5.75	5.10
INDIVIDUAL GROWTH NEED STRENGTH	6.15	5.60
BIOGRAPHICAL CHARACTERISTICS		
PERCENT MALE	82.00	87.00
PERCENT FEMALE	18.00	13.00
AVERAGE AGE	34.50	41.1
NUMBER OF RESPONDENTS	23	

| MOTIVATING POTENTIAL SCORE | 174.26 | 154.00 |

JOB DIAGNOSTIC SURVEY - JOB 02 - PERIPHERAL MACHINE OPERATOR

JOB DIMENSIONS	JOB	PROCESSING NORMS
SKILL VARIETY	1.67	4.20
TASK IDENTITY	3.00	4.30
TASK SIGNIFICANCE	5.33	5.30
AUTONOMY	5.33	4.50
FEEDBACK FROM THE JOB	2.33	4.70
EXPER. PSYCHOLOGICAL STATES		
MEANINGFULNESS OF WORK	3.25	5.00
RESPONSIBILITY FOR WORK	5.67	5.20
KNOWLEDGE OF RESULTS	2.50	5.10
AFFECTIVE RESPONSES TO JOB		
GENERAL SATISFACTION	2.00	4.60
INTERNAL WORK MOTIVATION	3.83	5.30
SPECIFIC SATISFACTIONS		
PAY SATISFACTION	1.45	4.50
SECURITY SATISFACTION	4.50	4.60
SOCIAL SATISFACTION	4.00	5.30
SUPERVISORY SATISFACTION	1.33	4.60
GROWTH SATISFACTION	5.25	4.70
INDIVIDUAL GROWTH NEED STRENGTH	2.15	4.60
BIOGRAPHICAL CHARACTERISTICS		
PERCENT MALE	68.00	77.00
PERCENT FEMALE	32.00	23.00
AVERAGE AGE	28.50	30.40
NUMBER OF RESPONDENTS	31	

MOTIVATING POTENTIAL SCORE	41.48	105.00

JOB DIAGNOSTIC SURVEY - JOB 03 - AIRCRAFT BRAKE ASSEMBLER

	JOB	MACHINE TRADES NORMS
JOB DIMENSIONS		
SKILL VARIETY	2.00	5.10
TASK IDENTITY	3.67	4.90
TASK SIGNIFICANCE	6.90	5.60
AUTONOMY	1.33	4.90
FEEDBACK FROM THE JOB	1.67	4.90
EXPER. PSYCHOLOGICAL STATES		
MEANINGFULNESS OF WORK	5.00	5.30
RESPONSIBILITY FOR WORK	2.17	5.40
KNOWLEDGE OF RESULTS	1.50	5.30
AFFECTIVE RESPONSES TO JOB		
GENERAL SATISFACTION	3.40	4.90
INTERNAL WORK MOTIVATION	3.83	5.60
SPECIFIC SATISFACTIONS		
PAY SATISFACTION	5.00	4.20
SECURITY SATISFACTION	6.50	5.00
SOCIAL SATISFACTION	4.00	5.50
SUPERVISORY SATISFACTION	5.00	4.60
GROWTH SATISFACTION	1.75	4.80
INDIVIDUAL GROWTH NEED STRENGTH	5.83	4.80
BIOGRAPHICAL CHARACTERISTICS		
PERCENT MALE	93.0	96.0
PERCENT FEMALE	7.0	4.0
AVERAGE AGE	45.1	43.2
NUMBER OF RESPONDENTS	14	

MOTIVATING POTENTIAL SCORE	9.31	136.00

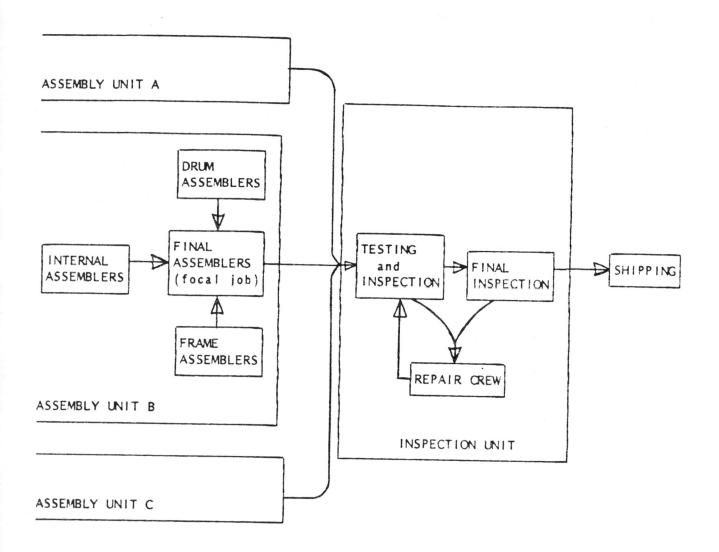

ASSEMBLY UNIT A

DRUM
ASSEMBLERS

INTERNAL
ASSEMBLERS

FINAL
ASSEMBLERS
(focal job)

FRAME
ASSEMBLERS

ASSEMBLY UNIT B

ASSEMBLY UNIT C

TESTING
and
INSPECTION

FINAL
INSPECTION

SHIPPING

REPAIR CREW

INSPECTION UNIT

AIRCRAFT BRAKE ASSEMBLY WORKFLOW

JOB 03: FINAL ASSEMBLERS: AIRCRAFT BRAKE ASSEMBLY

These workers perform the final assembly of wheel brakes for various types of aircraft. The basic workflow is shown in the attached diagram. Within each of the three assembly units (which produce brakes for three different types of aircraft), the basic workflow is the same.

The Final Assembler is the last work station in the Assembly Unit. He receives three components from other workers in his unit: (I) the internal assembly, which is the complex "heart" of the brake, and contains all hydraulic and electrical cricuits; (2) the drum assembly, which is a fairly simple device; and (3) the frame, which is larger, but also simple. The Final Assembler affixes the internal assembly and the drum assembly to the frame, following a step-by-step procedure that has been carefully engineered to minimize the possibility of error. An especially important part of the job is tightening various nuts to a specific torque criterion, with very low margin for error. Special tools are used in this process.

When the Final Assembler finishes work on a brake, he places it on a conveyor that takes it to a separate room where all brakes manufactured in the plant are tested, inspected, and prepared for shipping. There are two inspection stations in the Inspection Unit. If a brake is found faulty in any way it is given to a special Repair Crew in the Inspection Unit to be fixed. After repair, the brake again goes through the entire test and inspection process.

Each Assembly Unit is managed by a foreman who typically is highly competent in all technical matters having to do with brake assembly. If excessive numbers of brakes from one of the Assembly Units are found to be faulty by the Inspection Unit, the foreman is informed and is expected to identify and correct the problem. Often the difficulty turns out to be out-of-tolerance torque in the final assembly process, in which case the maintenance foreman is contacted and a maintenance worker is sent to re-adjust the tools used in the final assembly process.

CASE 15

EMPLOYEE INVOLVEMENT AT THE FORD WINDSOR PLANT

Employee Involvement at the Ford Windsor Plant

1. Analyse the EI program at the Windsor plant from an OD perspective. Look at such aspects of the program as:

- perceived need for change

- diagnosis of situation, causes of problems

- objectives for the change program

- development of the OD program

- implementation of the program

- tracking of progress, adaptations

- reinforcement, rewards

- long term evaluations

- changes in priorities, definitions of goals, problems

- changes in commitment, support

- development of reactionary forces

Specific information about all of these aspects may not be available in the case. Inferences may have to be drawn about some of the aspects.

2. From the limited information available about the Oakville plant, why do you think the QWL program at the Oakville plant was considered to be a fiasco?

In North America, the auto industry, like other industries, has traditionally been run along militaristic lines. Management made the decisions, and workers were expected to obey orders and keep their mouths shut. The result was unhappy, frustrated workers and, too often, inferior products. Then along came the Japanese with their quality-obsessed workers who, at Toyo-Kogyo Co. Ltd.'s Mazda plant in Hiroshima, for example, make an average of 130 suggestions for improvements each year.

While some would like to blame the North American auto industry's problems on the North American auto worker, management at Ford admits that much of the fault has been management's. In the past, says Jerry Steele, the ebullient American in charge of industrial relations at the five Windsor Ford plants, management took for granted that it had "the sole responsibility and the omnipotent power and knowledge. That's why we're in a lot of our troubles."

The impetus for EI comes from top management at Ford's world headquarters in Dearborn, Mich. Peter Pestillo, vice-president of labor relations, agreed to establish the program during negotiations with the United Auto Workers (UAW) in 1979. In Canada, the decision on whether to co-operate in EI is up to each individual union local. While the desirability of involving workers in their work seems self-evident, for Ford the EI program represents a major philosophical shift. A company once notorious for its poor labor relations is trying nothing less than to dismantle an adversarial system that took 80 years to construct. The problem is that many people, including some tough managers, union representatives jealous of their authority and workers accustomed to hating the company, have a stake in the adversarial system.

Changing the system isn't cheap, nor is it easy. Steele says that last year in the five Windsor plants, some 80,000 man-hours were spent in training people to lose the old ways. That cost the company more than $1 million, which, Steele promises skeptical controllers, will someday be repaid tenfold. The hourly workers are getting 20 hours of training in problem solving and another 20 hours in Statistical Process Control, a method that helps them inspect components as they're being produced rather than at the end of the line. Managers, meanwhile, are spending three days learning something called Teleometrics, a sort of sensitivity training to enable them to deal with the new phenomenon of involved employees. Explains Steele: "As a supervisor of people out on the floor, if you don't relate to their personal needs, if you aren't a good listener and if you don't understand that you have to be a different manager to different people, then you can't be effective in Employee Involvement."

Ford has claimed a 59% improvement in quality (measured by a reduction in customer warranty claims) since 1980, the year EI got underway. Steele says it's made a big difference in absenteeism. During November, 1982, some 400 Ford workers in Windsor were absent because of sickness or disability. Last November, although 1,100 additional workers had boosted the labor force at the five plants to 4,500, the number of workers absent during the month was down to 144. Equally significant, he says, is that at the same time Windsor's five plants had only 37 people on workers' compensation, while the Oakville, Ont., assembly plant, which has 1,400 fewer workers, had 125. Steele thinks the reasons are that Oakville has neither an Employee Involvement program nor the positive management-union relationship that Windsor has.

"The worker always knows what's wrong," says Leo Brown, manager of Ford's engine plants. "He wasn't being asked before"

The Oakville situation illustrates the problems involved in breaking free of the adversarial system. UAW Local 707 won't agree to introduce the program because, according to union representative Jim Donegan, a previous attempt to implement a similar program was a fiasco. The union went into the program, known as Quality of Work Life, in 1979 full of enthusiasm and dropped it in 1982 completely disillusioned.

A typical example of what went wrong, says Donegan, was an initiative by a group of workers to resolve some problems in a frame assembly operation. Their recommendations resulted in increased quality and saved money. The company's response was to cut the work force in the area by two, over the workers' opposition. "The workers felt betrayed," according to Donegan. "In some areas, management lost interest in it and some supervisors were making fun of the program, saying the union's getting too soft. At the end, we weren't talking quality of work life, we were solely talking quality of product."

At Windsor, both management and labor agree that quality of work life and quality of product go together. One reason for the more positive atmosphere in Windsor is the amazing success story of the EI team formerly chaired by Hank Hunt, which is credited with preventing the demise of Windsor Engine Plant 2.

In 1981 production of the 255-cu.-in. eight-cylinder engine was discontinued. Only 83 employees were left in the huge Engine Plant 2, working in a small stampings operation producing engine parts. Projected losses for the year were $1.6 million. Closing the plant seemed a logical step, and that is what the company announced it would do.

Jerry Steele observes that strong medicine, such as the threat of a plant closing, is "sometimes what's required to shake us from our sheeplike passivity." The EI team renamed itself SOS (Save Our Stampings) and got to work. But three months later, it hadn't come up with any suggestions, and suspicions were voiced that the members of the SOS gang were merely sheep headed for the slaughter. "We were conducting a survey," Hunt explains. "We'd been keeping records, facts and figures. We were out gauging steel. We did much of it on our own time."

They discovered that the steel being delivered by the supplier was of poor quality and insisted that it be brought up to standard. They developed a system to reduce rust that blows moisture off newly produced and washed parts. They obtained a stamping compound (the lubricant used to prepare steel for the presses) that works far better than the one they had been using.

Those improvements helped cut scrap to 3% from 23%, and that made the operation profitable. And because the doors were still open, management chose Engine Plant 2 when it was looking for a site to produce a 302-cu.-in. eight-cylinder engine. The result is that there are now more than 900 employees in a plant for which, Hunt enjoys recalling, "the padlocks had already been bought." Had the lights been turned off at Engine Plant 2, chances are they would never have come on again. Those 900 jobs might well have gone elsewhere, says Gary Lesperance, EI and training administrator at Ford's Windsor plants.

CASE 16

BAXTER CHEMICALS

Baxter Chemicals

A case study of the development of a new philosophy of management and a QWL program in a new petrochemical plant. The material for this case study is derived from a research project on The QWL Program at the XYZ Chemicals Plant, by D.A. Ondrack and M.G. Evans of the Faculty of Management Studies at the University of Toronto. The research project was funded by a research grant from the Employment Relations Branch, Labour Canada, Ottawa.

1. Introduction:

Baxter Chemicals is a large company which produces industrial chemicals and petrochemical-based consumer goods. As part of an overall expansion of production capacity, the firm decided to build a new petrochemical plant in Bradley, Ontario with some major innovations in process technology. It is a world-scale petrochemical plant representing an initial investment in plant and equipment of $200 million with a subsequent expansion approved for a further $40 million investment. It was expected that the original plant would employ some 270 persons which would mean a ratio of capital to labour of about $3/4 million per employee. Baxter chemicals had developed a new chemical refining process which would be used for the first time in this plant and it was hoped that the new process would give the plant a significant cost advantage over competitors.

In 1978, a second decision was made to improve further the competitive edge of the new Bradley plant. It had been the experience of some general managers at Baxter Chemicals that new plant start-ups were always characterized by an excellent employee relations climate. Start-ups had a strong spirit of enthusiasm, cooperation and teamwork which made new plants exciting places to work and frequently highly productive. Unfortunately this spirit often wore off after a start-up was completed and operations settled down to a routine. If only the start-up employee relations climate could be maintained, management reasoned, such a plant might be much more competitive and a nicer place to work. It was also hoped that a positive employee relation climate would allow the plant to remain non-union although the company intended to offer competitive wages and benefits.

The strategy chosen to achieve the desired employee relations climate was to try to introduce a new work system which would improve the quality of work life at the Bradley plant. Basically the QWL Program consisted of a plant employee relations philosophy which emphasized participative management and decision-making, an open climate of communications, operators organized into largely autonomous work teams, and a system of pay increases based on skill qualifications. In this system workers would be paid according to the number of skill modules they mastered and not necessarily for actual job duties. Skills based pay was intended to foster flexibililty of work assignments for operators within a team since each operator would be qualified for several tasks.

A manager from another Baxter Chemicals plant with a similar innovative work system was transferred to Bradley to head up the implementation of the new work system. It was his responsibility to translate much of the philosophy of the new work system into operational practices at Bradley. He was very enthusiastic about the opportunity to introduce such a system into a "green field" site with a completely new plant and work force.

2.   Goals of the New Work System:

1. The major goal was the maintenance of high productivity for the Bradley Plant. Participative management was intended to be the principle means to increase productivity in this high technology continuous process plant.

2. Baxter Chemicals wished to operate a plant which employees "have no need for third party (e.g. union) intervention". The reasoning here was that

participation and open communication would lead to greater fulfillment and satisfaction of employees' needs so that there would be little sense of frustration and therefore little demand for unionization. In terms of benefits and working conditions Baxter Chemicals (like other companies in the area) claimed to be competitive with industry standards so there would be no need for third party representation in these matters as well.

3. The new work system developed at the Bradley plant was intended to have three major changes to the employees' work:

   a. Increased operator control over day-to-day production flows and product specification controls.

   b. Increased worker control over working conditions.

   c. Increased opportunities for individual growth and the development of new skills and abililties.

It should also be noted that the general manager of the Petrochemicals Division and the plant manager were engaged in a risky enterprise. They were about to operate: a) a new plant, b) with a new and unfamiliar technology and c) using a new and untried (in Canada) work system (Baxter Chemicals was among the earliest of the petrochemical plants in Canada to embark upon a quality of work life program). Normally considerable apprehension exists about starting a new chemical plant, even with conventional technology, due to the enormous capital investment involved. When the new plant is based on a new and different type of technology, the apprehension is further magnified. With a new plant it is taken for granted that a long period of troubleshooting will be necessary before the plant can produce a product reliably and efficiently. Under such circumstances of uncertainty and pressure to start earning a return on the capital investment, it is very unusual for management to try at the same time an experiment in managerial style. However, it was felt that if the strong sense of employee involvement, participation and commitment normally associated with a plant start-up could be sustained, then the experiment would be worth the gamble.

3. Implementation of the New Work System

a) Selection and Recruitment

The supervisory staff at the Bradley Plant were hired about nine months prior to the start-up of the Utilities section of the plant and about 15 months prior the full start-up. There are about 60 managers and supervisors in the various areas of the plant. Of these, about 50% were recruited internally from other parts of Baxter Chemicals operations and the remainder were recruited from outside the firm.

Emphasis upon participative management was used during recruitment to attract those wishing to work in such an environment and to discourage those who would feel uncomfortable with participative management. Recruiting also included a post selection interview by all employees with the Plant Manager to reinforce the emphasis on participative management.

The first line supervisors basically had little prior supervisory experience in this new type of managerial environment. About 2/3 had some supervisory experience at conventional chemical plants while the remaining 1/3 were experienced high level operators from other Baxter plants. For this latter group, the Bradley Plant was their first supervisory position.

Despite the emphasis on the Bradley Plant management philosophy in recruiting, it would appear that supervisor selection was made principally on the basis of a person's technical competence, and to a lesser extent on a person's skills at managing participatively. It may have been assumed that the emphasis on the philosophy of the new work system during recruitment was sufficient for compatibility of values of new supervisors to be assured by a process of self-selection.

In addition, a number of technical experts (about 90) were brought to the plant site on two year start-up assignments who came from other plants with very different supervisory climates. It was not possible to select or train the start-up specialists in the philosophy or new work system at the Bradley Plant. As a result, new supervisors and operators at the Bradley plant were exposed to a variety of management styles and organizational climates during their training and work in the start-up period.

b)   Training and Induction in the new System

The next vehicle used for the implementation of the new work system was the initial socialization process at the Bradley Plant. Induction of new employees into the system was carried out in the following ways:

-   On being hired, each supervisor was interviewed by the plant manager, who explained the importance of participative management as laid out in the plant Philosophy Statement.

-   During training, supervisors and operators received a heavy input of experiential human relations and communication training (i.e., role playing, t-groups).

265

c) <u>Supervisor Training</u>

The details are not entirely clear of what supervisory training took place prior to start-up, in part due to earlier turnover among the training staff. It <u>is</u> clear that the outcomes of this training were not very satisfactory. Prior to their technical training, supervisors received a two week behavior theory course for familiarization with the philosophy of the new work system at the Bradley Plant coupled with intensive communications and behaviour training (such as transactional analysis). In the main, the behavioural material presented was rather theoretical, and little information of direct practical use was provided.

The two week course also contained a 3-day version of a standard company course on supervision involving the supervisory functions of planning, organizing, staffing and controlling. A lack of correspondence between the behavioral content and the supervision content of the training left the supervisory trainees somewhat confused about their role and what the appropriate supervisory style was to be at the Bradley Plant.

In particular they were not clear about their rights and duties as supervisors and they were not sure where participation left off and where permissiveness began. Further, as the plant was not yet in operation, their jobs were limited to those of writing manuals for operating procedures and later technical training of their subordinates. This situation increased their confusion as they had no actual supervisory role to perform prior to start-up.

d) <u>Operator Training</u>

Operators were hired three months prior to the start-up of the units to

266

which they were assigned. During this period extensive technical training
carried out by technical specialists and supervisors took place. Prior to
their technical training, each operator also went through a two week
orientation program for the new work system.

The orientation program had many "house-keeping" aspects (pay system,
fire and safety procedures, plant layout, etc.), and also placed heavy
emphasis on indoctrination into the plant philosophy
and new work system. This included extensive communications and role playing
behavioral training, such as feedback exercises, perception sensitivity
exercises, group decision making exercises, intergroup conflict exercises,
and team building exercises. By all accounts this was a powerful
indoctrination program and resulted in high expectations among operators
toward the new work system of the plant. These high expectations were
enhanced by the fact that the trainees were a relatively young group of
persons whom, it was felt, were the product of the relatively permissive
1960's schools and homes.

4.   Early Results

Despite the level of enthusiasm, the actual start up did not go well.
Considerable confusion developed over managerial rights and authority and
vast amounts of time were spent in unproductive meetings of operator teams.
The operators perceived participative management to mean that they had the
right to participate in every decision and that any directive issued by a
supervisor was not legitimate unless a meeting was held to discuss it.
Supervisors, whether experienced or not, were confused about their authority

in this new system and had several different interpretations of the meaning of participative management as well. Senior management were often inconsistent in their use of participative management by frequently giving orders to supervisors (i.e.: no participation), while telling supervisors that they had to be participative with their subordinates. Finally, the start-up technical specialists were used to having the authority of their technical expertise and had little patience with anybody's interests in participation.

The confusion about participative management, respective roles and responsibilities was soon translated into disappointing performance in meeting start-up targets. Various projects were not completed on time and trial runs of the new production process failed to produce any usable product. Out of frustration, some managers adopted a laissez-faire approach and let operators do pretty much what they wanted. Due to their lack of experience, few operators knew how to take over this responsibility and standards generally began to slip around the plant. The plant manager finally decided after three months of operations in late 1980 that further supervisory training was required to clear up the confusion and authorized the training department to develop a supplementary training course to reaffirm the principles of participative management and teamwork.

Accordingly, a new program of training was designed consisting of a repeat of the standard company three-day course on basic supervision principles, a two-day session on harmony in the workplace given by a big name external consultant; a two-day session on interpersonal communicatons; a five-day session on systematic problem-solving and decision-making; and a three-day session on writing job descriptions for subordinates.

No Contingency

Unfortunately the new three week course was in process in January 1981 when a plant safety audit conducted by Baxter Chemicals found the plant to be seriously deficient in several key areas of plant safety. Secondly, management from headquarters on a surprise visit, found several operational problems in the plant being unattended while supervisors were occupied in the supplementary training course. At this point, headquarters decided to intervene. All non-technical training programs were suspended, several of the training staff left and the plant manager was reassigned back to his former plant.

A new plant manager was transferred in and given the assignment to put the Bradley plant in order and get the plant back to basics again. He was also to make an assessment of what had happened to the new work system and to make a recommendation on whether it should be dropped or continued. If it was to be dropped, he had to assess the consequences to employee relations in terms of the expectations which had been built up. If it was to be continued, he had to figure out how to avoid the former mistakes and how to proceed from the present situation. As he was trying to assess the situation, he learned from the plant employee relations manager that the local chemical workers union was going to mount an organization drive on the Bradley plant.

The new plant manager, Ken Wilson, quickly did an audit of the employee relations climate in the plant by having informal talks with people at all levels of the organization. He concluded the following:

1. People's expectations are unrealistic about the new work system. They don't realize that the plant has to operate within several firm operating constraints, and participative decision making has to operate within those boundaries.

2. The philosophy statements about the new work system are too general and subject to many different interpretations.

3. Instead of clarifying the philosophy in operational terms and people's different roles and responsibilities, the earlier training sessions actually increased the confusion by being non-relevant and not practically focussed.

4. Top management at the plant were not clear in their own minds about how the new system was supposed to work and were inconsistent in their own directives, role models and guidance. This problem was aggravated by the presence of outside start-up specialists who were not involved in the new work system.

5. Management has tried to introduce too much too soon with the new work system, especially when it coincided with the pressures and difficulties of a new plant start-up plus a new process technology.

6. Supervisors do not yet trust the new work system and will revert back to a traditional authoritarian style of management under high pressure operations.

Despite the problems identified, Ken Wilson decided that too much had been invested in the new work system and that a severe crisis in employee relations would occur if the program was abandoned at this point. He decided to go ahead with trying to implement the new system even though it meant putting his neck on the line. Top management at headquarters would back him up only to a certain point, as they were now very concerned about what was hapening to their $250 million investment. The question now for Ken Wilson was how to proceed?

CASE 17

CAREER PLANNING EXERCISE

CAREER PLANNING

INTRODUCTION

Obviously, different occupations and professions require different strengths (skills, abilities, talents, etc.) of the people who are effective in their work. The skills and abilities required for a particular line of work reflect the activities that are involved in the job, that, in turn, are largely dictated by the "raw materials" involved in the work. Broadly speaking, all jobs require dealing with one or more of four types of raw materials: things, data, ideas, and people. Figure 1 suggests some of the elemental job activities required for each of these raw materials.

Some jobs seem to require the ability to deal with only one type of material: bookkeepers work mostly with data, carpenters with things, philosophers with ideas, and sales clerks with people. Most jobs require the ability to effectively deal with at least two types of material. For example, *all* managers deal with people, but the Controller also works with data, the Vice President of Engineering is heavily involved with data and things, and the Vice President of Marketing with ideas and data.

Individuals vary in their preferences and abilities for dealing with different types of work.   The purpose of this exercise is to give you a chance to evaluate your strengths and weaknesses in each of the four work areas. Effective planning of your career requires that you identify your personal strengths and find a line of work that will let you use those skills that you enjoy exercising the most. Once you have identified a particular vocational area that capitalizes on your strengths, it is also important that you identify any remediable deficiencies or weaknesses that may hinder you from achieving your full potential in your field. You will need to develop specific plans for moving into your chosen line of work (if you are not already in it) and for overcoming your weaknesses.

FIGURE 1
Four Categories of Job Activities

Things	Here are some activities involving *things:* Move, manipulate, machine (saw, drill, finish, etc.), adjust, assemble, design, operate, handle, construct, arrange, inspect, clean, deliver, store, drive, etc.
Data	Here are some job activities involving *data:* Compare, collect, copy, analyze, check, compile, organize, summarize, type, collate, store and retrieve, classify, schedule, observe, diagnose, etc.
People	Here are some job activities involving *people:* Counsel, assist, coach, teach, manage, persuade, interview, consult, advise, criticize, lead, communicate, request, encourage, sell, recruit, manage, arbitrate or mediate conflict, negotiate, speak in public, supervise, listen, help others to express themselves.
Ideas	Here are some job activities involving *ideas:* Create, compare, critique, publish, think about, argue, comprehend, decide, plan, interpret, define, establish goals, imagine, invent, synthesize, etc.

Developed by Donald D. Bowen.

PROCEDURE

Step 1

1. Take four blank sheets of lined 8½ × 11-inch notebook paper. Put a heading on each sheet, one sheet for each of the four basic areas of:

Things	People
Data	Ideas

2. On the first line of each sheet, write "Satisfying Skills." Beginning with *things*, think of and list all of the things you can do really well with physical materials and objects. Think, in particular, of skills that provide you with a deep sense of satisfaction when you exercise them.

   Figure 1 may be a helpful guide in suggesting ideas here.

3. When you have listed as many skills and abilities as you can think of for *things*, move on to the sheets labeled *people, data,* and *ideas*. Repeat the process until you feel you have listed all of your really important skills and abilities in each area.

Step 2

From your lists of "satisfying skills," which are the most important to you? On a fresh sheet of paper, make a list of your *five* most satisfying skills and abilities—those that you enjoy using the most (be careful to retain the "things" "people," etc., labels).

Step 3

Do a or b, below.

a. *For people who are not certain about their career interests:* What types of careers tend to require the exercise of your most important skills and abilities? Identify as many possibilities as you can before you select that alternative that seems to fit you best. (If you are not sure about some of the possibilities here, there are several ways to get more information. Most colleges and universities have placement and counseling centers that will be glad to discuss your interests with you. If you think certain vocations might be a good fit for you, talk to some people in these jobs—don't be afraid to call someone you don't even know. You might be surprised at how willing most people are to help. If you are really at a loss to think of anything, look up some jobs in the *Occupational Outlook Handbook* or *Dictionary of Occupational Titles* in the nearest library. Once you have identified some likely possibilities, check the card catalog for anything that may be written about these jobs.)

   As you begin to develop some specific feasible alternatives, pick up any information you can about how people get into this line of work. What are the educational, training and experience requirements you are going to have to fulfill? Is there a practical way for you to meet these requirements? How? Prepare notes on your findings and conclusions. You will need them in Step 5.

   You are now ready to establish a *tentative* career objective. The objective you set should have the characteristics shown in Figure 2.

   When you have stated your career objective, go on to Step 4.

b. *For people who are satisfied with career choices already made:* Where do you want to go in your occupation or profession? What does it mean to you to "advance" in your field? Don't restrict yourself to thinking only in terms of traditional measures such as salary and organizational level. For purposes of this activity, define advancement as *moving into a new position or redesign-*

FIGURE 2
Characteristics of a Good Career Objective

A good career objective is one that is:

Challenging: A good objective is one that you must stretch to achieve.

Realistic: While your objective should be challenging, it should also be one that you can realistically hope to achieve, given your strengths, weaknesses, needs, circumstances, values, problem solving styles, and so on.

Measurable and Concrete: Establish a time target for achieving your objective. Phrase the objective in specific terms; for example:

Poor I want to be an executive.
Better I'd like to be a vice-president of personnel within five years.
Best I'd like to be vice-president of manufacturing of a medium sized (200 to 500 employees) storm door company within 12 years. The position must pay at least $50,000 per year, and the company must place emphasis on quality manufacturing. Possibilities include...

Long Term: Your objective should represent a major career goal or milestone for you. You will probably want to think at least 5 to 10 years into the future.

Relevant: Achieving your objective should be deeply satisfying because it fulfills your most central needs and requires the exercise of those talents and abilities you enjoy using most.

_____

ing your present job so that it requires you to use even more of your most important and satisfying skills and abilities. Prepare a statement of your career objective that fulfills the criteria in Figure 2.

What would need to be done to make this possible? How can you initiate the process that will eventually have a high probability of achieving these changes? What additional experiences or training do you need? Are the opportunities available in your present organization? In other organizations? Prepare notes on your analysis for use in Step 5.

Step 4

Take the original four sheets ("Things," "Data," "People," "Ideas"). Turn them over and head up each sheet with, respectively, weaknesses/deficiencies—things, weaknesses/deficiencies—data, weaknesses/deficiencies—people, weaknesses/deficiencies—ideas (that is, you are to use one heading on each sheet).[1]

Things I do poorly: These are things you don't do well, but for some reason you want to or have to do them. Don't list things you have no interest in doing or don't need to do.
Things I would like to stop doing: We all have things we'd like to stop doing. These may or may not be things you have a reason for doing.
Things I would like to learn to do well: These are things you must do well and/ or things you want to do well.

Which of these deficiencies are most important *right now?* Which must you do something about first in order to begin moving toward the objective you set for yourself in Step 3? Select and rank-order the three most important on the piece of paper where you listed your five most satisfying skills and abilities.

Step 5

Prepare a brief written plan showing how you plan to move toward your career objective (from Step 3), and including your plans for dealing with the weaknesses that stand betweeen you and your objective.